Perennials
for OHIO

Debra Knapke
Alison Beck

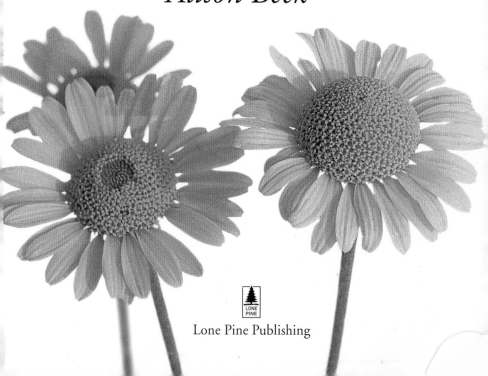

Lone Pine Publishing

The Publisher: Lone Pine Publishing

10145 – 81 Avenue
Edmonton, AB, Canada T6E 1W9
Website: www.lonepinepublishing.com

1808 – B Street NW, Suite 140
Auburn, WA, USA 98001

National Library of Canada Cataloguing in Publication Data

Knapke, Debra, 1955–
    Perennials for Ohio / Debra Knapke and Alison Beck.

    Includes index.
    ISBN 1-55105-386-1

    1. Perennials—Ohio. I. Beck, Alison, 1971– II. Title.
SB434.K52 2003   635.9'32'09771   C2002-911445-4

Editorial Director: Nancy Foulds
Project Editor: Dawn Loewen
Illustrations Coordinator: Carol Woo
Photo Editor: Don Williamson
Production Coordinator: Jennifer Fafard
Book Design: Heather Markham
Layout & Production: Ian Dawe, Elliot Engley, Arlana Anderson-Hale
Cover Design: Gerry Dotto
Image Editing: Elliot Engley, Jeff Fedorkiw, Lynett McKell, Arlana Anderson-Hale, Ian Dawe
Scanning, Separations & Film: Elite Lithographers Co.

Photography: all photos by Tim Matheson or Tamara Eder, except Karen Carriere, 117a, 199a, 327a&b; Elliot Engley, 43a, 44a,b&c; Anne Gordon, 76, 112, 135b, 223a, 311a; Joan de Grey, 132, 135a, 226, 227a; Horticolor, 227b; Debra Knapke, 12, 13, 17, 77a&b, 165a&b, 269a, 270b, 271a, 332b, 335b; Colin Laroque, 137c; Janet Loughrey, 115a, 133b, 134a&b, 194, 224a; Erika Markham, 46a&b; David McDonald, 150; Steve Nikkila, 270a, 271b; Kim O'Leary, 113a&b, 193a, 274b; Laura Peters, 95a; Robert Ritchie, 18a, 24, 55b, 59c, 63, 69c, 92, 93a&b, 103b, 141b, 212, 213, 247, 281a; Peter Thompstone, 173a, 176b, 177a, 183b, 208, 209b, 228, 246, 248a&b, 251b, 257c, 280b, 290, 291a, 326; Valleybrook Gardens, 164, 244a&b; Don Williamson, 315

Cover photos (clockwise from top left): by Tim Matheson, bleeding heart, campanula, Shasta daisy, hardy geranium, daylily; by Tamara Eder, clematis

Bug illustrations: Ian Sheldon

We acknowledge the financial support of the Government of Canada through the Book Publishing Industry Development Program (BPIDP) for our publishing activities.

Contents

Acknowledgments

We gratefully acknowledge all who were involved in this project, as well as the many gorgeous public and private gardens that provided the setting for photographs in this book. Special thanks are extended to the following individuals and organizations: Barbara and Douglas Bloom, Thea and Don Bloomquist, Heidi Clausen, Robert Ritchie, Peter Thompstone, Agriculture Canada Central Experimental Farm, Bordine Nursery, Casa Loma Gardens, Chicago Botanic Garden, Cranbrook Gardens, Cranbrook Garden Auxiliary, Cullen Gardens, Edwards Gardens, Inniswood Metro Gardens, Montréal Botanic Garden, Morton Arboretum, Niagara Parks Botanical Gardens and Royal Botanical Gardens.

I am extremely grateful to all the teachers, writers, horticulturists, botanists, photographers, gardeners and friends who have taught, guided and otherwise influenced me over the years. I wish to especially thank Steven Still; Denise Adams; Fred Hower; my husband, Tony; and our children, Sarah, John and Robert. —*Debra Knapke*

The Flowers at a Glance

Pictorial Guide in Alphabetical Order, by Common Name

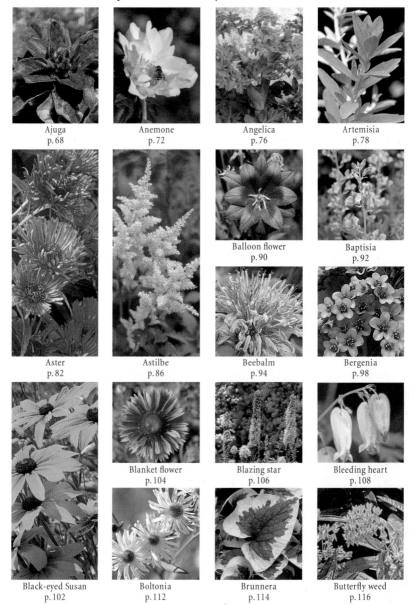

Ajuga
p. 68

Anemone
p. 72

Angelica
p. 76

Artemisia
p. 78

Aster
p. 82

Astilbe
p. 86

Balloon flower
p. 90

Baptisia
p. 92

Beebalm
p. 94

Bergenia
p. 98

Black-eyed Susan
p. 102

Blanket flower
p. 104

Blazing star
p. 106

Bleeding heart
p. 108

Boltonia
p. 112

Brunnera
p. 114

Butterfly weed
p. 116

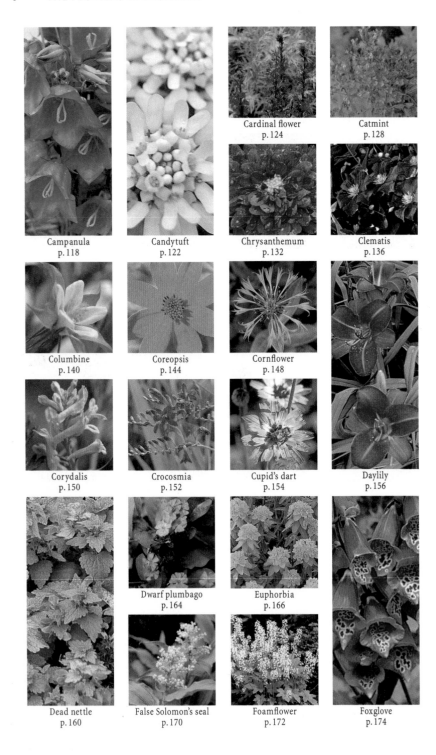

Campanula
p. 118

Candytuft
p. 122

Cardinal flower
p. 124

Catmint
p. 128

Chrysanthemum
p. 132

Clematis
p. 136

Columbine
p. 140

Coreopsis
p. 144

Cornflower
p. 148

Daylily
p. 156

Corydalis
p. 150

Crocosmia
p. 152

Cupid's dart
p. 154

Dwarf plumbago
p. 164

Euphorbia
p. 166

Foxglove
p. 174

Dead nettle
p. 160

False Solomon's seal
p. 170

Foamflower
p. 172

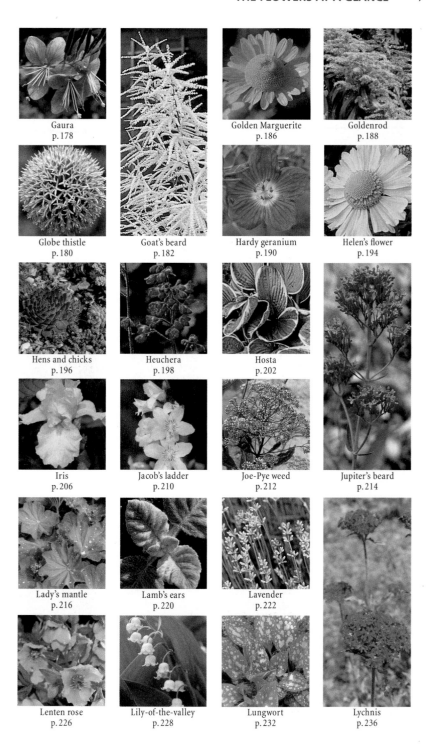

Gaura
p. 178

Golden Marguerite
p. 186

Goldenrod
p. 188

Globe thistle
p. 180

Goat's beard
p. 182

Hardy geranium
p. 190

Helen's flower
p. 194

Hens and chicks
p. 196

Heuchera
p. 198

Hosta
p. 202

Iris
p. 206

Jacob's ladder
p. 210

Joe-Pye weed
p. 212

Jupiter's beard
p. 214

Lady's mantle
p. 216

Lamb's ears
p. 220

Lavender
p. 222

Lenten rose
p. 226

Lily-of-the-valley
p. 228

Lungwort
p. 232

Lychnis
p. 236

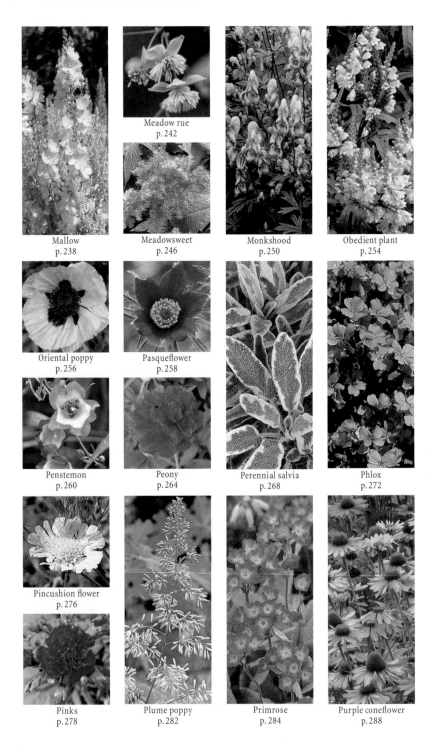

Mallow
p. 238

Meadow rue
p. 242

Meadowsweet
p. 246

Monkshood
p. 250

Obedient plant
p. 254

Oriental poppy
p. 256

Pasqueflower
p. 258

Penstemon
p. 260

Peony
p. 264

Perennial salvia
p. 268

Phlox
p. 272

Pincushion flower
p. 276

Pinks
p. 278

Plume poppy
p. 282

Primrose
p. 284

Purple coneflower
p. 288

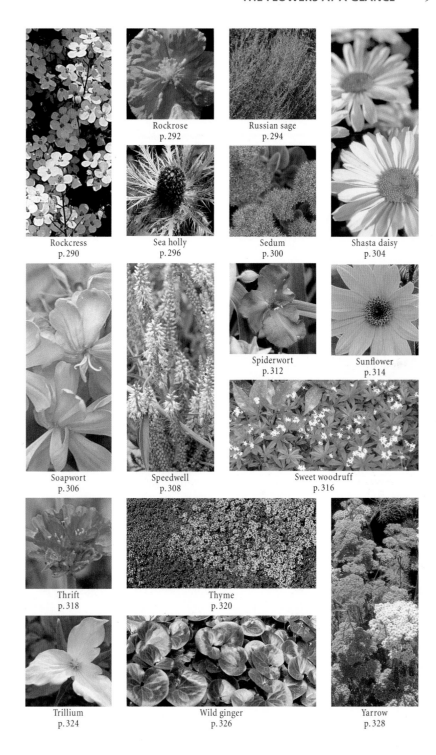

Rockcress
p. 290

Rockrose
p. 292

Russian sage
p. 294

Sea holly
p. 296

Sedum
p. 300

Shasta daisy
p. 304

Soapwort
p. 306

Speedwell
p. 308

Spiderwort
p. 312

Sunflower
p. 314

Sweet woodruff
p. 316

Thrift
p. 318

Thyme
p. 320

Trillium
p. 324

Wild ginger
p. 326

Yarrow
p. 328

Introduction

ALTHOUGH NEW JERSEY IS OFTEN CALLED THE GARDEN STATE, the nickname would apply just as well to Ohio. We have a rich horticultural history. In the 1800s, Ohio was situated at the edge of the 'east' and was the jumping-off point for expansion into the west. As a major crossroads for the nation, it became a hub for the green industry. Cincinnati was compared favorably to the cities of the east in many respects, not the least of which was its many gardens. Towns bordering Lake Erie—Toledo, Cleveland, Painesville and others—were prime growing areas for orchards, seed companies and plant nurseries. More recently, in 1983, Ohio became the birthplace of the Perennial Plant Association, a national organization devoted to the cultivation and use of herbaceous perennials. The interest in gardening and in perennials continues to increase, and our future looks as strong as our past.

Perennials are plants that take three or more years to complete their life cycle. This broad definition includes trees and shrubs. To narrow the sense for the garden, we use the term to refer to just herbaceous perennials. Herbaceous perennials live three or more years, but they generally die back to the ground at the end of the growing season and start fresh with new shoots each spring. Some plants grouped with perennials do not die back completely; the subshrubs, such as thyme, fall into this category. Still others remain green all winter; for example, pinks are evergreen perennials.

The temperate climate of Ohio, with its warm summers, cold winters and fairly dependable rainfall, is ideal for growing a wide range of perennials. The Ohioan gardener also has the benefit of many human resources. From one end of the state to the other, there are enthusiastic and creative individuals, growers, breeders, societies, schools, publications and public gardens devoted to the advancement and enjoyment of gardening in Ohio. These people are happy to provide information, encouragement and fruitful debate. They boast a knowledge of planting and propagation methods, a precision in identifying plants and a plethora of passionate opinions on what is best for any little patch of ground. Watch your local newspaper for the Home and Garden Show schedules and spring and fall flower festivals. For design ideas and inspiration, visit one of the many public gardens in Ohio. The list on p. 337 will help you plan your garden explorations.

The Ohio Environment

Two main factors influence gardening conditions in a region: climate and soil. Over the course of a year and across the state, Ohio gardens can be surprisingly diverse in these respects.

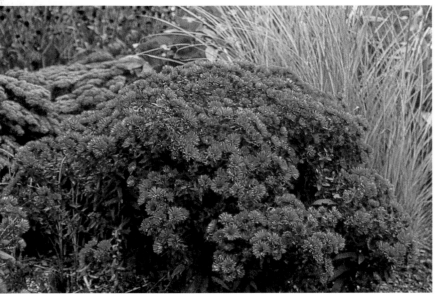

Early-fall Ohio garden with aster & sedum

Climate

The 1990 United States Department of Agriculture (USDA) plant hardiness map—the basis for the map on p. 15—places approximately two-thirds of the state in Zone 5 and one-third in Zone 6. These zones are based on average annual minimum temperatures. In Zone 5, the lowest winter temperatures average –10° to –20° F, and in warmer Zone 6, 0° to –10° F. In recent years, minimum winter temperatures have been higher, and the newly released National Arbor Day Foundation cold hardiness map (http://www.arborday.org/) proposes that approximately 90% of Ohio now

belongs in Zone 6. Only time will tell as to whether or not Ohio's winters are truly warming.

A few areas of Ohio experience very cold winter conditions. One area is along the western border of the state, where the flat topography allows cold winter winds to sweep across the landscape. In central Ohio, other cold spots periodically see minimum winter temperatures down in the Zone 4 range.

For the last spring frost date, averages across the state fall between April 14 and May 14. As one would expect, the earliest dates occur close to Lake Erie (Put-in-Bay and Sandusky) and close to the Ohio River (Portsmouth). The large cities also have early dates, probably because of a heat island effect.

At the end of the season, the average first frost dates fall between September 30 and October 25. The latest first frosts occur close to Lake Erie and the Ohio River, and in the large cities, so these areas have the longest growing seasons in the state.

Based on weather data from 1961 to 1990, Ohio yearly rainfall averages range from 32.8" in Wood County to 43.8" in Brown County. Rainfall during the growing season (May through September) averages 17–19" in northern Ohio, increasing to 23–25" in southern Ohio. Most of this rainfall comes in spring and fall. In early to mid-July, the amount and frequency of rain decreases significantly, and we can experience mild to severe drought conditions into September. The degree to which our plants are stressed depends on the maximum summer temperatures and nighttime temperatures. Days when the afternoon temperature exceeds 90° F and the nighttime temperature exceeds 70° F stress not only our plants, but us, too!

Ohio's average annual snowfall ranges from 20" along the Ohio River to a high of 100" in the 'snow belt' centered on the northeast corner of the state. Although parts of Ashtabula and Geauga counties can average 100" of snow per year, most of the snow belt receives about 50–70". About half of Ohio—the central portion—receives an average of only 30" of snow per year, but

Winter garden with sedum & ornamental grasses

snowfall has been extremely variable within the past ten years.

Snow provides a blanket for dormant and evergreen plants. Cold temperatures without snow cover are a major cause of winter damage and winterkill. Periodically, Ohioans will experience wet winters, especially in central and southern portions of the state, where it often rains more than it snows. This situation can be particularly dangerous for our plants: one of the leading causes of death of many perennials is 'wet feet' in winter. Although many plant deaths are attributed to winter cold, it is often the winter wet that does them in. As you peruse the plant selections in

An outdoor room provides shelter for you and your plants.

this guide, please note that many require a well-drained site.

Also characteristic of Ohio's weather are the frequent freeze-thaw cycles that occur from December through February. It is not uncommon for the mercury to drop into the teens in mid-December and then climb to a balmy 40°–50° F by the end of the month. Such freeze-thaw cycles frequently occur in late January and early February. For some plants, such as the subshrubs, short periods of warmth are a signal to start growing. When the temperature drops below freezing again, this premature growth stops, but not without a cost to the plant in wasted food reserves.

Topography & Soil

Ohio has a varied topography that is intersected by many rivers and streams. The eastern portion is part of the Appalachian Plateau, with rolling hills and dramatic ridges throughout the area. Hocking Hills State Park near Logan is representative of what you will see in the Appalachian Plateau region. Ohio becomes flatter as you travel west into the Central Lowlands. This area of Ohio is known for its agricultural history. Its rich soils attracted early immigrants who farmed the land.

As the topography changes from east to west, so does the pH of the soil. State Route 23, running north to south, approximates the dividing line between the more acidic soils of the east and the more neutral to alkaline soils of the west. There are exceptions, especially in the northern two-thirds of the state covered by glaciers in our geologic past, but this generalization holds true through a good part of Ohio.

If you get a group of gardeners together, the conversation will eventually turn to a discussion of soils and the Herculean efforts required to develop each garden. The dominant soil type of Ohio is clay, which is wonderful for holding water and nutrients, but it drains poorly when wet and when it does dry becomes almost as hard as the rock it came from. See pp. 22 and 25 for suggestions on how to amend your soil.

Local topography in the garden creates microclimates, small areas that may be more or less favorable for growing different plants. Microclimates may be created, for example, in the lee of a nearby building, in a low, cold hollow or at the top of a windswept knoll (see 'Getting Started,' p. 19, for more information on assessing conditions in your garden).

Microclimates give gardeners almost everywhere the possibility of growing that one perennial everyone says won't ever grow here. The challenge of gardening with plants that are borderline hardy is part of the fun of growing perennials, so don't let information about climate zones and perennial hardiness limit your experimentation. Unlike trees and shrubs, perennials are relatively inexpensive and easy to share with friends and neighbors. The more varieties you try, the more likely you'll be to discover what loves to grow in your garden. When it comes to perennials, the best advice is to dig in and just 'grow for it'!

Hardiness Zones Map

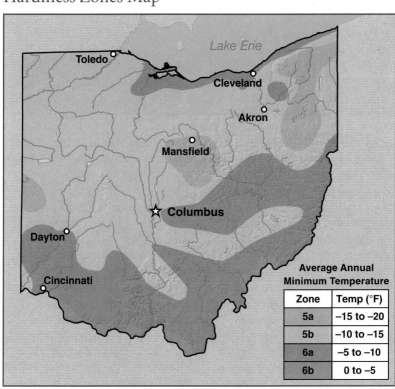

Zone	Temp (°F)
5a	−15 to −20
5b	−10 to −15
6a	−5 to −10
6b	0 to −5

Average Annual Minimum Temperature

Perennial Gardens

Perennials can be included in any type, size or style of garden. From the riot of color in a cottage garden, to the cool, soothing shades of green in a woodland garden, to a welcoming cluster of pots on a front doorstep, perennials open up a world of design possibilities for even the most inexperienced gardener.

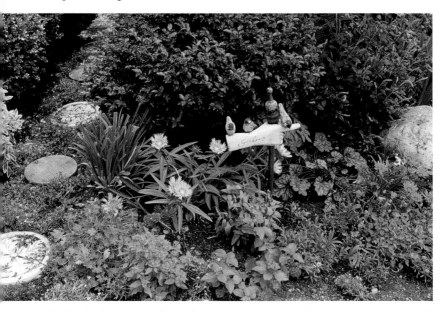

Perennials can stand alone in a garden or combine with other plants. They form a bridge between the temporary color provided by annuals and the permanent structure provided by trees and shrubs. Perennials often require less care and are less prone to pests and diseases than annuals, and in many cases they flower longer and grow to mature size more quickly than shrubs.

It is very important when planning your garden to decide what you like. If you enjoy the plants that are in your garden, you will be more likely to take proper care of them.

Decide what style of garden you like as well as what plants you like. Think about the gardens you have most admired in your neighborhood, in books or while visiting friends. Use these ideas as starting points for planning your own garden.

Select perennials that flower at different times in order to have some part of your garden flowering all season. In Ohio it is possible to have perennials blooming from mid-February (e.g., Lenten rose) to early November (e.g., chrysanthemums). Each perennial entry in this book indicates blooming seasons;

you will also find the Quick Reference Chart on pp. 338–343 handy when trying to select plants that bloom at different times.

Consider not just the flowers but also the foliage of the perennials you want to use. Leaves can be bold or flimsy, coarse or refined; they can be big or small, light or dark; their color can vary from any multitude of greens to yellow, gray, blue or purple; and they can be striped, splashed, edged, dotted or mottled. Their surfaces can be shiny, fuzzy, silky, rough or smooth. The famous white gardens at Sissinghurst, England, were designed, not to showcase a haphazard collection of white flowers, but to remove the distraction of color and allow the eye to linger on the foliage, to appreciate its subtle appeal. Flowers may come and go, but a garden planned with careful attention to foliage will always be interesting.

As well, consider the size and shape of the perennials you choose. Pick a variety of forms to make your garden more diverse. The size of your garden influences these decisions, but do not limit a small garden to small perennials or a large garden to large perennials. Use a balanced combination of plant sizes that are in scale with their specific location. (See individual entries and Quick Reference Chart, p. 338.)

Color . . . tomes have been written on the subject of color in art and design. We tend to focus on color because it is often the first thing we notice in a garden. Choose a variety of flower and foliage colors for your garden. Keep in mind that different colors have different effects on our

Hosta provides foliage interest.

senses. Cool colors like blue, purple and green are soothing. They make small spaces seem bigger because they appear to move away from the viewer. Warm colors like red, orange and yellow are more stimulating; they appear to advance and fill larger spaces. (See individual entries and Quick Reference Chart, p. 338.)

Textures can also create a sense of space. Large leaves are considered bold or coarse in texture. Their visibility from a greater distance makes spaces seem smaller and more shaded. Small leaves, or those that are finely divided, are considered fine in texture. They create a sense of greater space and light. Some gardens have been designed solely on the basis of texture.

Bold-Textured Perennials

Angelica
Bergenia
Goat's beard
Hosta
Joe-Pye weed
Lungwort
Purple coneflower
Sedum 'Autumn Joy'

Joe-Pye weed

Fine-Textured Perennials

Artemisia
Astilbe
Bleeding heart
Clematis
Columbine
Coreopsis
Meadow rue
Thyme

Bleeding heart

Finally, decide how much time you will have to devote to your garden. With good planning and preparation, you can enjoy a relatively low-maintenance perennial garden. Consider using plants that perform well with little care and those that generally resist pest and disease problems.

Low-Maintenance Perennials

Ajuga*
Beebalm*
Catmint
Cornflower*
Daylily*
Dead nettle*
Foxglove
Hardy geranium
Heuchera
Hosta
Mallow
Pinks
Russian sage
Sedum 'Autumn Joy'
may become invasive

Dead nettle with pink verbena

Getting Started

Once you have some ideas about what you want in your garden, consider the growing conditions. Plants grown in ideal conditions, or conditions as close to ideal as possible, are healthier and less prone to pest and disease problems than plants growing in stressful conditions. Some plants considered high maintenance become low maintenance when grown in the right conditions.

Avoid trying to make your garden match the growing conditions of the plants you like. Instead, choose plants suited to your garden conditions. The levels of light, the type of soil and the amount of exposure in your garden provide guidelines that make plant selection easier. A sketch of your garden, drawn on graph paper, may help you organize the various considerations you want to keep in mind for planning. Start with the garden as it exists, marking areas that are shaded, boggy, windy and so on. Knowing your growing conditions can prevent costly mistakes—plan ahead rather than correct later.

Light

Buildings, trees, fences and the time of day influence the amount of light that gets into your garden. There are four basic categories of light in the garden: full sun, partial shade, light shade and full shade. Various plants are adapted to each of these light levels, and some can tolerate a wide range of light conditions.

Full sun locations receive direct sunlight all or most of the day (more than six hours). An example would be a location along a south-facing wall. **Partial shade,** or partial sun, locations receive direct sun for part of the day (four to six hours) and shade for the rest. An east- or west-facing wall gets only partial sun. **Light shade** locations receive shade most or all of the day, but some sun gets through to ground level. The ground under a small-leaved tree is often lightly shaded, with small dapples of sun visible beneath the tree. **Full shade** locations receive no direct sunlight. The north side of a house is considered to be in full shade.

It is important to remember that the intensity of full sun can vary. For example, between buildings in a city, heat can become trapped and magnified, baking all but the most heat-tolerant plants in a concrete oven. Conversely, that shaded, sheltered hollow that protects your heat-hating plants in summer may become a frost trap in winter, killing tender plants that should otherwise survive.

Full sun garden

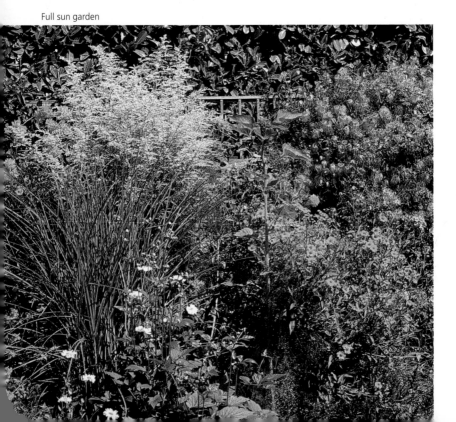

Perennials for Full Sun
Artemisia
Coreopsis
Daylily
Mallow
Phlox
Russian sage
Sedum
Thyme

Perennials for Full Shade
Astilbe
Bleeding heart
Dead nettle
Hosta
Lily-of-the-valley
Lungwort
Monkshood
Primrose
Sweet woodruff
Wild ginger

Phlox cultivar

Lily-of-the-valley

Soil

Plants and the soil they grow in have a unique relationship. Many plant functions go on underground. Soil holds air, water, nutrients, organic matter and a variety of beneficial organisms. Plants depend upon these resources, and the roots use soil as an anchor to hold the plant body upright. In turn, plants influence soil development by breaking down large clods with their roots and by increasing soil fertility when they die and decompose.

Soil is made up of particles of different sizes. Sand particles are the largest. Sand has lots of air space and doesn't compact easily; unfortunately, water drains quickly out of sandy soil and nutrients are quickly washed away. Clay particles are the smallest, visible only through a microscope. Water penetrates clay very slowly and drains very slowly. Clay holds the most nutrients, but it compacts easily because there is very little room between the particles for air. Most soil is made up of a combination of different particle sizes. These soils are called loams.

Particle size is one influence on the drainage properties of your soil; slope is another. Rocky soil on a hillside will probably drain very quickly and should be reserved for those plants

Globe thistle

that prefer a very well-drained soil. Low-lying areas retain water longer, and some areas may rarely drain at all. Moist areas suit plants that require a consistent water supply, and areas that stay wet can be used for plants that prefer boggy conditions.

Drainage can be improved in very wet areas by adding organic matter to the soil and by building raised beds. Water retention in sandy soil can be improved through the addition of organic matter. Some perennials thrive in difficult conditions and may be useful to you, because amending soils can be a long process.

Another aspect of soil to consider is its pH—the measure of acidity or alkalinity. A pH of 7 is neutral; higher numbers (up to 14) indicate alkaline conditions, and lower numbers (down to 0) indicate acidic conditions. Soil pH influences nutrient availability for plants. Although some plants prefer acid or alkaline soils, most grow best in a mid-range pH of between 5.5 and 7.5.

Soils in Ohio run the gamut from acidic to alkaline. You can test your soil's pH using testing kits available at most garden centers, and then decide whether or not you want to try amending the soil.

Perennials for Sandy Soil
Artemisia
Baptisia
Cornflower
Euphorbia
Globe thistle
Rose campion
Russian sage
Thyme

Perennials for Clay Soil
Ajuga
Black-eyed Susan
Blazing star
Foamflower
Hardy geranium
Hosta
Lily-of-the-valley
Purple coneflower
Yarrow

Blazing star

Ajuga, yarrow & hardy geranium

Soil can be made more alkaline by adding horticultural lime. Soil can be made more acidic by adding sulfur, peat moss, pine needles or chopped oak leaves. Altering the pH of your soil takes a long time, often many years, and it is not easy. If you are trying to grow only one or two plants that require a more or less acidic soil than that in your garden, consider growing them in a container or raised bed. There it will be easier to control and amend the pH as needed.

Siberian iris

Perennials for Moist Soil
Astilbe
Bleeding heart
Cardinal flower
Goat's beard
Hosta
Iris
Lady's mantle
Lungwort
Meadowsweet
Monkshood
Primrose

Perennials for Dry Soil
Artemisia
Butterfly weed
Euphorbia
Lamb's ears
Lavender
Moss phlox
Pinks
Russian sage
Sedum
Thrift
Yarrow

Lamb's ears, zinnia & thyme

Exposure

Finally, consider the exposure in your garden. Wind, heat, cold and rain are some of the elements your garden is exposed to, and some plants are better adapted to handle these forces than others. Buildings, walls, fences, hills, hedges and trees all influence your garden's exposure.

Wind in particular can cause extensive damage to your plants. Plants become dehydrated in windy locations if they aren't able to draw water out of the soil fast enough to replace the moisture lost through their leaves. Tall, stiff-stemmed perennials can be knocked over or broken by strong winds. Some plants that do not require staking in a sheltered location may need to be staked in a more exposed one.

Use plants that are recommended for exposed locations, or temper the effect of the wind with a hedge or trees. A solid wall creates turbulence on the leeward side, while a looser structure, such as a hedge, breaks up the force of the wind and protects a larger area.

No matter what conditions you have in your garden, there are perennials that will flourish and provide you with a variety of colors, sizes and forms.

Perennials for Exposed Locations
Candytuft
Columbine
Creeping phlox
Euphorbia
Penstemon
Sedum (groundcover species)
Thrift
Thyme
Yarrow

Columbine

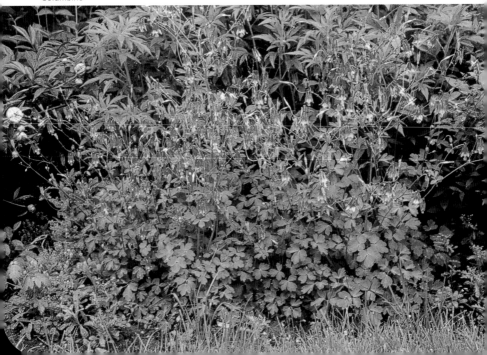

Preparing the Garden

Before you plant your perennials, take the time to properly prepare your flowerbeds. Doing so will save you time and effort later on. The first step is to remove the weeds, preferably by thoroughly digging over the beds and picking out all weeds by hand. Next, you'll want to amend the soil with organic matter.

Turning compost into beds

Removing weeds & debris

Organic Soil Amendments

All soils benefit from the addition of organic matter. Not only does this material contribute nutrients, it improves the structure of the soil. Organic matter improves heavy clay soils by loosening them and allowing air and water to penetrate. It improves sandy or light soils by increasing their ability to retain water, which allows plants to absorb nutrients before they are leached away.

Some of the best organic additives are compost, well-rotted manure and composted hemlock bark mulch. Granulated, composted chicken or barnyard manure is a wonderful product that is available from suppliers of organic gardening products. Composted horse manure is also an excellent additive and is usually available from stables, often in a seemingly endless supply. If you have access to fresh manure, compost it first or use it sparingly because roots that come in contact with fresh manure will suffer fertilizer burn. Incorporate it into beds at least two weeks before—or better yet, the season before—planting. Avoid using it in vegetable beds at all to prevent the potential spread of fecal-borne diseases.

Mix your organic matter into the soil with a garden fork. If you are

Compost worms

Wooden compost bins (above)

Plastic compost bins

Material for compost

adding just one or two plants and do not want to prepare an entire bed, dig holes twice as wide and deep as the rootball of each plant. Add a slow-release organic fertilizer or composted manure mixed with peat moss to the backfill of soil that you spread around the plant.

Within a few months, earthworms and other decomposer organisms will break down the organic matter, releasing nutrients for plants. At the same time, the activities of these decomposers will help keep the soil from compacting.

Composting

In forests and meadows, organic debris, such as leaves and other plant bits, breaks down where it falls on the soil surface, and the nutrients are gradually made available to the plants growing there. In the home garden, pests and diseases may be a problem, and untidy debris isn't practical. Still, we can easily acquire the same nutrient benefits by composting. Compost is a great regular additive for your garden, and good composting methods will help reduce pest and disease problems.

Compost can be made in a pile, in a wooden box or in a purchased composter bin, and the process is not complicated. A pile of kitchen scraps, grass clippings and fall leaves will eventually break down if simply left alone. Such 'passive' or cool composting may take one to two seasons for all the materials to break down. You can speed up the process and create an 'active' or hot compost pile by following a few simple guidelines.

Use dry as well as fresh materials, with a higher proportion of dry matter than fresh green matter. Appropriate dry matter includes chopped straw, shredded leaves and sawdust. Green matter may consist of vegetable scraps, grass clippings and pulled weeds. The green matter breaks down quickly and produces nitrogen, which composting organisms use to break down dry matter. Spread the green materials evenly throughout the pile by layering them between dry materials.

An active (hot) compost bin

As well, add layers of soil or finished compost in order to introduce the organisms necessary to break down the compost pile properly. If the pile seems dry, add a bit of water as you layer. The pile needs to be moist but not soggy: about as wet as a wrung-out sponge.

Turn the pile over or poke holes in it with a pitchfork every week or two. Air must get into the pile in order to speed up decomposition. Well-aerated compost piles will generate a lot of heat. A thermometer attached to a long probe, similar to a meat thermometer, will be able to take the temperature near the middle of the pile. Compost can easily reach 160° F while decomposing. At this temperature, weed seeds are destroyed and many damaging soil organisms killed. Most beneficial soil organisms, on the other hand, are not killed unless the compost temperature exceeds 160° F. Once your compost reaches that temperature, turn the pile to aerate it and keep the temperature stable.

Avoid putting diseased, pest-ridden plant material or pet waste into your compost pile, or you will risk spreading problems throughout your entire garden. If you must put questionable material in the pile, put it as near the center as possible, where temperatures are highest. Never put such material into a passive compost pile because the internal temperatures do not rise high enough to kill pests and diseases.

Your compost has reached the end of its cycle when you can no longer recognize the matter you added initially, and when the temperature no longer rises when you turn the pile. It may take as little as one month to reach this stage. Your compost is now ready to spread onto your perennial garden. It will have a good mixture of nutrients and be rich in beneficial organisms.

Finished compost

Selecting Perennials

Perennials can be purchased or started from seed. Purchased plants often begin flowering the same year they are planted, while plants started from seed may take several years to mature. Starting from seed is more economical if you want large numbers of plants. (See 'Propagating Perennials,' p. 43, to learn how to start seeds.)

Plant on left is rootbound, plant on right healthy.

Get your perennials from a reputable source, and check to make sure the plants are not diseased or pest-ridden. Garden centers, mail-order catalogs and friends and neighbors are excellent sources of plants and seeds. A number of garden societies promote the exchange of seeds, and many public gardens sponsor plant sales and sell seeds of rare plants.

Gardening clubs are also a great source of rare and unusual plants.

Purchased plants generally come in one of two forms. **Potted** perennials are growing in pots, usually the ones they were raised in. **Bare-root** perennials consist of pieces of root packed in moist peat moss or sawdust. These roots are typically dormant, although some of the previous year's growth may be evident or there may be new growth starting. Sometimes the roots appear to have no evident growth, past or present. Both potted and bare-root perennials are good purchases, and in each case there are things to look for to make sure you are getting a plant of the best quality.

Potted plants come in many sizes, and though a larger plant may appear more mature, a smaller one will suffer less from the shock of being transplanted. Most perennials grow quickly once they are planted in the garden, so the initial size won't matter too much. Select plants that seem to be a good size for the pot they are in. When a plant is tapped lightly out of the pot, the roots should be visible but not winding and twisting around the inside of the pot.

The leaves should be a healthy color. If they appear to be chewed or damaged, check carefully for insects or diseases. If you find any pests on a plant, don't purchase it unless you are willing to cope with the hitchhikers before you move the plant into the garden, where the pest could spread. If the plant looks diseased, do not purchase it.

Once you get your potted plants home, water them if they are dry and keep them in a lightly shaded location until you plant them. Remove any damaged growth and discard it. Plant your new perennials into the garden as soon as possible.

Bare-root plants are most commonly sold through mail order, but some are available in garden centers, usually in spring. If you're buying at a garden center, look for roots that are dormant (without top growth). A plant that has been trying to grow in the stressful conditions of a plastic bag may not have enough energy to recover, or it may take longer to establish.

Cut off any damaged parts of the roots with a very sharp knife. Bare-root perennials need to be planted more quickly than potted plants because they will dehydrate rapidly out of soil. Soak the roots in lukewarm water for one to two hours to rehydrate them. Do not leave them in water longer than that, or you may encourage root or crown rot. Plant them directly in the garden or into pots with good-quality potting soil until they can be moved to the garden.

It is often difficult to distinguish the top from the bottom of bare-root plants. Usually there is a telltale dip or stub from which the plant grew. If you can't find any distinguishing characteristics, lay the root on its side and the plant will send the roots down and the shoots up.

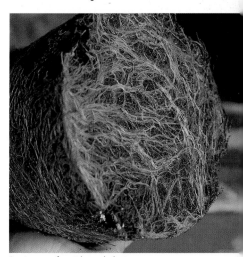

Root mass of root-bound plant

Planting Perennials

Once you have your garden planned, the soil well prepared and the perennials purchased, it's time to plant. If your perennials came with identification tags, be sure to poke them into the soil next to the new plants. Next spring, the tags will help you with identification and remind you that there is indeed a plant in that bare patch of soil. A diagram of the plants is also helpful.

Potted Perennials

Perennials in pots are convenient because you can arrange them across the bed before you start to dig. To prevent the roots from drying out, do not unpot the plants until just before you transplant.

To plant potted perennials, start by digging a hole about the width and depth of the pot. Remove the perennial from the pot. If the pot is small enough, you can hold your hand across the top of the pot, letting your fingers straddle the stem, and then turn it upside down. Never pull on the stem or leaves to get a plant out of

a pot. It is better to cut a difficult pot off than risk damaging the plant.

If you have taken advantage of an end-of-season sale, you will probably have to deal with root-bound plants. Before planting them, you will need to tease apart or cut into the roots if they are winding around the rootball. If there is a solid mat at the bottom of the rootball, remove it, because such roots will not be able to spread out and establish themselves in the soil.

Gently spread out the roots as you plant. The process of cutting into the bottom half of the rootball and spreading the two halves of the mass outward like a pair of wings is called 'butterflying' and is an effective way to promote fast growth of pot-bound perennials.

Place the plant in the prepared hole. It should be planted at the same level that it was at in the pot, or a little higher, to allow for the soil to settle. If the plant is too low in the ground, it may rot when rain collects around the crown. Fill the soil in and firm it down. Water the plant well as soon as you have planted it, and water regularly until it has become established.

Fall-planted perennials may be subject to frost heaving if they did not have enough time to establish a good root system. When the ground cools—after several frosts and extended cool temperatures—you may want to mulch plants that were planted out in fall, to avoid heaving. Do not mulch before the ground cools because the trapped heat in the soil will prevent the perennials from entering complete winter dormancy. As well, mulch placed around plants that are still above ground will trap moisture and promote rot and other diseases. Mulching after the ground cools or freezes will help modify the effect of Ohio's freeze-thaw cycles, particularly for the top 4" of soil where the roots of your newly planted perennials reside.

Bare-Root Perennials

Before planting, bare-root perennials should not be spaced out across the bed unless you planted them in temporary pots. Roots dry out quickly.

Support plant as you remove pot (above photos).

Loosen rootball before planting.

If you want to visualize your spacing, you can poke sticks into the ground or put rocks down to represent the locations of your perennials.

If you have been keeping your bare-root perennials in potting soil, you may find that the roots have not grown enough to knit the soil together and that all the soil falls away from the root when you remove it from the pot. Don't be concerned. Just follow the regular root-planting instructions. If the soil does hold together, plant the root the way you would a potted perennial.

The type of hole you need to dig will depend on the type of roots the perennial has. Plants with **fibrous roots** need a mound of soil in the center of the planting hole over which the roots can be spread out evenly. The hole should be dug as deep as the longest roots. Mound the soil into the center of the hole up to ground level. Spread the roots out around the mound and cover them with loosened soil.

Plants with a **taproot** need a hole that is narrow and about as deep as the root is long. The job is easily done with the help of a trowel: open up a suitable hole, tuck the root into it and fill it in again with the soil around it. If you can't tell which end is up, plant the root on its side.

Some plants have roots that may appear to be taproots, but the shoot seems to be growing off the side of the root, rather than upwards from one end. These roots are actually modified stems called **rhizomes.** Most irises, for example, have rhizomes. Rhizomes should be planted horizontally in a shallow hole and covered with soil.

In most cases, you should try to get the crown at or just above soil level and loosen the soil that surrounds the planting hole. Keep the roots thoroughly watered until the plants are well established.

Whether the plants are potted or bare-root, leave them alone for a period of time to let them recover from the stress of planting. In the first month, you will need only to water the plant regularly, weed it and watch for pests. A mulch will keep in moisture and control weeds.

If you have prepared your beds properly, you probably won't have to fertilize in the first year. If you do wish to fertilize, wait until your transplants have started healthy new growth, and apply only a weak fertilizer to avoid damaging the sensitive new roots.

Planters

Perennials can also be grown in planters for compact, movable displays. Planters can be used on patios or decks, in gardens with very poor soil or in areas where kids and dogs might destroy a perennial bed.

Use a good-quality potting mix or soil mix intended for containers. Garden soil can quickly lose its structure and become a solid lump in a container, preventing air, water and roots from penetrating. Perennials will never thrive in small containers if planted entirely in garden soil. Replace the potting mix each year, or add some new peat and compost before replanting.

With larger containers (top diameter at least 36"), you may not want to replace the growing medium annually. Consider using some garden soil to create a healthier long-term growing environment. Many of the soil-less mixes will compact over time, and mixes that contain vermiculite can become slimy and impermeable to water and air after one growing season. The addition of some garden soil to a container, approximately one-third of the total volume, can extend the 'life' of the medium.

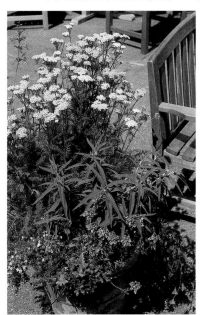
Mixed container planting

Many perennials, such as hostas and daylilies, can grow in the same container without any fresh potting soil for five or six years. Be sure, though, to fertilize and water perennials in planters more often than those growing in the ground. Dig your finger deep into the soil around the perennial to make sure it needs water. Too much water in a planter causes root rot.

When designing a planter garden, you can either keep one type of perennial in each planter and display many different planters together, or mix different perennials in large planters together with annuals and bulbs. The latter choice results in a dynamic bouquet of flowers and foliage. Keep the tall upright perennials, such as yarrow, in the center of the planter; the rounded or bushy types, such as coreopsis, around the sides; and low-growing or draping perennials, such as candytuft (the species), along the edges. Perennials that have long bloom times or attractive foliage often work well in planters.

Choose hardy perennials that are able to tolerate difficult conditions. Planters are exposed to extremes of our variable weather—baking hot in summer and freezing cold in winter. The soil in planters dries out quickly in hot weather and becomes waterlogged after a couple of rainy days. The more invasive perennials often make good choices for these extreme conditions; they'll be tough to kill, and their otherwise aggressive spread will be controlled.

Perennials in planters are more susceptible to winter damage because the exposed sides of the container provide very little insulation for roots against fluctuations in temperature. The container itself may even crack when exposed to a deep freeze. Don't despair—it's not difficult to get planters through a tough Ohio winter in great shape. The simplest thing to do is to move the planter to a sheltered spot when winter arrives. Most perennials do require some cold in order to flower the next year, so find a spot that is cold but not exposed. An unheated garage or enclosed porch is a good place, and even your garden shed will offer plants more protection than they would get outdoors, open to the elements on all sides.

If you lack the space or access to these places, consider your basement window wells. These sheltered, below-ground spaces also offer some heat from the windows. Layer straw at the bottom of the well, sit your pots on the straw, then cover them with more straw. Wait until the pots freeze before placing them in the wells, in order to prevent rot and problems with mice. Mice find the straw makes a comfortable home and the perennial roots a tasty treat, but they can't dig as easily in frozen soil. If mice are a problem, try Styrofoam insulation instead of straw; it may be less appealing to rodents.

You can winterproof the pots themselves before planting your perennials. Place a layer of Styrofoam insulation, packing 'peanuts' or commercial planter insulation at the bottom of the pot and around the inside before you add your soil and plants. Make sure excess water can still drain freely from the container. This technique is particularly useful for high-rise dwellers with balcony or rooftop gardens. The insulation has the added benefit of protecting the roots from overheating in summer.

Planters can also be buried in the garden for the winter. Find an open space in a flowerbed, and dig a hole deep enough to allow you to sink the planter up to its rim. This job can be messy, though, particularly in spring when you dig up the planter. It also requires a good deal of empty space in the garden. Large planters may require extensive excavation, making this technique impractical for all but the smallest containers.

Perennials for Planters
Artemisia
Astilbe
Candytuft
Daylily
Dead nettle
Goat's beard
Hardy geranium
Heuchera
Hosta
Iris
Lady's mantle
Pinks
Salvia
Thyme
Yarrow

Lady's mantle

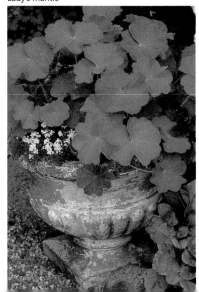

Caring for Perennials

Many perennials require little care, but all benefit from a few maintenance basics. Weeding, mulching, watering and pruning are some of the chores that, when done on a regular basis, keep major work to a minimum.

Weeding

Controlling weeds is one of the most important things you will do in your garden. Weeds compete with your perennials for light, nutrients and space, and they can also harbor pests and diseases.

Many weed seeds, especially those of annual weeds, need light to germinate. Therefore, try to prevent weeds from germinating by blocking their access to light with a layer of mulch. As your garden matures, the perennials themselves will also suppress weeds by blocking the light.

Pull out weeds that do germinate while they are still small—before they have a chance to flower, set seed and start a whole new generation of problems. Weeds can be pulled out by hand or with a hoe. Quickly scuffing across the soil surface with a hoe will pull out small weeds and sever larger ones from their roots.

Mulching

Mulches are an important gardening tool. As mentioned, they prevent weed seeds from germinating by blocking out the light. As well, soil temperatures remain more consistent and more moisture is retained under a layer of mulch. Mulches also

Mulched garden

Lay down fresh mulch, up to 3–4" thick, once the ground freezes in fall to protect plants over the winter. This fall mulch is particularly important if you can't depend on a steady layer of snow to cover your garden in winter, as is the case in much of central and southern Ohio. You can cover the plants themselves as well at this time with dry material, such as chopped straw, pine needles or shredded leaves.

Keep in mind that as the ground freezes, so too may your pile of potential mulch, making it difficult to spread. One solution is to cover most of the bed with mulch, leaving only the plants exposed, before the ground freezes. Put extra mulch, enough to cover the plants, in a large bag or your wheelbarrow, and move it somewhere that will take longer to freeze, perhaps in your garage or garden shed. Once the ground is completely frozen, you can use your supply of spreadable mulch to cover the plants.

In late winter or early spring, once the weather starts to warm, pull the mulch layer off the plants and see if they have started growing. If they have, pull the mulch back, but keep it nearby in case you need to replace it to protect the tender new growth from a late frost. Once your plants are well on their way and you're no longer worried about frost, remove the protective mulch completely from the plant crowns. Spread some around the bed for your spring and summer mulch, and compost the rest or use it elsewhere to start a new garden bed.

prevent soil erosion during heavy rain or strong winds.

Organic mulches include compost, bark chips, shredded leaves and grass clippings. Organic mulches are desirable because they improve the soil and add nutrients as they break down. Inorganic mulches, such as gravel, tend to compress soil and prevent free movement of beneficial soil organisms.

In spring, spread a couple of inches of mulch over your perennial beds around your plants. Keep the area immediately around the crown or stem of each plant clear (2–4" clearance). Mulch that is too close to your plants can trap moisture and prevent good air circulation, encouraging disease. If the layer of mulch disappears into the soil over the summer, replenish it.

Watering

Watering is another basic of perennial care. Once established, many perennials need little supplemental watering if they have been planted in their preferred conditions and are given a moisture-retaining mulch. Planting perennials with similar water requirements together makes watering easier.

The golden rule of watering is to water thoroughly and infrequently. If you water lightly and frequently, you will be wetting only the very top layer of soil. Plant roots will then stay near the surface instead of growing down, causing problems when Ohio's summer dry period hits and the surface roots can't take advantage of deeper soil moisture. So, when you do water, make sure the water penetrates several inches into the soil. One inch of water will infiltrate about 4" of soil.

Installing soaker hoses in your perennial beds is one of the most efficient ways to water.

Fertilizing

Generally, if you prepare your beds well and add new compost to them each spring, you should not need to add extra fertilizer. Many perennials, in fact, thrive in poor to average soil. If overfed, these perennials overgrow and become maintenance headaches. On the other hand, some plants are heavy feeders that do need additional supplements throughout the growing season.

If you have a limited amount of compost, you can mix a slow-release fertilizer into the soil around your perennials in spring. Many organic and chemical fertilizers are available at garden centers. Never use more than the recommended quantity because too much fertilizer will do more harm than good. Roots can be burned by fertilizer that is applied in high concentrations. Problems are more likely to be caused by chemical fertilizers because they are more concentrated than organic types. Keep in mind, too, that most fertilizer instructions recommend a higher rate than is necessary for good plant growth.

For perennials it is important to support good root development in the first year or two of growth. Phosphorus is the nutrient that promotes root growth, so if you lack compost, look for fertilizers high in phosphorus while plants are establishing. The typical fertilizer formula is N : P : K (Nitrogen : Phosphorus : Potassium). In the years after plants establish, nitrogen becomes important for leaf development, and potassium for flower and seed development.

Grooming

Many perennials benefit from a bit of grooming. Healthy, resilient plants with plentiful blooms and compact growth are the signs of a well-groomed garden. Thinning, pinching, disbudding and deadheading are pruning techniques used to enhance the beauty of a perennial garden. The methods are simple, but you may have to experiment to get the right effect in your own garden.

Thinning is done to clump-forming perennials such as black-eyed Susan, purple coneflower and beebalm early in the year, when shoots have just emerged. These plants have stems in a dense clump that allows very little air or light into the center of the plant. Remove half of the shoots when they first emerge

to increase air circulation and prevent diseases such as powdery mildew. The increased light will also encourage compact growth and more flowers. Throughout the growing season, thin any stems that are weak, diseased or growing in the wrong direction.

Pinching or **trimming** perennials is a simple procedure, but timing it correctly and achieving just the right look can be tricky. Early in the year, before the flower buds appear, trim the plant to encourage new side shoots. Remove the tip and some stems of the plant just above a leaf or pair of leaves. You can trim stem by stem, but if you have a lot of plants you can also trim off the tops with your hedge shears to one-third of the height you expect the plants to reach. The growth that begins to emerge can be pinched again. You can achieve beautiful layered effects by staggering the trimming times by a week or two.

Give plants enough time to set buds and flower. Continual pinching will encourage very dense growth but also delay flowering. Most spring-flowering plants cannot be pinched back or they will not flower. Early-summer or mid-summer bloomers should be pinched only once, as early in the season as possible. Late-summer and fall bloomers can be pinched several times but should be left alone past June. Don't pinch a plant if flower buds have formed—it may not have enough energy or time left in the year to develop a new set of buds. Experimenting and keeping detailed notes will improve your pinching skills.

Shasta daisy

therefore seedlings, around the garden; it often prolongs blooming; and it helps prevent pest and disease problems. The flowers can be pinched off by hand or snipped off with hand pruners. Bushy plants, and particularly ones with a short bloom period, such as dead nettle, can be more aggressively pruned back with garden shears when they are finished flowering. In some cases, as with moss phlox, shearing will promote new growth and possibly blooms later in the season.

Perennials to Pinch Early in the Season
Artemisia
Aster
Beebalm
Black-eyed Susan
Boltonia
Catmint
Chrysanthemum
Helen's flower
Mallow
Purple coneflower
Sedum 'Autumn Joy'
Shasta daisy

Perennials to Shear Back After Blooming
Campanula
Candytuft
Coreopsis
Creeping phlox
Dead nettle
Golden Marguerite
Hardy geranium
Rockcress
Sweet woodruff
Thyme
Yarrow

Disbudding is the final grooming stage before a plant blooms. It refers to the removal of some flower buds to encourage the remaining ones to produce larger flowers. This technique is popular with peony, dahlia and rose growers.

Deadheading, the removal of flowers once they have finished blooming, serves several purposes. It keeps plants looking tidy; it prevents them from spreading seeds, and

Campanula

Deadheading is not necessary for every plant. Some plants have attractive seedheads that can be left in place to provide interest in the garden over the winter. Other plants are short-lived, and by leaving some of the seedheads in place you will encourage future generations to replace the old plants. Blanket flower is one example of a short-lived perennial that re-seeds. In some cases the self-sown seedlings do not possess the attractive features of the parent plant; deadheading may be required in these cases.

Deadheading asters

Poppy and other seedheads

Corydalis

Perennials with Interesting Seedheads
Angelica
Baptisia
Blanket flower
Clematis
Columbine
False Solomon's seal
Goat's beard
Meadowsweet
Oriental poppy
Pasqueflower
Purple coneflower
Russian sage
Sea holly
Sedum 'Autumn Joy'

Perennials That Self-Seed
Ajuga (variable seedlings)
Bleeding heart (variable seedlings)
Cardinal flower
Columbine (variable seedlings)
Corydalis
Foxglove
Lady's mantle
Mallow
Pinks
Rose campion

Staking

Staking, the use of poles, branches or wires to hold plants erect, can often be avoided by astute thinning and pinching, but a few plants always need a bit of support to look their best. Three types of stakes are used for the different growth habits that need support.

Plants that develop tall spikes, such as some foxgloves, require each spike to be staked individually. A strong, narrow pole such as a bamboo stick can be pushed into the ground early in the year and the spike tied to the stake as it grows. A forked branch can also be used to support single-stemmed plants.

Many plants, such as peonies, get top-heavy as they grow and tend to flop over once they reach a certain height. A wire hoop, sometimes called a peony ring, is the most unobtrusive way to hold up such a plant. When the plant is young, the legs of the peony ring are pushed into the ground around it, and as the plant grows up, it is supported by the wire ring. At the same time, the bushy growth hides the ring. Wire tomato cages can also be used to support these types of plants.

Other plants, such as coreopsis, form a floppy tangle of stems. These plants can be given a bit of support with twiggy branches inserted into the ground around young plants; the plants then grow up into the twigs.

Some people consider stakes to be unsightly no matter how hidden they seem. As well as thinning and pinching, there are other steps you can take to reduce the need for staking. First, grow plants in the right

Spiral stakes

conditions. Don't assume a plant will do better in a richer soil than is recommended; very rich soil causes many plants to produce weak, leggy growth that is prone to lodging (falling over). Similarly, a plant that likes full sun will become stretched out and leggy if grown in the shade. Second, keep in mind that plants can give each other some support. Mix in plants that have a stable structure between the plants that need support. The weaker plants may still fall over slightly, but only as far as their neighbors will allow. Third, you can often find compact varieties that don't require staking.

Finally, keep in mind that not every plant needs to be ramrod straight. Graceful arching adds another element of interest to the garden.

Propagating Perennials

Learning to propagate your own perennials is an interesting and challenging aspect of gardening that can save you money, but it also requires time and space. Seeds, cuttings and division are the three methods of increasing your perennial population. Each method has advantages and disadvantages.

A cold frame is a wonderful gardening aid regardless of which methods of propagation you use. It can be used to protect tender plants over the winter, to start vegetable seeds early in spring, to harden plants off before moving them to the garden, to protect fall-germinating seedlings and young cuttings or divisions, and to start seeds that need a cold treatment. This mini-greenhouse structure is built so that ground level on the inside of the cold frame is lower than on the outside, so the soil around the outside insulates the plants within. The angled, hinged lid is fitted with glass. The lid lets light in and collects some heat during the day, and it prevents rain from damaging tender plants. If the interior gets too hot, the lid can be raised for ventilation.

A hot frame is insulated and has heating coils in the floor to prevent the soil from freezing or to maintain a constant soil temperature for germinating seeds and rooting cuttings.

Seeds

Starting perennials from seed is a great way to propagate a large number of plants at a relatively low cost. You can purchase seeds or collect them from your own or a friend's perennial garden. All the work involved in growing plants from seed is worth it when you see plants you raised from tiny seedlings finally begin to flower.

Shade cloth over cold frame

Seeding has some limitations. Some cultivars and varieties don't pass on their desirable traits to their offspring. Other perennials take a very long time to germinate, if they germinate at all, and an even longer time to grow to flowering size. Many perennials, however, grow easily from seed and flower within a year or two of being transplanted into the garden.

Specific propagation information is given for each plant in this book, but there are a few basic rules for starting all seeds. Some seeds can be started directly in the garden (direct sown), but it is easier to control temperature and moisture levels

and to provide a sterile environment if you start the seeds indoors. Seeds can be started in pots or, if you need a lot of plants, flats. Use a sterile soil mix intended for starting seeds. The soil will generally need to be kept moist but not soggy. Most seeds germinate in moderately warm temperatures of about 57°–70° F.

Seed-starting supplies are available at garden centers. Many supplies aren't necessary, but some, such as seed-tray dividers, are useful. Often called plug trays, these dividers are made of plastic and prevent the roots of seedlings from tangling and being disturbed during transplanting. Heating coils or pads can also come in handy to keep the soil at a constant temperature.

Fill your pot or seed tray with the soil mix and firm it down slightly—not too firmly or the soil will not drain. Wet the soil before planting your seeds because they may wash into clumps if watered immediately afterwards.

Large seeds can be planted individually and spaced out in pots or trays. If you have divided inserts for your trays, plant one or two seeds

Filling cell packs

Using folded paper to plant small seeds (above)

Spray bottle provides gentle mist

Prepared seed tray

per section. Small seeds may have to be sprinkled in a bit more randomly. Fold a sheet of paper in half and place the small seeds in the crease. Gently tap the underside of the fold to bounce or roll the seeds off the paper in a controlled manner. Some seeds are so tiny that they look like dust. These seeds can be mixed with a small amount of very fine sand and spread on the soil surface. Tiny seeds may not need to be covered with any more soil. The medium-sized seeds can be lightly covered, and the large seeds can be pressed into the soil and then lightly covered. Do not cover seeds that need to be exposed to light in order to germinate; these types of seeds are indicated as such in the plant descriptions later in the book.

Plant only one type of seed in each pot or flat. Each species has a different rate of germination, and the seedlings will require different conditions than the seeds that have yet to germinate.

Water the seeds using a very fine spray if the soil starts to dry out. A hand-held spray bottle will moisten the soil without disturbing the seeds. To keep the environment moist, you can place pots inside clear plastic bags. Change the bags or turn them inside out once condensation starts to build up and drip. Plastic bags can be held up with stakes or wires poked in around the edges of the pot. Many seed trays come with clear plastic covers that can be placed over the flats to keep the moisture in. Remove the plastic once the seeds have germinated.

Most seeds do not require a lot of light in order to germinate, so pots or trays can be kept in any warm, out-of-the-way place. Once the seeds have germinated, place them in a bright location but out of direct sun. Seedlings should be transplanted to individual pots once they have three or four true leaves. True leaves are the ones that look like the mature leaves. (The first one or two leaves are the cotyledons, or seed leaves.) Plants in plug trays can be left until neighboring leaves start to touch each other. At this point the plants will be competing for light and should be transplanted to individual pots.

Young seedlings do not need to be fertilized. Fertilizer causes seedlings to produce soft, spindly growth that is susceptible to attack by insects and diseases. The seed itself provides all the nutrition the seedling will need. A fertilizer diluted to one-quarter or one-half strength can be used once seedlings have four or five true leaves.

All seedlings are susceptible to a problem called **damping off,** which is caused by soil-borne fungi. An afflicted seedling looks as though someone has pinched the stem at soil level, causing the plant to topple over. The pinched area blackens and the seedling dies. Sterile soil mix, good air circulation and evenly moist soil will help prevent this problem.

Many seeds sprout easily as soon as they are planted. Some, however, have protection devices that prevent them from germinating when conditions are not favorable or from germinating all at once. Some seeds bear thick seed coats, and others produce poisonous chemicals in the seed coats to deter insects. In the wild, such strategies improve the chances of survival, but you will have to lower the defenses of these types of seeds before they will germinate.

Clematis

Perennials to Start from Seed
Boltonia
Clematis
Columbine
Corydalis
Foxglove
Lady's mantle
Lavender
Mallow
Pinks
Rose campion

Foxglove

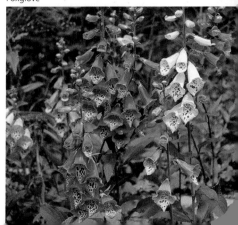

Seeds can be tricked into thinking the conditions are right for sprouting. Some thick-coated seeds can be soaked for a day or two in a glass of water to promote germination. This soaking mimics the beginning of the rainy season, which is when the plant would germinate in its natural environment. The water softens the seed coat and in some cases washes away the chemicals that have been preventing germination. Lavender is an example of a plant with seeds that need to be soaked before they will germinate.

Other thick-coated seeds need to be scarified (scratched) to allow moisture to penetrate the seed coat and prompt germination. In nature, birds scratch the seeds with the gravel in their craws and acid in their stomachs. Nick the seeds with a knife or gently rub them between two sheets of sandpaper. Leave the scratched seeds in a dry place for a day or so before planting them, to give them a chance to prepare for germination before they are exposed to water. Anemones are plants with seeds that need their thick coats scarified.

Scratching seed coats with sandpaper

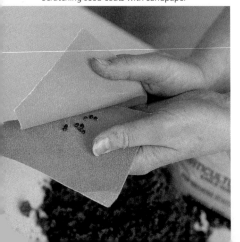

Plants from northern climates often have seeds that wait until spring before they germinate. These seeds must be given a cold treatment, which mimics winter, before they will germinate. Yarrows, primroses and bergenias have seeds that respond to cold treatment.

One method of cold treatment is to plant the seeds in a pot or tray and place them in the refrigerator for up to two months. Check the container regularly and don't allow the seeds to dry out. This method is fairly simple but not very practical if your fridge is as crowded as mine.

A less space-consuming method is to mix the seeds with some moist sand, peat moss or sphagnum moss. Place the mix in a sealable sandwich bag and pop it in the refrigerator for up to two months, again being sure the sand or moss doesn't dry out. The seeds can then be planted in a pot or tray. Spread the seeds and the

Mixing seeds with moist peat for cold treatment

moist sand or moss onto the prepared surface and press it down gently.

As noted in certain entries in this book, some plants have seeds that must be planted when freshly ripe. These seeds cannot be stored for long periods of time.

Cuttings

Cuttings are an excellent way to propagate varieties and cultivars that you really like but that don't come true from seed or don't produce seed at all. Each cutting will grow into a reproduction (clone) of the parent plant. Cuttings are taken from the stems of some perennials and the roots or rhizomes of others.

Stem cuttings are generally taken in spring and early summer. During this time plants produce a flush of fresh, new growth, either before or after flowering. Avoid taking cuttings from plants that are in flower.

Perennials to Start from Stem Cuttings

Artemisia
Aster
Boltonia
Bleeding heart
Campanula
Candytuft
Catmint
Coreopsis
Euphorbia
Helen's flower
Penstemon
Pinks
Rockcress
Sedum 'Autumn Joy'
Thyme
Yarrow

Aster

Catmint

A) Removing lower leaves

B) Dipping in rooting hormone

C) Firming cutting into soil

D) Newly planted cuttings

E) Healthy roots

Plants that are blooming or about to bloom are busy trying to reproduce; plants that are busy growing, by contrast, are already full of the right hormones to promote quick root growth. If you do take cuttings from plants that are flowering, be sure to remove the flowers and buds to divert the plant's energy back into growing roots and leaves.

Because cuttings need to be kept in a warm, humid place to root, they are prone to fungal diseases. Providing proper sanitation (sterile soil mix, clean tools and containers) and encouraging quick rooting will increase the survival rate of your cuttings, but be sure to plant a lot of them to make up for any losses.

Debate exists over what size cuttings should be. Some gardeners claim that smaller cuttings are more likely to root and to root more quickly. Other gardeners claim that larger cuttings develop more roots and become established more quickly when planted in the garden. You may wish to try different sizes to see what works best for you. A small cutting is 1–2" long, and a large cutting is 4–6" long.

Size of cuttings is partly determined by the number of leaf nodes on the cutting. You will want at least three or four nodes on a cutting. The node is where the leaf joins the stem, and it is from here that the new roots will grow. The base of the cutting should be just below a node. Strip the leaves gently from the first and second nodes and plant them below the soil. The above-ground parts of the new plants will grow from the nodes above the soil; keep the leaves in place on these nodes. Some plants have a lot of space between nodes, so that your cutting may be longer than the 1–2" or 4–6" guideline. Conversely, some plants have almost no space at all between nodes. Cut these plants according to the length guidelines, and gently remove the leaves from the lower half of the cutting. Plants with closely spaced nodes often root quickly and abundantly.

Always use a sharp, sterile knife to take cuttings. Cuts should be made straight across the stem. Once you have stripped the leaves, you can dip the end of the cutting into a rooting-hormone powder intended for softwood cuttings. Sprinkle the powder onto a piece of paper and dip the cuttings into it. Discard any extra powder left on the paper to prevent the spread of disease. Tap or blow the extra powder off the cutting. Cuttings caked with rooting hormone are more likely to rot than to root, and they do not root any faster than those that are lightly dusted.

Your cuttings are now prepared for planting. The sooner you plant, the better. The less water the cuttings lose, the less likely they are to wilt and the more quickly they will root. Cuttings can be planted much like seeds. Use a sterile soil mix, intended for seeds or cuttings, in pots or trays. You can also root cuttings in sterilized sand, perlite, vermiculite or a combination of the three.

Firm the soil down and moisten it before you start planting. Poke a hole in the soil with a pencil or similar object, tuck the cutting in and gently firm the soil around it.

Make sure that the lowest leaves do not touch the soil. The cuttings should be spaced far enough apart that adjoining leaves do not touch each other.

Cover the pots or trays with plastic to keep in the humidity. The rigid plastic lids that are available for trays may not be high enough to fit over cuttings, in which case you will have to use a plastic bag. Push stakes or wires into the soil around the edge of the pot or tray so that the plastic will be held off the leaves.

Keep the cuttings in a warm place, about 65°–70° F, in bright indirect light. Keep the soil moist. Use a hand-held mister to gently moisten the soil without disturbing the cuttings. Turn the bag inside out when condensation becomes heavy. A few holes poked in the bag will allow for some ventilation.

Most cuttings require from one to four weeks to root. After two weeks, give the cutting a gentle tug. You will feel resistance if roots have formed. If the cutting feels as though it can pull out of the soil, gently push it back down and leave it longer. New growth is also a good sign that your cutting has rooted. Some gardeners simply leave the cuttings alone until they can see roots through the holes in the bottoms of the pots. Uncover the cuttings once they have developed roots.

When the cuttings are showing new leaf growth, apply a foliar feed using a hand-held mister. Plants quickly absorb nutrients through the leaves, and feeding that way lets you avoid stressing the newly formed roots. Your local garden center should have foliar feeds and information about applying them.

Once your cuttings have rooted and have had a chance to establish, they can be potted individually. If you rooted several cuttings in one pot or tray, you may find that the roots have tangled together. If gentle pulling doesn't separate them, take the entire clump that is tangled together and try rinsing some of the soil away. Enough roots should become freed that you can separate the plants.

Pot the young plants in sterile potting soil. They can be moved into a sheltered area of the garden or a cold frame and grown in pots until they are mature enough to fend for themselves in the garden. The plants may need some protection over the first winter. Keep them in the cold frame if they are still in pots, or give them an extra layer of mulch if they have been planted out.

Basal cuttings involve removing the new growth from the main clump of a plant and rooting it in the same manner as stem cuttings. Many plants send up new shoots or plantlets around their bases. Often, the plantlets will already have a few roots growing. Once separated, these young plants develop quickly and may even grow to flowering size the first summer.

Treat these cuttings in much the same way you would stem cuttings. Use a sterile knife to cut out the shoot. You may have to cut back some of the top growth of the shoot, because the tiny developing roots may not be able to support all of it. Sterile soil mix and humid conditions are preferred. Pot plants individually or place them in soft soil in the garden until new growth appears and roots have developed; then you can transplant to any desired location.

Hens and chicks
Pincushion flower

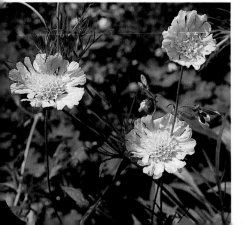

Perennials to Start from Basal Cuttings

Ajuga
Beebalm
Campanula
Catmint
Dead nettle
Euphorbia
Hardy geranium
Hens and chicks
Phlox
Pincushion flower
Sedum

Root cuttings can also be taken from some plants. Dandelions are well known for their ability to propagate this way: even the smallest piece of root left in the ground can sprout a new plant, foiling attempts to eradicate the weed from lawns and flowerbeds. But there are desirable perennials that share this ability.

Cuttings can be taken from the fleshy roots of certain perennials that do not propagate well from stem cuttings. These cuttings should be taken in early or mid-spring when the ground is just starting to warm up and the roots are about to break dormancy. At this time, the roots are full of nutrients, which the plants stored the previous summer and fall, and hormones are initiating growth. You may have to wet the soil around the plant to loosen it enough to get to the roots.

You do not want very young or very old roots. Very young roots are usually white and quite soft; very old ones are tough and woody. The roots you should use will be tan in color and still fleshy.

To prepare your root, cut out the section you will be using with a sterile knife. Cut the root into pieces 1–2" long. Remove any side roots before planting the sections in pots or planting trays. Roots must be planted in a vertical, not horizontal, position, and they need to be kept in the orientation they held when attached to the parent plant. People use different tricks to help them remember which end is up. One method is to cut straight across the tops and diagonally across the bottoms.

You can use the same type of soil mix as you would for starting seeds and stem cuttings. Poke the pieces vertically into the soil, leaving a tiny bit of the end poking up out of the soil. Remember to keep the pieces the right way up. Keep the pots or trays in a warm place out of direct sunlight. They will send up new shoots once they have rooted and can be planted in the same manner as stem cuttings (see p. 49).

The main difference between starting root cuttings and starting stem cuttings is that the root cuttings must be kept fairly dry; they can rot very easily. Keep the roots slightly moist but not wet while you are rooting them, and avoid overwatering as they establish.

Perennials to Start from Root Cuttings

Anemone
Black-eyed Susan
Bleeding heart
Oriental poppy
Phlox
Plume poppy
Primrose

Oriental poppy

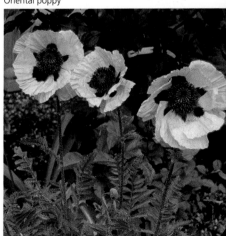

Rhizome cuttings are the easiest means of propagating plants from underground parts. In addition to true roots, some plants have rhizomes, which are thick, fleshy modified stems that grow horizontally underground. A rhizome sends up new shoots at intervals along its length, and in this way the plant spreads. It is easy to take advantage of this feature.

Dig up a section of rhizome when the plant is growing vigorously, usually in late spring or early summer. If you look closely at the rhizome, you will see that it appears to be growing in sections. The places where these sections join are the nodes. It is from these nodes that small, stringy feeder roots extend downwards and new shoots sprout upwards. You may even see small plantlets already sprouting.

Cut your chunk of rhizome into pieces. Each piece should have at least one node in it.

Fill a pot or planting tray to about 1" from the top with perlite, vermiculite or seeding soil. Moisten the soil and let the excess water drain away. Lay the rhizome pieces flat on top of the mix, and almost cover them with more of the soil mix. If you leave a small bit of the top exposed to the light, it will encourage the shoots to sprout. The soil does not have to be kept wet; to avoid having your rhizome rot, moisten it only when it dries out.

Once your rhizome cuttings have established, they can be potted individually and then grown in the same manner as stem cuttings (see p. 49).

Perennials to Propagate from Rhizomes
Bergenia
Campanula
Hardy geranium
Iris
Lily-of-the-valley
Wild ginger

Bergenia

Iris

Division

Division is perhaps the easiest way to propagate perennials. As most perennials grow, they form larger and larger clumps. Dividing this clump periodically will rejuvenate the plant, keep its size in check and provide you with more plants. If a plant you really want is expensive, consider buying only one, because within a few years you may have more than you can handle.

How often, or whether, a perennial needs dividing varies. Some perennials, like astilbes, need dividing almost every year to keep them vigorous. Others, like peonies, should never be divided. They may have a single crown from which the plant grows, or they may simply dislike having their roots disturbed. Still other perennials are content to remain in one spot for a long time, though they can be successfully divided for propagation purposes if desired.

Each entry in this book gives recommendations for division. You can also watch for several signs that indicate a perennial may need dividing:

- the center of the plant has died out
- the plant is no longer flowering as profusely as it did in previous years
- the plant is encroaching on the growing space of other plants sharing the bed.

It is relatively easy to divide perennials. Begin by digging up the entire clump and knocking any large clods of soil away from the rootball. The clump can then be split into several pieces. A small plant with

Digging up perennials for division (above & center)

Clump of stems, roots & crowns (below)

Pulling a clump apart

Cutting apart and dividing tuberous perennials

fibrous roots can be torn into sections by hand. A large plant can be pried apart with a pair of garden forks inserted back to back into the clump. Plants with thicker tuberous or rhizomatous roots can be cut into sections with a sharp, sterile knife. In all cases, cut away any old sections that have died out and replant only the newer, more vigorous sections.

Once your clump has been divided into sections, replant one or two of them into the original location. Take the opportunity to work organic matter into the soil before replanting. The other sections can be moved to new spots in the garden or potted and given away.

Get the sections back into the ground as quickly as possible to prevent the exposed roots from drying out. Plan where you are going to plant your divisions and have the spots prepared before you start digging the plant up. Plant your perennial divisions in pots if you aren't sure where to put them all.

The larger the sections of the division, the more quickly the plant will re-establish and grow to blooming size again. For example, a perennial divided into four sections will bloom sooner than the same one divided into eight sections. Very small divisions may benefit from being planted in pots until they are bigger and better able to fend for themselves in the garden.

Newly planted divisions will need extra care and attention. Water them thoroughly and keep them well watered until they re-establish. As well, for the first few days after planting, give them shade from direct sunlight. A light covering of burlap or damp newspaper should be sufficient to shelter garden transplants for this short period. Divisions that have been planted in pots should be kept in a shaded location.

There is some debate about the best time to divide perennials. Some gardeners prefer to divide perennials while they are dormant, whereas others believe perennials establish more quickly if divided when they are growing vigorously. Still others decide when to divide on the basis of when the plant blooms. These gardeners divide fall bloomers in spring, and divide spring and summer bloomers after they bloom or in fall. You may wish to experiment with dividing at different times of the year to see what works best for you.

Monkshood (above)

Perennials That Should Not Be Divided

Angelica
Baptisia
Butterfly weed
Clematis
Euphorbia
Gaura
Lavender
Meadow rue
Monkshood
Pasqueflower
Perennial salvia
Pinks
Rockrose
Russian sage
Sea holly

Baptisia

Euphorbia

Problems & Pests

Perennial gardens are both an asset and a liability when it comes to pests and diseases. Perennial beds often contain a mixture of different plant species. Many insects and diseases attack only one species of plant, so mixed beds make it difficult for pests and diseases to find their preferred hosts and establish a population. At the same time, because the plants are in the same spot for many years, any problems that do develop can become permanent. Yet, if allowed, beneficial insects, birds and other pest-devouring organisms can also develop permanent populations.

For many years, pest control meant spraying or dusting with the goal to eliminate every insect—the good and the bad—in the garden. A more moderate approach is often advocated today. The goal is now to maintain problems at levels at which negligible damage is done.

Chemicals should be used only as a last resort because they do more harm than good. They endanger the gardener and his or her family, and they kill the good organisms along with the bad, leaving the garden vulnerable to even worse attacks.

A responsible, organic pest-management program has four steps. Cultural controls are the most important. Physical controls should be attempted next, followed by biological controls. Chemical controls should be used only when the first three possibilities have been exhausted.

Cultural controls are the gardening techniques you use in the day-to-day care of your garden. To prevent pest and disease problems, one essential such technique is growing perennials in the conditions they prefer. As well, many diseases can be prevented or even cured by establishing a vigorous microbial population in the soil. Adding compost to the soil annually is an excellent way to keep soil healthy. It also helps to spray compost 'tea' onto the plants' foliage; make compost tea by simply soaking some compost in a bucket of water and then straining it out.

Most cultural controls are simple and straightforward. Choose resistant varieties of perennials that are not prone to problems. Space perennials so that they have good air circulation around them and are not stressed from competing for light, nutrients and space. Remove plants from the garden if they are constantly decimated by the same pests every year. Remove and destroy diseased foliage. Prevent the spread of disease by keeping your gardening tools clean and by tidying up fallen leaves and dead plant matter at the end of the growing season.

Physical controls are generally used to combat insect and mammal pest problems. An example of such a control is picking insects off plants by hand, which is not as daunting a solution as it seems if you catch the problem when it is just beginning. Other physical controls include traps, barriers, scarecrows and natural repellants that make a plant taste or smell bad to pests. Garden centers offer a wide array of such devices. Physical control of diseases usually necessitates removing the infected plant or parts of the plant in order to keep the problem from spreading.

Biological controls make use of populations of natural predators.

Frogs eat many insect pests.

Such animals as birds, snakes, frogs, spiders, lady beetles and certain bacteria can help keep pest populations at a manageable level. Encourage these creatures to take up permanent residence in your garden. A birdbath and birdfeeder will encourage birds to enjoy your yard and feed on a wide variety of insect pests. Beneficial insects are probably already living in your garden, and you can encourage them to stay and multiply by planting appropriate food sources. For example, many beneficial insects eat nectar from flowers such as yarrow and daisies.

Chemical controls should rarely be necessary in a perennial garden, but if you feel you must use them, some 'organic' options should be available at local garden centers. Organic sprays are no less dangerous than synthetic chemical ones, but they are made from natural sources and will eventually break down into harmless compounds. The main drawback to using any chemicals is that they also kill the beneficial insects you have been trying to attract to your garden. Make sure when using chemicals to apply them in the recommended amounts (more is not better), and to use them to combat only the pests listed on the package. Proper and early identification of problems is vital in finding a quick solution.

Glossary of Pests & Diseases

Anthracnose

Fungus. Yellow or brown spots on leaves; sunken lesions and blisters on stems; can kill plant.

What to Do: Choose resistant varieties and cultivars; keep soil well drained; thin out stems to improve air circulation; avoid handling wet foliage. Remove and destroy infected plant parts; clean up and destroy debris from infected plants at end of growing season.

Aphids

Tiny, pear-shaped insects, winged or wingless; green, black, brown, red or gray. Cluster along stems, on buds and on leaves. Suck sap from plants; cause distorted or stunted growth. Sticky honeydew forms on surfaces and encourages sooty mold growth. Woolly adelgids are a type of aphid.

What to Do: Squish small colonies by hand; dislodge with brisk water spray; encourage predatory insects and birds that feed on aphids; spray serious infestations

Green aphids

with insecticidal soap or neem oil
according to package directions.

Aster Yellows
see Viruses

Beetles
Many types and sizes; usually
rounded in shape with hard, shell-
like outer wings covering mem-
branous inner wings. Some are
beneficial, e.g., ladybird beetles
('ladybugs'). Others, e.g., Japanese
beetles, blister beetles, leaf
skeletonizers and weevils, eat
plants. Larvae: see Borers, Grubs.
Leave wide range of chewing damage: make small or large holes in or
around margins of leaves; consume
entire leaves or areas between leaf
veins ('skeletonize'); may also chew
holes in flowers. Some beetles carry
deadly plant diseases.

What to Do: Pick beetles off at
night and drop them into an old
coffee can half filled with soapy
water (soap prevents them from
floating and climbing out).

Blight
Fungal diseases, many types; e.g.,
leaf blight, snow blight, tip blight.
Leaves, stems and flowers blacken,
rot and die.

What to Do: Thin stems to
improve air circulation; keep mulch
away from base of plants; remove
debris from garden at end of growing season. Remove and destroy
infected plant parts.

Borers
Larvae of some moths, wasps and
beetles; among the most damaging

Ladybird beetle

Beneficial ladybird beetle larva

Japanese beetles

Beneficial predatory ground beetle

Lygus bug may disfigure flowers.

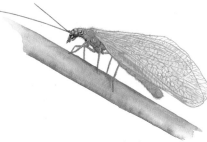

Green lacewing is a beneficial predator in the garden.

Harlequin bug is a garden pest.

plant pests. Worm-like; vary in size and get bigger as they bore through plant. Burrow into stems, leaves and/or roots, destroying conducting tissue and structural strength; leave tunnels that create sites for infection.

What to Do: Keep plants as healthy as possible with proper fertilizing and watering; control parent populations before eggs laid; may be able to squish within leaves. Remove and destroy infected plant parts; may need to remove entire plant.

Bugs (True Bugs)

Small insects, up to $1/2$" long; green, brown, black or brightly colored and patterned. Many beneficial; a few pests, such as lace bugs, pierce plants to suck out sap. Toxins may be injected that deform plants; sunken areas left where pierced; leaves rip as they grow; leaves, buds and new growth may be dwarfed and deformed.

What to Do: Remove debris and weeds from around plants in fall to destroy overwintering sites. Spray plants with insecticidal soap or neem oil according to directions.

Canker

Swollen or sunken lesions, often on stems, caused by many different bacterial and fungal diseases. Most canker-causing diseases enter through wounds.

What to Do: Maintain plant vigor; avoid causing wounds; control borers and other tissue-dwelling pests. Prune out and destroy infected plant parts. Sterilize pruning tools before and after use.

Caterpillars

Larvae of butterflies, moths, sawflies. Include bagworms, budworms, case bearers, cutworms, leaf rollers, leaf tiers, loopers. Chew foliage and buds; can completely defoliate plant if infestation severe.

What to Do: Removal from plant is best control. Use high-pressure water and soap or pick caterpillars off small plants by hand. Control biologically using the naturally occurring soil bacterium *Bacillus thuringiensis* var. *kurstaki* or *B.t.* for short (commercially available), which breaks down gut lining of caterpillars.

Clubroot

see Galls

Damping Off

see p. 45

Galls

Unusual swellings of plant tissues; may be caused by insects, such as *Hemerocallis* gall midge, or diseases. Can affect leaves, buds, stems, flowers, fruit. Often a specific gall affects a single genus or species.

What to Do: Cut galls out of plant and destroy them. Galls caused by insects usually contain the insect's eggs and juvenile stages. Prevent such galls by controlling insects before they lay eggs; otherwise try to remove and destroy infected tissue before young insects emerge. Generally insect galls are more unsightly than damaging to plant. Galls caused by diseases often require destruction of plant. Avoid placing

Caterpillar eating flowers

other plants susceptible to same disease in that location.

Gray Mold

Fuzzy gray fungus that coats flowers or fruits. Common in wet weather.

What to Do: Prevent disease by encouraging good air circulation; avoid handling wet plants; remove infected plant material.

Grubs

Larvae of different beetles, commonly found below soil level; usually curled in C-shape. Body white or gray; head may be white, gray, brown or reddish. Problematic in lawns; may feed on roots of perennials. Plant wilts despite regular watering; may pull easily out of ground in severe cases.

What to Do: Toss any grubs found while digging onto a stone path, driveway or patio for birds to devour; apply parasitic nematodes or milky spore to infested soil (ask at your local garden center).

Leaf Blotch

see Leaf Spot

Spittle mass can be washed away.

Leafhoppers & Treehoppers

Small, wedge-shaped insects; green, brown, gray or multi-colored. Example: spittlebugs. Jump around frantically when disturbed. Suck juice from leaves, cause distorted growth, carry diseases such as aster yellows.

What to Do: Encourage predators by planting nectar-producing species like yarrow. Wash insects off with strong spray of water; spray with insecticidal soap or neem oil according to package directions.

Leaf Miners

Tiny, stubby larvae of some butterflies and moths; may be yellow or

Leaf miner tunnels

green. Tunnel within leaves leaving winding trails; tunneled areas lighter in color than rest of leaf. Unsightly rather than major risk to plant.

What to Do: Remove debris from area in fall to destroy overwintering sites; attract parasitic wasps with nectar plants such as yarrow. Remove and destroy infected foliage; can sometimes squish by hand within leaf.

Leaf Spot

Two common types. *Bacterial:* small brown or purple spots grow to encompass entire leaves; leaves may drop. *Fungal:* black, brown or yellow spots; leaves wither; e.g., scab, tar spot, leaf blotch.

What to Do: Bacterial infection more severe; must remove entire plant. For fungal infection, remove and destroy infected plant parts. Sterilize removal tools; avoid wetting foliage or touching wet foliage; remove and destroy debris at end of growing season.

Mealybugs

Tiny crawling insects related to aphids; appear to be covered with white fuzz or flour. Sucking damage stunts and stresses plant. Excrete honeydew that promotes growth of sooty mold.

What to Do: Remove by hand from smaller plants; wash plant off with soap and water; wipe off with alcohol-soaked swabs; remove heavily infested leaves; encourage or introduce natural predators such as mealybug destroyer beetle and parasitic wasps (available at garden centers); spray with insecticidal soap. *Note:* larvae of mealybug destroyer beetles look like very large mealybugs.

Mildew
Two types, both caused by fungus, but with slightly different symptoms. *Downy mildew:* yellow spots on upper sides of leaves and downy fuzz on undersides; fuzz may be yellow, white or gray. *Powdery mildew:* white or gray powdery coating on leaf surfaces, doesn't brush off.

What to Do: Choose resistant cultivars; space plants well; thin stems to encourage air circulation; tidy any debris in fall. Remove and destroy infected leaves or other parts.

Powdery mildew

Mites
Tiny, eight-legged relatives of spiders; do not eat insects, but may spin webs. Almost invisible to naked eye; red, yellow or green; usually found on undersides of plant leaves. Examples: bud mites, spider mites. Suck juice out of leaves. May see fine webbing on leaves and stems; may see mites moving on leaf undersides; leaves become discolored and speckled, then turn brown and shrivel up.

What to Do: Wash off with strong spray of water daily until all signs of infestation are gone; introduce predatory mites available from garden centers; spray plants with insecticidal soap.

Nematodes
Tiny worms that give plants disease symptoms. One type infects foliage and stems; the other infects roots. *Foliar:* yellow spots that turn brown on leaves; leaves shrivel; problem starts on lowest leaves and works up plant. *Root-knot:* plant is stunted, may wilt; yellow spots on leaves; roots have tiny bumps or knots.

What to Do: Mulch soil; add organic matter; clean up debris in fall; don't touch wet foliage of infected plants. Can add parasitic nematodes to soil. Remove infected plants in extreme cases.

Rot
Several different fungi that affect different parts of plant and can kill plant. *Crown rot (stem rot):* affects base of plant, causing stems to blacken and fall over and leaves to yellow and wilt. *Root rot:* leaves yellow and plant wilts; digging up plant shows roots rotted away. *White rot:* a 'watery decay fungus' that affects any part of part; cell walls appear to break down, releasing fluids.

What to Do: Keep soil well drained; don't damage plant if you are digging around it; keep mulches away from plant base. Destroy plant if whole plant affected.

Snail eating leaf

Rust

Fungi. Pale spots on upper leaf surfaces; orange, fuzzy or dusty spots on leaf undersides. Examples: blister rust, hollyhock rust.

What to Do: Choose rust-resistant varieties and cultivars; avoid handling wet leaves; provide plant with good air circulation; clear up garden debris at end of season. Remove and destroy infected plant parts.

Scale Insects

Tiny, shelled insects that suck sap, weakening and possibly killing plant or making it vulnerable to other problems. Once female scale insect has pierced plant with mouthpart, it is there for life. Juvenile scale insects are called crawlers.

What to Do: Wipe off using alcohol-soaked swabs; spray with water to dislodge crawlers; prune heavily infested branches; encourage natural predators and parasites; spray dormant oil in spring before bud break.

Slugs & Snails

Both mollusks; slugs lack shells, snails have spiral shells. Up to 8" long, many smaller. Slimy, smooth skin; gray, green, black, beige, yellow or spotted. Leave large, ragged holes in leaves and silvery slime trails on and around plants.

What to Do: Attach strips of copper to wood around raised beds or to smaller boards inserted around susceptible groups of plants; slugs and snails get shocked if they try to cross copper surfaces. Pick off by hand in the evening and squish with your boot or drop in can of soapy water. Spread wood ash or diatomaceous earth (available in garden centers) on ground around plants; it will pierce their soft bodies and dehydrate them. Slug baits containing iron phosphate are not harmful to humans or animals and control slugs very well when used according to package directions. If slugs damaged garden last season, begin controls as soon as new green shoots appear in spring.

Smut

Fungus. May cause galls or streaking on leaves.

What to Do: Treat as for rust.

Sooty Mold

Fungus. Thin black film forms on leaf surfaces and reduces amount of light getting to leaf surfaces.

What to Do: Wipe mold off leaf surfaces; control insects like aphids, mealybugs, whiteflies (honeydew they deposit on leaves encourages mold growth).

Thrips

Tiny, slender insects, difficult to see; may be visible if you disturb them by blowing gently on an infested flower. Yellow, black or brown; narrow, fringed wings. Suck juice out of plant cells, particularly in buds and flowers, causing mottled petals and leaves, dying buds, distorted and stunted growth.

What to Do: Remove and destroy infected plant parts; encourage native predatory insects with nectar plants like yarrow; spray severe infestations with insecticidal soap or neem oil according to package directions.

Viruses

Plant may be stunted and leaves and flowers distorted, streaked or discolored. Examples: aster yellows, mosaic virus, ringspot virus.

What to Do: Viral diseases in plants cannot be treated. Control insects that spread disease, such as aphids, leafhoppers and whiteflies. Destroy infected plants.

Weevils

see Beetles

Whiteflies

Flying insects that flutter up into the air when plant is disturbed. Tiny, moth-like, white; live on undersides of plant leaves. Suck juice out of leaves, causing yellowed leaves and weakened growth; deposit sticky honeydew on leaves, encouraging sooty mold.

What to Do: Destroy weeds where insects may live. Attract native predatory beetles and parasitic wasps with nectar plants like yarrow; spray severe cases with insecticidal soap. Can make a sticky flypaper-like trap by mounting tin can on stake; wrap can with yellow paper and cover with clear plastic bag smeared with petroleum jelly; replace bag when covered in flies.

Wilt

If watering doesn't help wilted plant, one of two wilt fungi may be at fault. *Fusarium* wilt: plant wilts, leaves turn yellow then die; symptoms generally appear first on one part of plant before spreading. *Verticillium* wilt: plant wilts; leaves curl up at edges; leaves turn yellow then drop off; plant may die.

What to Do: Both wilts difficult to control. Choose resistant plant varieties and cultivars; clean up debris at end of growing season. Destroy infected plants; solarize (sterilize) soil before replanting (may help if entire bed of plants lost to these fungi)—contact local garden center for assistance.

You can make your own insecticidal soap at home. Mix 1 tsp of mild dish detergent or pure soap (biodegradable options are available) with 1 qt of water in a clean spray bottle. Spray the surfaces of your plants and rinse well within an hour of spraying to avoid foliage discoloration.

About This Guide

The perennials in this book are organized alphabetically by their most familiar common names. Additional common names and scientific names appear after the primary reference. The illustrated **Flowers at a Glance** at the beginning of the book allows you to become familiar with the different flowers quickly, and it will help you find a plant if you're not sure what it's called.

Clearly indicated at the beginning of each entry are height and spread ranges, flower colors, blooming times and hardiness zones. At the back of the book, you will find a **Quick Reference Chart** that summarizes different features and requirements of the plants; you will find this chart handy when planning diversity in your garden.

Each entry gives clear instructions and tips for planting and growing the perennial, and it recommends many of our favorite species and varieties. *Note:* If height or spread ranges or hardiness zones are not given for a recommended plant, assume these values are the same as the ranges at the beginning of the entry. Keep in mind, too, that many more hybrids, cultivars and varieties are often available. Check with your local greenhouses or garden centers when making your selection.

Pests or diseases commonly associated with a perennial, if any, are also listed for each entry. Consult the 'Problems & Pests' section of the introduction for information on how to solve these problems.

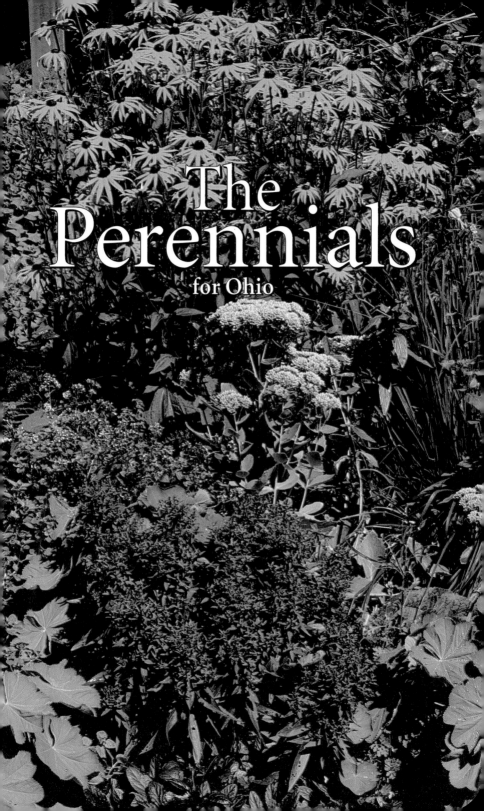

The Perennials
for Ohio

Ajuga
Bugleweed
Ajuga

Height: 3–12" **Spread:** 6–36" **Flower color:** purple, blue, pink, white; plant grown for foliage **Blooms:** late spring to early summer **Zones:** 3–8

WHY HAVE GRASS WHEN YOU CAN COVER THE GROUND WITH these lovely ramblers? Often labeled as rampant runners, ajugas are best used where they can roam freely. I have found that they can easily be removed from places they aren't wanted. The new cultivar *A. reptans* 'Chocolate Chip' is a wonderful edging plant with slightly better manners than its aggressive cousins. In my garden I have interplanted the sweetly scented Petrel daffodil with *A. reptans* 'Burgundy Glow.' The ajuga's variegated foliage and blue flowers combine beautifully with the white daffodil in spring.

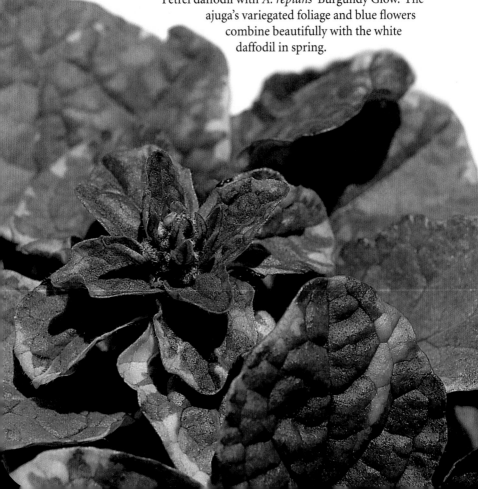

Planting

Seeding: Not recommended; foliage often reverts to green in seedlings

Planting out: Spring, summer or fall

Spacing: 12–18"

Growing

Ajugas develop the best leaf color in **partial or light shade** but tolerate full shade. The leaves may become scorched when exposed to too much sun. Any **well-drained** soil is suitable. Winter protection, such as evergreen branches laid across the plants, is recommended if snow cover isn't dependable in your garden. Divide these vigorous plants any time during the growing season.

Remove any new growth or seedlings that don't show the hybrid leaf coloring.

Tips

Ajugas make excellent groundcovers for difficult sites, such as exposed slopes and dense shade. They are also attractive groundcovers in shrub borders, where their dense growth will prevent the spread of all but the most tenacious weeds.

If you plant ajugas next to a lawn, you may soon be calling them weeds. Because they spread

A. reptans 'Chocolate Chip'

An ajuga syrup has been used to cure hangovers.

A. reptans with *Achillea filipendulina*

A. genevensis

A. reptans cultivars

A. reptans *is widely used in homeopathic remedies for throat and mouth irritations.*

A. reptans with Antirrhinum

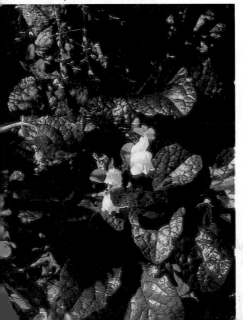

readily by stolons (creeping, above-ground shoots), these plants can easily invade a lawn, and their low growth escapes mower blades. The spread of ajugas may be somewhat controlled by the use of bed-edging materials. If an ajuga does start to take over, however, it is easy to rip out, and the soil it leaves behind will be soft and loose from the penetrating roots. Use an ajuga as a scout plant to send ahead and prepare the soil before you plant anything fussier in a shaded or woodland garden.

If you're not obsessive about edging beds, plant these aggressive growers in areas bordered by brick or cement. Close spacing and regular watering helps these plants spread quickly and fill in, preventing weeds from springing up among the groundcover.

Recommended

A. genevensis (Geneva bugleweed) is an upright, noninvasive species that grows 6–12" tall and spreads 18". The spring flowers are blue, white or pink. Because this species is less invasive than *A. reptans,* it is more suitable for a rock garden or near a lawn.

A. pyramidalis 'Metallica Crispa' (upright bugleweed) is a very slow-growing plant with bronzy, crinkly foliage. It grows to 3–5" tall and spreads to 6–10" in three years. The violet blue flowers contrast beautifully with the foliage. This plant prefers a shady, moist spot in the garden.

A. reptans is the ajuga most people plant. It is a low, quick-spreading groundcover that grows about 6" tall and spreads 18–24". **'Braunherz'** ('Bronze Heart') is an excellent, purple-bronze cultivar with bright blue flowers. It remains compact and richly colored all year. **'Burgundy Glow'** has variegated foliage in shades of bronze, green, white and pink. The habit is dense and compact. **'Caitlin's Giant'** has large, bronze leaves. It bears short spikes of bright blue flowers in spring. **'Chocolate Chip'** has a low, creeping form, 6" tall and up to 36" in spread, with chocolaty bronze, teardrop-shaped leaves. It bears spikes of blue flowers in early summer. **'Multicolor'** ('Rainbow,' 'Tricolor') is a vigorous spreader. Its bronze leaves are splashed with pink and white. **'Variegata'** is dense and slow growing. The green leaves have silver margins.

A. reptans (this page)

Problems & Pests

Occasional problems with crown rot, leaf spot and root rot can be avoided by providing good air circulation and by ensuring the plant is not standing in water for extended periods.

According to European folk myths, ajugas could cause fires if brought into the house.

Anemone
Windflower
Anemone

Height: 3"–5' **Spread:** 6–24" **Flower color:** white, pink, blue
Blooms: spring, summer, early fall **Zones:** 5–8

ALL THE ANEMONES LEND A SENSE OF REFINEMENT TO THE GARDEN.
These modest plants often serve as backdrops for showier plants. The white
species and cultivars sparkle as their petals reflect the light of the sun. The
early Grecian windflower signals the beginning of spring, first with ferny
mounds of foliage and then with delicate, short-lived blooms. Near the end
of the growing season, the Japanese anemone blooms as the days shorten.
This hybrid and its cultivars bear more substantial foliage and flowers, as if
in preparation for the coming winter.

Planting

Seeding: Not recommended

Planting out: Spring

Spacing: 4–18"

Growing

Anemones prefer **partial or light shade** but tolerate full sun with adequate moisture. The soil should be of **average to high fertility, humus rich** and **moist**. Grecian windflower prefers a light, sandy soil. Meadow anemone needs regular watering when first planted in order to become established. While dormant, anemones should have dry soil. Mulch Japanese anemone the first winter to help it establish.

Divide Grecian windflower in summer and other anemones in spring or fall.

Deadhead only to keep a tidy look, because removing spent flowers will not extend the bloom. A few anemones produce small, fluffball-like seedheads, which add another point of interest to the garden.

A. x hybrida (this page)

A. x hybrida

*The name anemone
(a-nem-o-nee) comes from
the Greek anemos, 'wind.'
It may refer to the windswept
mountainside habitat of some
species or to the plumed seeds
that float on the breeze.*

A. canadensis

Tips

Anemones make beautiful additions
to lightly shaded borders, woodland
gardens and rock gardens. Be careful
with *A. canadensis,* because it tends
to spread. It is best used as a groundcover in a well-mannered perennial
garden, not as an edging plant.

Recommended

A. blanda (Grecian windflower) is a
low, spreading, tuberous species that
bears blue flowers in spring. It grows
6–8" tall, with an equal spread. '**Pink
Star**' has pink flowers with yellow
centers. '**White Splendor**' is a vigorous plant with white flowers.

A. canadensis (meadow anemone) is
a spreading native plant with slightly
invasive tendencies. It grows 12–24"
tall and wide. The white flowers have
yellow centers and are borne in late
spring and early summer.

A. x *hybrida* (Japanese anemone,
hybrid anemone) is an upright,
suckering hybrid. It grows 2–5' tall,
spreads about 24" and bears pink or

white flowers from late summer to early fall. Many cultivars are available. '**Honorine Jobert**,' one of the oldest cultivars, has plentiful white flowers. '**Max Vogel**' has large pink flowers. '**Pamina**' has pinkish red double flowers. '**Whirlwind**' has white, semi-double flowers.

A. nemerosa (wood anemone) is a low, creeping perennial that grows 3–10" tall and spreads 12" or more. The spring flowers are white, often flushed with pink. '**Flore Pleno**' has double white flowers. '**Rosea**' has red-purple flowers.

Problems & Pests

Rare but possible problems include leaf gall, downy mildew, smut, fungal leaf spot, powdery mildew, rust, nematodes, caterpillars, slugs and flea beetles.

A. x *hybrida*

A. blanda 'White Splendor'

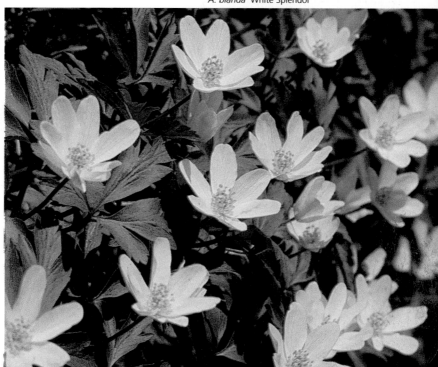

Angelica
Angelica

Height: 3–8' **Spread:** 1–4' **Flower color:** yellow-green, white, purple
Blooms: summer **Zones:** 4–8

BOLD IS THE WORD FOR THESE TOWERING, STATELY PLANTS.
Angelicas' large, intricately dissected leaves complement large clusters of
green to deep maroon flowers. *A. gigas* is a showstopper with deeply colored
stems and flowers. Plant it in combination with garden heliotrope *(Valeriana
officinalis)*, and enjoy the interplay of the angelica's maroon flowers and
stems with the heliotrope's white blooms. *A. archangelica* is a bit more sub-
dued but still very effective when combined with herbs and perennials that
tolerate shadier conditions.

Planting

Seeding: Start freshly
ripened seed in a cold
frame in fall or early
spring

Planting out: Spring

Spacing: 2–5'

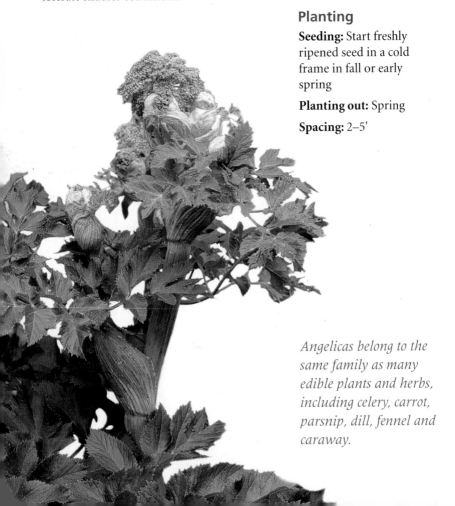

*Angelicas belong to the
same family as many
edible plants and herbs,
including celery, carrot,
parsnip, dill, fennel and
caraway.*

Growing

Angelicas grow well in **full sun** or **partial shade,** preferring some afternoon shade. The soil should be **fertile** and **moist,** though some drought is tolerated. These plants develop a long taproot and resent being moved or divided. Plant out the seedlings while they are still small.

A. archangelica may live for several years but will die once it has flowered and set seed. Remove the flowerheads before seed sets to extend the plant's life, or allow the plant to set seed and self-sow.

Tips

Angelicas' dense clump of attractive, scented foliage and affinity for moist soil make these excellent plants to use near a water feature. If kept well watered, they will thrive in a mixed or herbaceous border or in a woodland garden. Angelicas make wonderful additions to a shady herb garden.

Recommended

A. archangelica (angelica, European angelica) grows 3–8' tall, with a spread of up to 4'. It forms a mound of large, deeply cut foliage, with yellow-green flowers in large, rounded clusters atop tall, strong stems. It flowers the second year from seed in early to mid-summer.

A. atropurpurea (wild angelica, American angelica) is a clump-forming North American native. It grows 4–6' tall and spreads about 3'. The stems are purple and the early-summer flowers are white or greenish white.

A. gigas (Korean angelica) forms a large clump of foliage. It grows 5–6' tall and spreads 3–4'. Tall red stems bear clusters of purple flowers in mid- and late summer.

Problems & Pests

Occasional problems with powdery mildew, spider mites, aphids, leaf miners and leaf spot can occur.

A. archangelica (this page)

All parts of A. archangelica *have a licorice scent. The plant is edible as a potherb, and the stems can be candied and used to decorate cakes. The species has a long history of use in Chinese medicine.*

Artemisia
Wormwood, Sage, Dusty Miller
Artemisia

Height: 6"–6' **Spread:** 12–36" **Flower color:** white or yellow, generally inconspicuous; plant grown for foliage **Blooms:** late summer, mid-fall
Zones: 3–8

MOST OF THE ARTEMISIAS ARE VALUED FOR THEIR SILVERY FOLIAGE, not for their flowers. Silver is the ultimate blending color in the garden, seeming to enhance every other hue combined with it. One of my first artemisias was the tough, low-mounded *A. schmidtiana* 'Nana.' It survived hot, dry summers and cold winters in poor soil and looked great. But when I moved it to a better location, it died. This was Mother Nature's lesson: leave well enough alone! The giant of this genus is *A. lactiflora*. Its showy plumes of white flowers look beautiful in the back of the perennial border. Unfortunately, the deer in my neighborhood consider it a delicacy and routinely eat it to the ground in late spring.

Planting
Seeding: Not recommended

Planting out: Spring, summer or fall

Spacing: 10–36"

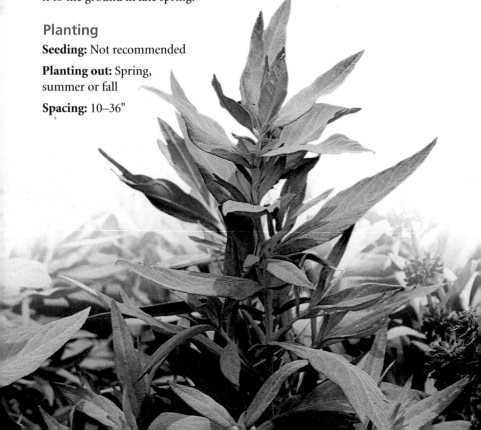

Growing

Artemisias grow best in **full sun**. The soil should be of **low to average fertility** and **well drained**. These plants dislike wet, humid conditions.

Artemisias respond well to pruning in late spring. If you prune before May, frost may kill any new growth. Whenever artemisias begin to look straggly, they may be cut back hard to encourage new growth and maintain a neater form. Divide every one or two years when plants appear to be thinning in the centers.

Tips

Use artemisias in rock gardens and borders. Their silvery gray foliage makes them good backdrop plants to use behind brightly colored flowers. They are also useful for filling in spaces between other plants. Smaller forms may be used to create knot gardens.

Some species can become invasive. If you want to control horizontal spreading of a rhizomatous artemisia, plant it in a bottomless container. Sunk into the ground, the hidden container prevents the plant from spreading beyond the container's edges. You can maintain good drainage by removing the bottom of the container.

Recommended

A. absinthium (common wormwood) is a clump-forming, woody-based perennial that grows 24–36" tall and about 24" in spread. It has aromatic, hairy gray foliage and bears inconspicuous yellow flowers

A. ludoviciana cultivar

A. absinthium *lent its name and its flavor to the liqueur absinthe, which was once popular in France. Absinthe containing the wormwood toxin thujone is illegal to sell in the U.S.*

A. schmidtiana 'Nana'

A. ludoviciana 'Valerie Finnis'

There are almost 300 species of Artemisia *distributed around the world.*

A. ludoviciana with *Phlox & Malva*

in late summer. '**Lambrook Silver**' has attractive, silver gray foliage. (Zones 4–8)

A. lactiflora (white mugwort) is an upright, clump-forming species 4–6' tall and 24–36" in spread. It is one of the few artemisias to bear showy flowers; its attractive, creamy white blooms appear from late summer to mid-fall. The foliage of this hardy species is dark green or gray-green. '**Guizho**' is an outstanding cultivar with dark green foliage and reddish stems that contrast well with its creamy flowers. (Zones 3–8)

A. ludoviciana (white sage, silver sage) is an upright, clump-forming plant. It grows 2–4' tall and 24" in spread. The foliage is silvery white and the flowers are inconspicuous. The species is not grown as often as the cultivars. '**Silver Frost**' has narrow leaves that give the plant a soft, feathery appearance. It grows 18–24" tall, with an equal spread. '**Valerie Finnis**' is a good choice for hot, dry areas. It has very wide, silvery leaves, is less invasive than the species and combines beautifully with many other perennials. (Zones 4–8)

A. '**Powis Castle**' is compact, mounding and shrubby, reaching 24–36" in height and spread. It has feathery, silvery gray foliage and inconspicuous flowers. This cultivar is reliably hardy to Zone 6, but with winter protection in a sheltered site it is worth trying in colder regions.

A. schmidtiana (silvermound artemisia) is a low, dense, mound-forming perennial 12–24" tall and 12–18" wide. The foliage is feathery, hairy and silvery gray. 'Nana' (dwarf silver-mound) is very compact and grows only half the size of the species. This cultivar is extremely hardy, but highly susceptible to crown rot in wet soils. (Zones 3–8)

A. stelleriana 'Silver Brocade' is a low, somewhat spreading cultivar about 6" tall and up to 18" in spread. Its soft, pale gray leaves have rounded lobes. This cultivar is very hardy. Plant several, as it is a favorite food of American lady butterfly larvae. (Zones 3–8)

Problems & Pests
Rust, downy mildew and other fungi can cause problems for artemisias.

A. *lactiflora*

A. *ludoviciana* cultivar

Aster

Aster

Height: 10"–5' **Spread:** 18–36" **Flower color:** red, white, blue, purple, pink; often with yellow centers **Blooms:** late summer to mid-fall **Zones:** 3–8

AMONG THE LAST PLANTS TO BLOOM BEFORE THE SNOW FLIES, asters are often the last meal for migrating butterflies. Many garden asters are native to the United States. English and German gardeners have so loved our asters that they imported them, improved them and then sold them back to us! The flower colors range from bright purples and magentas to cool whites. One of my favorites is *A. novae-angliae* 'Purple Dome.' Combine it with *Sedum* 'Autumn Joy' and maiden grass (*Miscanthus sinensis* 'Malepartus'), and you have a beautiful fall scene. Most of the asters are sun lovers, but the white wood aster prefers shade. It is lovely combined with *Anemone* x *hybrida* 'Honorine Jobert' for a white garden in late summer to fall.

Planting

Seeding: Not recommended

Planting out: Spring or fall

Spacing: 18–36"

Growing

Asters prefer **full sun** but tolerate **partial shade.** The soil should be **fertile, moist** and **well drained.** Pinch or shear these plants back in early summer to promote dense growth and reduce disease problems. Mulch in winter to protect plants from temperature fluctuations. Divide every two to three years to maintain vigor and control spread.

Tips

Asters can be used in the middle of borders and in cottage gardens. These plants can also be naturalized in wild gardens.

A. novi-belgii (this page)

These old-fashioned flowers were once called starworts because of the many petals that radiate out from the center of the flowerhead.

Recommended

Some *Aster* species have recently been reclassified under the genus *Symphyotrichum*. You may see both names at garden centers.

A. divaricatus (white wood aster) is a spreading aster that tolerates shade. It grows 12–24" tall and spreads to 36". The flowers are tiny white stars with yellow centers. The stems tend to sprawl, but they can be controlled by pruning them by half in early to mid-June.

A. novae-angliae (Michaelmas daisy, New England aster) is an upright, spreading, clump-forming perennial that grows to 5' and spreads 24". It bears yellow-centered purple flowers. 'Alma Potschke' bears bright salmon pink or cherry red flowers. It grows 3–4' tall and spreads 24". The dwarf 'Purple Dome' bears dark purple flowers. It grows 18–24" tall and spreads 24–30". This cultivar is resistant to mildew.

A. novae-angliae
A. novi-belgii

A. novi-belgii (Michaelmas daisy, New York aster) is a dense, upright, clump-forming perennial with purple flowers. It grows 3–4' tall and spreads 18–36". **'Alice Haslam'** is a dwarf plant with bright pink flowers. It grows 10–18" tall and spreads 18". **'Chequers'** is a compact plant with purple flowers.

Problems & Pests

Powdery mildew, aster wilt, aster yellows, aphids, mites, slugs and nematodes can cause trouble.

What looks like a single flower of an aster, or of other daisy-like plants, is actually a cluster of many tiny flowers. Look closely at the center of the flowerhead and you will see all the individual florets.

A. novae-angliae
A. novi-belgii

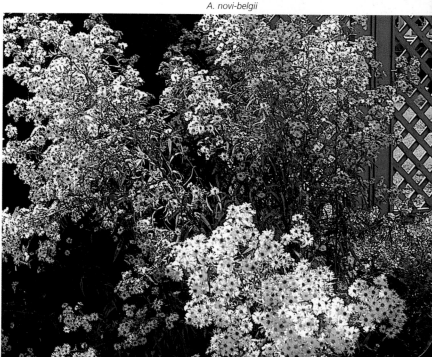

Astilbe
Astilbe

Height: 10"–4' **Spread:** 8–36" **Flower color:** white, pink, peach, purple, red
Blooms: late spring, summer **Zones:** 3–9

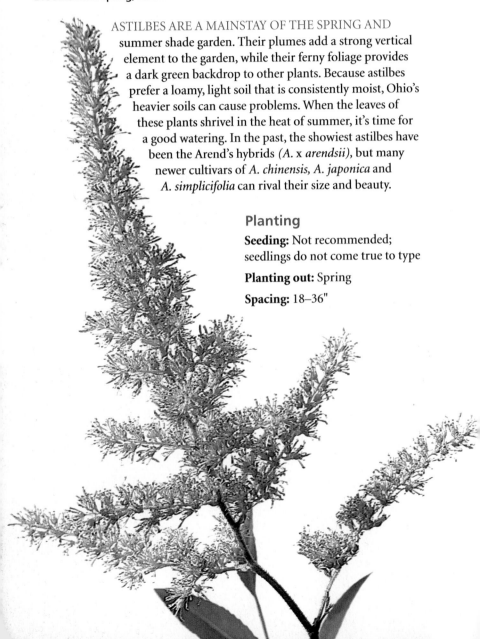

ASTILBES ARE A MAINSTAY OF THE SPRING AND summer shade garden. Their plumes add a strong vertical element to the garden, while their ferny foliage provides a dark green backdrop to other plants. Because astilbes prefer a loamy, light soil that is consistently moist, Ohio's heavier soils can cause problems. When the leaves of these plants shrivel in the heat of summer, it's time for a good watering. In the past, the showiest astilbes have been the Arend's hybrids (*A.* x *arendsii*), but many newer cultivars of *A. chinensis, A. japonica* and *A. simplicifolia* can rival their size and beauty.

Planting

Seeding: Not recommended; seedlings do not come true to type

Planting out: Spring

Spacing: 18–36"

Growing

Astilbes enjoy **light or partial shade** and tolerate full shade, though flowering is reduced in deep shade. The soil should be **fertile, humus rich, acidic, moist** and **well drained.** Astilbes like to grow near water sources, such as ponds and streams, but they dislike standing in water. Provide a mulch in summer to keep the roots cool and moist.

Divide every three years in spring or fall to maintain plant vigor.

Tips

Astilbes can be grown near the edges of bog gardens or ponds, in woodland gardens and in shaded borders.

The root crown of an astilbe tends to lift out of the soil as the plant grows bigger. This problem can be solved by applying a top dressing of rich soil as a mulch when the plant starts lifting or by lifting the entire plant and replanting it deeper into the soil.

A. x *arendsii* (this page)

In late summer, transplant seedlings found near the parent plant for plumes of color throughout the garden.

A. x *arendsii* (above & next page)
A. japonica 'Deutschland'

Astilbe flowers fade to various shades of brown. Deadheading will not extend the bloom, so the choice is yours whether to remove the spent blossoms. Astilbes self-seed easily, and their flowerheads look interesting and natural in the garden well into fall. Self-seeded plants are unlikely to resemble the parent plant.

Recommended

A. x *arendsii* (astilbe, false spirea, Arend's astilbe) grows 18"–4' tall and spreads 18–36". Many cultivars are available from this group of hybrids, including the following selections. 'Avalanche' bears white flowers in late summer. **'Bressingham Beauty'** bears bright pink flowers in mid-summer. 'Cattleya' bears reddish pink flowers in mid-summer. **'Fanal'** bears red flowers in early summer and has deep bronze foliage. **'Weisse Gloria'** bears creamy white flowers in mid- to late summer.

A. chinensis (Chinese astilbe) is a dense, vigorous perennial that tolerates dry soil better than other astilbe species. It grows about 24" tall, spreads 18" and bears fluffy white, pink or purple flowers in late summer. **Var.** *pumila* is more commonly found than the species. This plant

With their fern-like foliage and showy, plume-like flowers, astilbes are favorite summer-flowering perennials.

forms a low groundcover 10" tall and 8" in spread. It bears dark pink flowers. **'Superba'** is a tall form with lavender purple flowers produced in a long, narrow spike.

A. japonica (Japanese astilbe) is a compact, clump-forming perennial. The species is rarely grown in favor of the cultivars. **'Deutschland'** grows 20" tall and spreads 12". It bears white flowers in late spring. **'Etna'** grows 24–30" tall and spreads 18–24". It bears dark red flowers in early summer. **'Peach Blossom'** bears peach pink flowers in early summer. It grows about 20" tall.

A. simplicifolia (star astilbe) is a compact astilbe with glossy, dark green leaves. The flower plumes are more airy and open than those of the other species and hybrids. **'Hennie Graafland'** grows to 16" tall and produces rosy flowers in mid-summer. **'Sprite'** is as cute as its name suggests. It grows 12–16" tall, and its blush pink flower cluster ages well, maturing to an interesting rust-colored seedhead.

Problems & Pests

A variety of pests, such as whiteflies, black vine weevils and Japanese beetles, occasionally attack astilbes. Powdery mildew, bacterial leaf spot and fungal leaf spot can also present problems.

Astilbes make great cut flowers, and if you leave the plumes in a vase as the water evaporates, you'll have dried flowers to enjoy all winter.

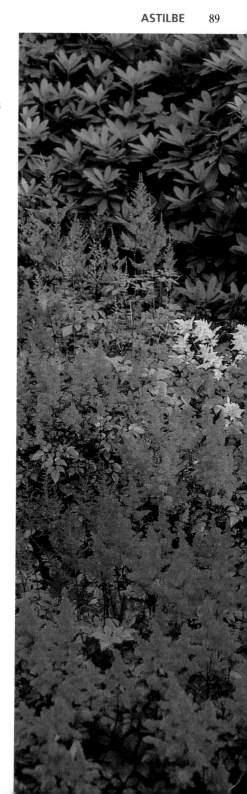

Balloon Flower

Platycodon

Height: 24–36" **Spread:** 12–18" **Flower color:** blue, pink, white
Blooms: summer **Zones:** 3–8

I REMEMBER POPPING MATURE BUDS OF BALLOON FLOWER IN MY nana's garden when I was a child, and even now it is difficult to resist the temptation in my garden. If you squeeze the bud gently you will not damage the petals. My favorite balloon flowers are the deep blue cultivars. The blue is a true blue—not violet, not purple, but blue. There is also a beautiful shell pink cultivar named 'Fuji Pink.' It is not as vigorous as the blues, but it looks wonderful in combination with annual larkspur *(Consolida)*.

Planting

Seeding: Start indoors in late winter or direct sow in spring; plants bloom second year after seeding

Planting out: Spring

Spacing: 12–18"

When using these lovely flowers in arrangements, singe the cut ends with a lit match to prevent the milky white sap from running.

Growing

Balloon flower grows well in **full sun** or **partial shade**. The soil should be of **average to rich fertility, light, moist** and **well drained**. This plant dislikes wet soil.

You should rarely need to divide your balloon flower. It resents having its roots disturbed and can take a long time to re-establish after dividing. Propagate by gently detaching and replanting the side shoots that sprout up around the plant. Balloon flower also self-seeds, and the seedlings, when still small, can be moved to new locations if desired.

Deadhead to improve appearance and prolong the blooming period.

Tips

Use balloon flower in borders, rock gardens and cottage gardens. It resents being crowded, so make sure to give it enough space.

This plant sprouts late in spring. To avoid accidentally damaging it, be sure to mark where it is in fall.

Recommended

P. grandiflorus is an upright, clump-forming perennial 24–36" tall and 12–18" in spread. It bears blue flowers in summer. The cultivars tend to be lower and more rounded in habit. **Var. *albus*** bears white flowers, often veined with blue. **'Double Blue'** is a compact plant with purple-blue double flowers. **'Fuji Blue'** from Japan has deep blue flowers, excellent for cutting. **'Fuji Pink'** bears pink flowers. **'Mother of Pearl'** bears pale pink flowers. **'Sentimental Blue'** is a new dwarf form that is good for containers; it has intense blue flowers.

Problems & Pests

Without well-drained soil, balloon flower will succumb to crown rot, especially in wet winters.

'Double Blue' (above)

Var. *albus* (center)
P. grandiflorus (below)

Baptisia
False Indigo
Baptisia

Height: 3–5' **Spread:** 2–4' **Flower color:** purple-blue, white
Blooms: late spring, early summer **Zones:** 3–9

BAPTISIAS CAN BE CONSIDERED THREE-SEASON PLANTS. THEY produce spikes of beautiful pea-blossom flowers in spring and interesting brown 'pea pods' for summer and fall. Throughout the growing season they provide a lovely foliage backdrop for other plants. *B. australis* and *B. alba* are both native Midwest prairie plants. They survive by creating a fleshy taproot that tries to grow to China, which explains why they are difficult to divide. Fortunately, baptisias will self-seed if you let the pods mature, and young seedlings are easily transplanted. Combine baptisias with other late-spring bloomers, such as hardy geraniums, daylilies and coreopsis.

Planting

Seeding: Sow indoors in early spring or direct sow in late summer; protect plants for the first winter

Planting out: Spring

Spacing: 24–36"

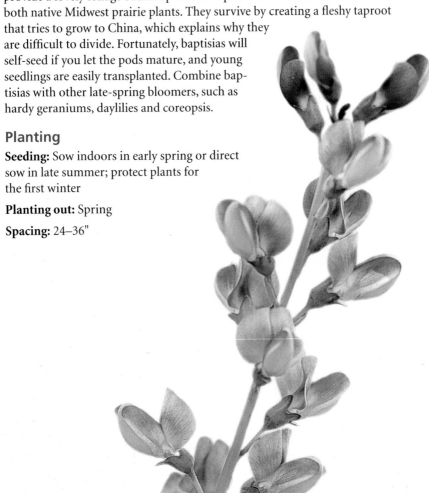

Growing

Baptisias prefer **full sun** but tolerate partial shade. Too much shade results in lank growth that causes the plants to split and fall. The soil should be of **average or poor fertility, sandy** and **well drained.** Baptisias are happy to remain in the same place for a long time and often resent being divided. Divide carefully in spring, and only when you desire more plants.

Staking may be required if your plant is not getting enough sun. To prevent having to worry about staking or moving the plant, place it in the sun and give it lots of space to spread.

The hard seed coats may need to be penetrated before the seeds can germinate. Scratch the seeds with sandpaper before planting them.

Tips

Baptisias can be used in an informal border or cottage-type garden. Use them in a natural planting, on a slope or in any well-drained, sunny spot. When first planted, baptisias may not look too impressive, but once established they are long-lived, attractive and dependable.

Recommended

B. alba is similar in size and form to *B. australis* (the more commonly grown baptisia). *B. alba* bears white flowers and is more tolerant of partial shade.

B. australis is an upright or somewhat spreading, clump-forming plant that bears spikes of purple-blue flowers. '**Purple Smoke**' bears lighter purple flowers.

B. australis (this page)

Problems & Pests

Minor problems with mildew, leaf spot and rust can occur.

If you've had difficulties with lupines, try the far less demanding baptisias instead.

Beebalm
Bergamot, Oswego Tea
Monarda

Height: 2–4' **Spread:** 12–24" **Flower color:** red, pink **Blooms:** late summer
Zones: 3–9

ONE COMMON NAME FOR THIS PLANT, OSWEGO TEA, REFERS TO
its use as a tea substitute after colonists dumped the imported black tea into
Boston Harbor back in 1773. It was introduced to the colonists by the
Oswego Indians. The brew is refreshing, but very different from black tea
(Camellia sinensis). In the garden, the flowers are some of the busiest 'cafés' for
insects. Like many of its cousins in the mint family, beebalm produces abundant nectar for bees, wasps, butterflies, moths and
colorful flies. One of my favorites
is the taller 'Jacob Cline,' which
has not developed powdery
mildew in my garden.

Planting

Seeding: Start seed outdoors in cold frame or indoors in early spring

Planting out: Spring or fall

Spacing: 18–24"

Growing

Beebalm grows well in **full sun, partial shade** or **light shade**. The soil should be of **average fertility, humus rich, moist** and **well drained**. Dry conditions encourage mildew and loss of leaves, so regular watering is a must. Divide every two or three years in spring just as new growth emerges.

In June, cut back some of the stems by half to extend the flowering period and encourage compact growth. Thinning the stems in spring also helps prevent powdery mildew. If mildew strikes after flowering, cut the plants back to 6" to increase air circulation.

M. didyma

The genus name honors Spanish botanist and physician Nicholas Monardes (1493–1588).

'Marshall's Delight'

M. *didyma* (this page)

Tips

Use beebalm beside a stream or pond, or in a lightly shaded, well-watered border. It will spread in moist, fertile soils, but like most mints, the roots are close to the surface and can be removed easily.

The fresh or dried leaves may be used to make a refreshing, minty, citrus-scented tea. Put a handful of fresh leaves in a teapot, pour boiling water over them and let steep for at least five minutes. Sweeten with honey to taste.

Beebalm attracts bees, butterflies and hummingbirds to your garden. Avoid using pesticides, which can seriously harm or kill these creatures and which will prevent you from using the plant for culinary or medicinal purposes.

Recommended

M. didyma is a bushy, mounding plant that forms a thick clump of stems with red or pink flowers. 'Gardenview Scarlet' bears large scarlet flowers and is less susceptible to powdery mildew. 'Jacob Cline' is a taller beebalm that should be cut back by half in June to prevent flopping. It bears deep blue-red flowers and is very resistant to powdery mildew. 'Marshall's Delight' doesn't come true to type from seed; it must be propagated by cuttings or divisions. It is very resistant to powdery mildew and bears pink flowers. 'Panorama' is a group of hybrids with flowers in scarlet, pink or salmon.

Problems & Pests

Powdery mildew is often the worst problem, but rust, leaf spot and leafhoppers can also cause trouble. Don't allow beebalm to dry out for extended periods.

The alternative name bergamot comes from the similarity of this plant's scent to that of Italian bergamot orange (Citrus bergamia), *used in aromatherapy and to flavor Earl Grey tea.*

M. didyma (this page)

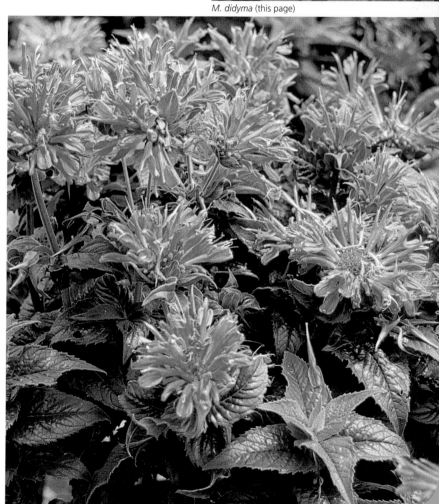

Bergenia
Pigsqueak
Bergenia

Height: 12–24" **Spread:** 12–24" or more **Flower color:** red, purple, light to dark pink, white; plant also grown for foliage **Blooms:** spring **Zones:** 3–8

THE LARGE, BOLD LEAVES OF BERGENIAS ARE EVERGREEN TO semi-evergreen in Ohio, with foliage of a few species and cultivars changing to a bronzy color in fall and winter. In areas of consistent snow cover, the leaves survive winter in better shape. Bergenias' bold, glossy leaves contrast beautifully when interplanted with heucheras and variegated hostas in a partial-shade garden. They also provide winter interest when the heucheras and hostas go dormant.

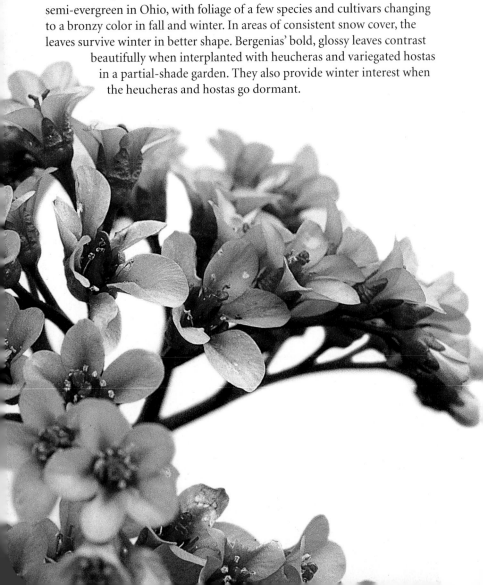

Planting

Seeding: Seeds may not come true to type. Fresh, ripe seeds should be sown uncovered, either indoors or in the garden. Keep soil temperature at 69°–70° F.

Planting out: Spring

Spacing: 10–20"

Growing

Bergenias grow best in **partial shade**. If grown in the sun, a western exposure should be avoided. The soil should be of **average to rich fertility** and **well drained**. A moist soil is preferable, especially when plants are grown in sunnier areas; however, bergenia is fairly drought tolerant once established. Divide every two to three years when the clump begins to die out in the middle.

Propagating by seed can be risky; you may not get what you hoped for. A better way to maximize your plants' potential is to propagate them with root cuttings. Bergenias spread just below the surface by rhizomes, which may be cut off in pieces and grown separately as long as a leaf shoot is

B. x schmidtii

B. cordifolia

'Bressingham White'

These plants are also called elephant ears, because of their large leathery leaves, and pigsqueak, for the unusual sound made when a leaf is rubbed briskly between thumb and forefinger.

B. cordifolia

attached to each section. Apply compost in spring if rhizomes appear to be lifting out of the soil.

Tips

These versatile, low-growing, spreading plants can be used as groundcovers, as edging along borders and pathways, as part of woodland rock gardens and in mass plantings under trees and shrubs.

Once flowering is complete, bergenias remain a beautiful addition to the garden with their thick, glossy, leathery leaves. With its expanse of green, a planting of bergenia provides a soothing background for other flowers. Many varieties turn attractive shades of bronze and purple in fall and winter.

Recommended

B. **'Bressingham White'** grows about 12" tall and has white flowers.

B. ciliata (winter bergenia) grows 18–24" tall, with an equal spread. Its flowers are white or light pink.

B. cordifolia (heart-leaved bergenia) grows about 24" tall, with an equal or greater spread. Its flowers are deep pink, and the foliage turns bronze or

purple in fall and winter. '**Purpurea**' has magenta-purple flowers and red-tinged foliage.

B. '**Evening Glow**' ('Abendglut') grows about 12" tall and spreads 18–24". The flowers are a deep magenta-crimson. The foliage turns red and maroon in winter.

B. purpurascens (purple bergenia) grows about 18" tall and spreads about 12". The young leaves are red, as are the undersides of the mature leaves. In winter the foliage turns purple or red again. Deep purple flowers are borne in mid- to late spring.

B. x *schmidtii* is a compact plant that grows 12" tall and spreads 24". The flowers are pink.

B. '**Winter Fairy Tale**' ('Wintermärchen') grows 12–18" tall and spreads 18–24". The flowers are rose red, and the dark green leaves are touched with red in winter.

Problems & Pests

Rare problems with fungal leaf spot, root rot, weevils, slugs, caterpillars and foliar nematodes are possible.

B. cordifolia

B. x *schmidtii*

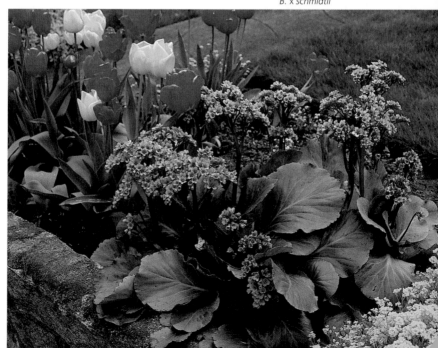

Black-Eyed Susan
Rudbeckia, Coneflower
Rudbeckia

Height: 18"–10' **Spread:** 12–36" **Flower color:** yellow or orange, with brown or green centers **Blooms:** mid-summer to fall **Zones:** 3–9

THE DAISY FAMILY RULES THE SUMMER GARDEN, WITH THE GENUS *Rudbeckia* providing much of the show. Everyone knows black-eyed Susan because it is a favorite pass-along plant among gardeners. Some may say it is overused, but a large drift of these golden flowers always elicits a smile. And you don't have to work hard to create a drift of *R. fulgida* var. *sullivantii* 'Goldsturm'; it self-seeds liberally and also spreads by rhizomes. For a 'green-eyed' Susan, try *R. nitida* 'Herbstsonne.' This tall beauty needs space to grow. Combine it with other giants in the summer garden, such as Joe-Pye weed and cup plant *(Silphium perfoliatum),* to create a display that can be seen from quite a distance.

Planting

Seeding: Start seed in a cold frame or indoors in early spring; soil temperature should be about 61°–64° F

Planting out: Spring

Spacing: 12–36"

The genus Rudbeckia *includes annual, biennial and perennial species, all native to North America.*

Growing

Black-eyed Susans grow well in **full sun** or **partial shade**. The soil should be of **average fertility** and **well drained**. Fairly heavy clay soils are tolerated, with several *Rudbeckia* species touted as 'claybusters.' Regular watering is best, but established plants are drought tolerant.

Pinch plants in June to encourage shorter, bushier growth. Divide in spring or fall every three to five years.

Tips

Use black-eyed Susans in wildflower or naturalistic gardens, borders and cottage-style gardens. They are best planted in masses and drifts.

Deadheading early in the flowering season keeps the plants flowering vigorously. Leave seedheads in place later in the season to add late-fall and winter interest and to provide food for birds.

Recommended

R. fulgida is an upright, spreading plant. It grows 18–36" tall and spreads 12–24". The orange-yellow flowers have brown centers. **Var.** *sullivantii* 'Goldsturm' bears large, bright golden yellow flowers.

R. laciniata (cutleaf coneflower) forms a large, open clump. It grows 4–10' tall and spreads 24–36". The yellow flowers have green centers. The popular cultivar **'Goldquelle'** grows 36" tall and has bright yellow double flowers.

R. nitida is an upright, spreading plant 3–6' tall and 24–36" in spread.

R. fulgida with *Echinacea*

The yellow flowers have green centers. **'Autumn Glory'** has golden yellow flowers. **'Herbstsonne'** ('Autumn Sun') has bright golden yellow flowers.

Problems & Pests

Rare problems with slugs, aphids, rust, smut and leaf spot are possible.

R. laciniata

Blanket Flower
Gaillardia

Height: 12–36" **Spread:** 12–24" **Flower color:** combinations of red, yellow **Blooms:** early summer to early fall **Zones:** 3–10

BLANKET FLOWER BLOOMS LONGER THAN MOST PERENNIALS, especially if deadheaded regularly. This plant will bloom its heart out, which may explain its limited life span of only about two to three years. Luckily, it self-seeds, and the seed lasts a long time in the soil. In an old garden area of mine that has become a patio, blanket flower has popped up along the perimeter. Because of the sand base and gravel fill, the area is exceptionally well drained—perfect for blanket flower, which doesn't like wet feet. My original plants were 'Kobold,' a diminutive cultivar. The seedlings have reverted back to the taller hybrid, but they are welcome nonetheless.

Most Gaillardia *species are native to the United States and are found growing wild on the prairies.*

Planting

Seeding: Start seed indoors or direct sow in early spring. Don't cover the seeds because they need light to germinate. Cultivars are best propagated from cuttings.

Planting out: Spring

Spacing: 18"

Growing

Blanket flower grows best in **full sun**. The soil should be **fertile, light** and **well drained**. Poor soils are tolerated, but plants won't overwinter in heavy, wet soil. Deadheading encourages blooming all summer. Cut the plants back to within 6" of the ground in late summer to encourage new growth and promote the longevity of these often short-lived plants.

Tips

Blanket flower is a North American prairie plant whose multi-colored flowers will add a fiery glow to cottage gardens, wildflower gardens or meadow plantings. It is also attractive planted in clumps of three or four in a mixed or herbaceous border. Drought tolerant, it is ideal for neglected and rarely watered parts of the garden. Dwarf varieties make good container plantings.

Recommended

G. x *grandiflora* is a bushy, upright plant 24–36" tall and 12–24" in spread. It bears daisy-like flowers all summer long and into early fall. The petals have yellow tips and red bases. '**Burgundy**' is 24–36" tall, with dark red flowers. '**Kobold**' ('Goblin') is a compact cultivar only 12" tall. The flowers are variegated red and yellow, like those of the parent species.

Problems & Pests

Powdery mildew, downy mildew, leaf spot, rust, aster yellows and leafhoppers are possible problems but rarely cause much trouble.

The name Gaillardia *honors Gaillard de Charentonneau, an 18th-century French patron of botanical research.*

G. x grandiflora with Echinops

Blazing Star
Spike Gayfeather, Gayfeather
Liatris

Height: 18–36" **Spread:** 18–24" **Flower color:** purple, white
Blooms: summer **Zones:** 3–9

THE INTENSE PURPLE TO fuchsia color of its flowers and a curious blooming sequence—top to bottom—make *Liatris* a notable perennial. The tall flower spikes contrast wonderfully with the blooms of the daisy family. The strong vertical line of blazing star draws your attention to the sky, while the rounded flowers of the daisies keep your feet firmly on the ground. Combine the purple and white cultivars of blazing star with black-eyed Susan, purple coneflower and native grasses to create a meadow or prairie garden.

Blazing star is an eye-catching perennial that will attract butterflies to the garden.

Planting

Seeding: Direct sow in fall; plants may take two to four years to bloom from seed

Planting out: Spring

Spacing: 18–24"

Growing

Blazing star prefers **full sun**. The soil should be of **average fertility, sandy** and **humus rich**. Water well during the growing season, but don't allow the plants to stand in water during cool weather. Mulch during summer to prevent moisture loss.

Trim off the spent flower spikes to promote a longer blooming period and to keep blazing star looking tidy. Divide every three or four years in fall. The clump will appear crowded when it is time to divide.

Tips

Use this plant in borders and meadow plantings. Plant in a location that has good drainage to avoid root rot in winter. Blazing star does well when grown in planters.

The spikes make excellent, long-lasting cut flowers.

Recommended

L. spicata is a clump-forming, erect plant. The flowers are pinkish purple or white. **'Floristan Violet'** has purple flowers. **'Floristan White'** has white flowers. **'Kobold'** has deep purple flowers.

Problems & Pests

Slugs, stem rot, root rot, rust and leaf spot are possible problems.

'Floristan White'

'Kobold'

Bleeding Heart
Dicentra

Height: 1–4' **Spread:** 12–36" **Flower color:** pink, white, red
Blooms: spring, summer **Zones:** 3–9

BLEEDING HEART IS A WELL-LOVED MAINSTAY OF THE VICTORIAN or old-fashioned garden. Picture it next to the gate, welcoming you into the garden. Enjoy it in spring, because it usually goes dormant to avoid Ohio's hot, dry summers. For a longer season of interest, try *D. exima* or *D. formosa* and their hybrids. In a recent extended fall, fringed bleeding heart took a rest in my garden in September and then bloomed intermittently in October and November. The blue-green, ferny foliage of the smaller bleeding hearts contrasts well with European wild ginger, hostas and Lenten rose *(Helleborus* x *hybridus).*

Planting

Seeding: Start freshly ripened seed in cold frame; plants self-seed in the garden

Planting out: Spring

Spacing: 18–36"

Growing

Bleeding hearts prefer **light shade** but tolerate partial or full shade. The soil should be **humus rich, moist** and **well drained**. Though these plants prefer soil to remain evenly moist, they tolerate drought quite well, but only when the weather isn't too hot. Very dry summer conditions cause the plants to die back, but they will revive in fall or the following spring. It is most important for bleeding hearts to remain moist while blooming in order to prolong the flowering period. Regular watering will keep the flowers coming until mid-summer.

D. exima and *D. spectabilis* rarely need dividing. *D. formosa* can be divided every three years or so.

Tips

Bleeding hearts can be naturalized in a woodland garden or grown in a border or rock garden. They make excellent early-season specimen plants and do well near a pond or stream.

D. formosa

These delicate plants are the perfect addition to a moist woodland garden. Plant them next to a shaded pond or stream.

D. spectabilis

All bleeding hearts contain toxic alkaloids, and some people develop allergic skin reactions from contact with these plants.

Recommended

D. 'Adrian Bloom' forms a compact clump of dark gray-green foliage. It grows about 12" tall and spreads about 18". Bright red flowers bloom in late spring and continue to appear intermittently all summer.

D. exima (fringed bleeding heart) forms a loose, mounded clump of lacy, fern-like foliage. It grows 15–24" tall and spreads about 18". The pink or white flowers are borne mostly in spring but may be produced sporadically over summer. Unless kept well watered, the plant will go dormant during hot, dry weather.

D. formosa (western bleeding heart) is a low-growing, wide-spreading plant. It grows about 18" tall and spreads 24–36". The pink flowers fade to white as they mature. This plant is likely to self-seed. The most drought tolerant of the bleeding hearts, it is the most likely to continue flowering all summer. It can become invasive. **Var.** *alba* has white flowers.

D. formosa

D. spectabilis 'Alba'

D. '**Luxuriant**' is a low-growing hybrid with blue-green foliage and red-pink flowers. It grows about 12" tall and spreads about 18". Flowers appear in spring and early summer.

D. spectabilis (common bleeding heart, Japanese bleeding heart) forms a large, elegant mound up to 4' tall and about 18" in spread. It blooms in late spring and early summer. The inner petals are white and the outer petals are pink. This species is likely to die back in summer heat and prefers light dappled shade. '**Alba**' has entirely white flowers. '**Goldheart**' has chartreuse foliage.

D. '**Stuart Boothman**' is a spreading perennial with blue-gray foliage. It grows about 12" tall, with an equal or greater spread. Dark pink flowers are produced over a long period from spring to mid-summer.

Problems & Pests

Slugs, downy mildew, *Verticillium* wilt, viruses, rust and fungal leaf spot can cause occasional problems.

Enjoy these showy blooms in the garden, because they don't work well as cut flowers.

D. exima (this page)

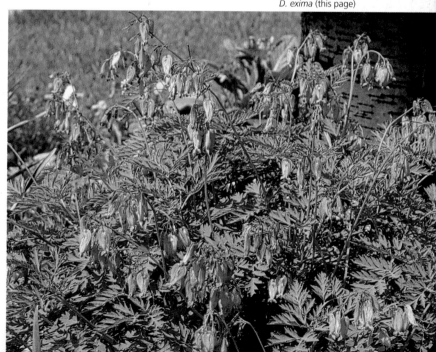

Boltonia

Boltonia

Height: 3–6' **Spread:** 4' or more **Flower color:** white, mauve or pink, with yellow centers **Blooms:** late summer and fall **Zones:** 4–9

IN LATE AUGUST AND INTO OCTOBER, BOLTONIA IS COVERED WITH tiny white stars. It is a tough native plant that doesn't need much care once it is established. Boltonia quickly forms large clumps, so it is a perfect pass-along plant for sharing. I purchased my original plant in a quart container. After eight years in my garden, it has developed into a drift 7' long. Pieces have found their way into many friends' gardens.

Planting

Seeding: Start seed in a cold frame in fall

Planting out: Spring or fall

Spacing: 36"

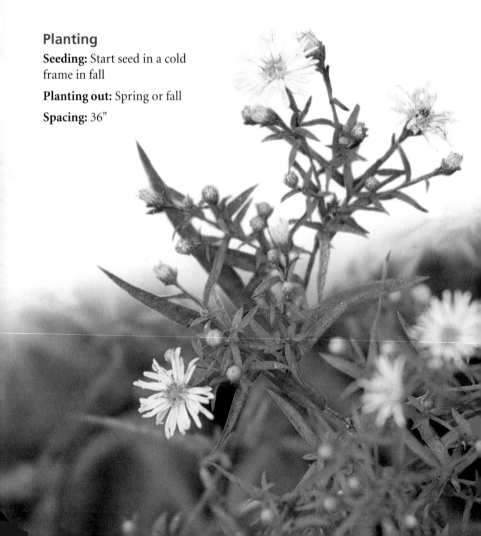

Growing

Boltonia grows best in **full sun** but tolerates partial shade. It prefers soil that is **fertile, humus rich, moist** and **well drained** but adapts to less fertile soils and tolerates some drought. Divide in fall or early spring when the clump becomes overgrown or begins to die out in the middle.

Staking may be required, particularly in partially shaded areas. Use twiggy branches or a peony hoop to provide support. If installed while the plant is young, the stakes will be hidden by the growing branches. Alternatively, cut the plant back by one-third in June to reduce the height and prevent flopping.

Tips

This large plant can be used in the middle or at the back of a mixed border, in a naturalized or cottage-style garden or near a pond or other water feature.

A good alternative to the Michaelmas daisies, boltonia is less susceptible to powdery mildew.

Recommended

B. asteroides is a large, upright perennial with narrow, grayish green leaves. It bears many white or slightly purple daisy-like flowers with yellow centers. **'Pink Beauty'** has a looser habit and bears pale pink flowers. It is less vigorous than **'Snowbank,'** which has a denser, more compact habit and bears more plentiful white flowers than the species.

Problems & Pests

Boltonia has rare problems with rust, leaf spot and powdery mildew.

Boltonia is native to the eastern and central United States.

Brunnera
Siberian Bugloss
Brunnera

Height: 12–18" **Spread:** 18–24" **Flower color:** blue **Blooms:** spring
Zones: 3–8

BRUNNERA HAS OFTEN BEEN CALLED FALSE FORGET-ME-NOT ON account of its tiny, baby blue flowers. It is in the same plant family as forget-me-not, so there are indeed some similarities. Brunnera does best in the shade, but it will tolerate sun if watered. In my garden, one plant seeded itself into a sunny area that does not get watered. Although the plants look awful by the end of the summer, they have come back every spring for seven years. Use brunnera as a medium- to bold-textured contrast to ferns, bleeding hearts and hostas. The cultivar 'Langtrees' has silver marks between the leaf veins, simulating the effect of sun breaking through the trees to shine on the plants below.

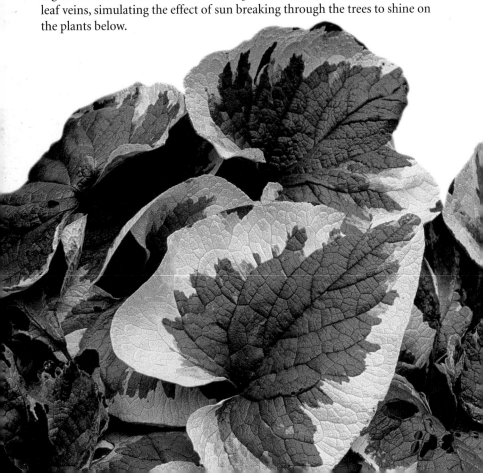

Planting

Seeding: Start seed in cold frame in early fall or indoors in early spring

Planting out: Spring

Spacing: 12–18"

Growing

Brunnera prefers **light shade** but tolerates morning sun with consistent moisture. The soil should be of **average fertility, humus rich, moist** and **well drained**. The species and its cultivars do not tolerate drought.

Cut back faded foliage mid-season to produce a flush of new growth. Divide in spring when the center of the clump begins to die out.

Tips

Brunnera makes a great addition to a woodland or shaded garden. Its low, bushy habit makes it useful as a groundcover or as an addition to a shaded border.

Recommended

B. macrophylla forms a mound of soft, heart-shaped leaves and produces loose clusters of blue flowers all spring. **'Dawson's White'** ('Variegata') has large leaves with irregular creamy patches. **'Hadspen Cream'** has leaves with creamy margins. **'Langtrees'** has silvery marks on the leaves. Grow variegated plants in light or full shade to avoid scorched leaves.

This reliable plant rarely suffers from any problems.

B. macrophylla

Brunnera is related to borage and forget-me-nots.

'Dawson's White'

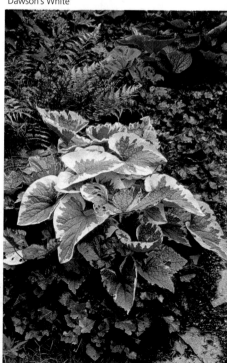

Butterfly Weed
Milkweed, Pleurisy Root
Asclepias

Height: 18–36" **Spread:** 12–24" **Flower color:** orange, yellow, white, red, pink, light purple **Blooms:** late spring, summer, early fall **Zones:** 4–9

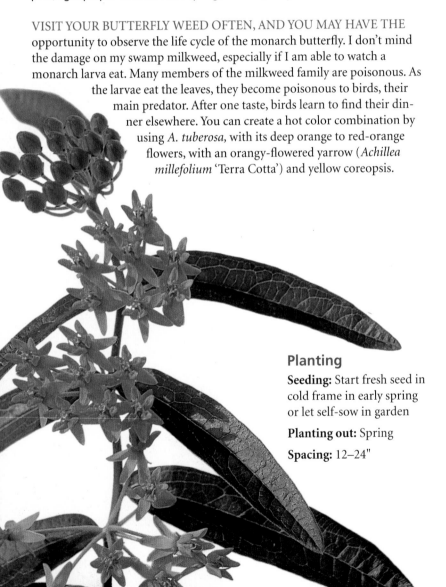

VISIT YOUR BUTTERFLY WEED OFTEN, AND YOU MAY HAVE THE opportunity to observe the life cycle of the monarch butterfly. I don't mind the damage on my swamp milkweed, especially if I am able to watch a monarch larva eat. Many members of the milkweed family are poisonous. As the larvae eat the leaves, they become poisonous to birds, their main predator. After one taste, birds learn to find their dinner elsewhere. You can create a hot color combination by using *A. tuberosa*, with its deep orange to red-orange flowers, with an orangy-flowered yarrow (*Achillea millefolium* 'Terra Cotta') and yellow coreopsis.

Planting

Seeding: Start fresh seed in cold frame in early spring or let self-sow in garden

Planting out: Spring

Spacing: 12–24"

Growing

Butterfly weeds prefer **full sun.** The soil should be **fertile, moist** and **well drained,** though A. *tuberosa* is drought tolerant.

To propagate, remove the seedlings that will sprout up around the base of these plants. The deep taproot makes division very difficult.

Deadhead to encourage a second blooming.

Tips

Use A. *tuberosa* in meadow plantings and borders, on dry banks, in neglected areas and in wildflower, cottage and butterfly gardens. Use A. *incarnata* in moist borders and in bog, pondside or streamside plantings.

Butterfly weeds are slow to start in spring. Place a marker beside each plant in fall so you won't forget the plant is there and inadvertently dig it up.

Recommended

A. *incarnata* (swamp milkweed) grows about 36" tall and spreads up to 12". It bears clusters of pink, white or light purple flowers in late spring or early summer. Although it naturally grows in moist areas, it appreciates a well-drained soil in the garden. 'Ice Ballet' bears white flowers.

A. *tuberosa* (butterfly weed) forms a clump of upright, leafy stems. It grows 18–36" tall and spreads 12–24". It bears clusters of orange flowers from mid-summer to early fall. 'Gay Butterflies' bears orange, yellow or red flowers.

Problems & Pests

Aphids and mealybugs can cause occasional problems.

A. tuberosa with *Liatris* & *Eupatorium*

Native to North America, the butterfly weeds are a major food source for the monarch butterfly and will attract butterflies to your garden.

A. tuberosa

Campanula
Bellflower, Harebell
Campanula

Height: 4"–6' **Spread:** 12–36" **Flower color:** blue, white, purple
Blooms: summer, early fall **Zones:** 3–7

MY LOVE AFFAIR WITH CAMPANULAS STARTED IN 1993, AND IN THE ensuing years I have managed to grow many of the species, hybrids and cultivars. With their wide range of heights and habits, it is possible to put a campanula almost anywhere in the garden. I wish I could say that I've always been successful, but some campanulas will not deal with hot, humid weather and heavy soils. One of my favorite ramblers is the Serbian bellflower. It is considered invasive, but the conditions in my rock garden hold it in check. It is planted under a dwarf golden false cypress, where its blue flowers complement the conifer's golden leaves.

Planting

Seeding: Not recommended because germination can be erratic; if necessary, direct sow in spring or fall

Planting out: Spring or fall

Spacing: 12–36"

Growing

Campanulas grow well in **full sun, partial shade** or **light shade**. The soil should be of **average to high fertility** and **well drained**. These plants appreciate a mulch to keep their roots cool and moist in summer and protected in winter, particularly if snow cover is inconsistent. It is important to divide campanulas every few years in early spring or late summer to keep plants vigorous and to prevent them from becoming invasive.

Deadhead to prolong blooming. For the upright campanulas, consider cutting back sections of the plant one at a time. Doing so allows for new buds to form on the pruned sections, which will bloom as the uncut sections finish blooming.

Campanulas can be propagated by basal, new-growth or rhizome cuttings.

Tips

Upright and mounding campanulas can be used in borders and cottage gardens. Low, spreading and trailing campanulas can be used in rock gardens and on rock walls. You can also edge beds with the low-growing varieties.

C. persicifolia

Prompt deadheading keeps campanulas looking tidy and extends their bloom time.

C. carpatica

C. lactiflora

For a cottage-garden effect, plant a drift of peach-leaved bellflower, then let it self-seed and intermingle with other plants.

C. poscharskyana

Recommended

C. x **'Birch Hybrid'** is low growing and spreading. It bears light blue to mauve flowers in summer.

C. carpatica (Carpathian bellflower, Carpathian harebell) is a spreading, mounding perennial. It grows 10–12" tall, spreads 12–24" and bears blue, white or purple flowers in summer. **'Blue Clips'** is a smaller, compact plant with large blue flowers. **'Bressingham White'** is a compact plant with large white flowers. **'Jewel'** is low growing, only 4–8" tall. It has deep blue flowers. **'Kent Belle'** is a stately new hybrid with large, deep violet blue bells on arching stems.

C. glomerata (clustered bellflower) forms a clump of upright stems. It grows 12–24" tall, with an equal or greater spread. Clusters of purple, blue or white flowers are borne over most of the summer. **'Superba'** has dark purple flowers.

C. lactiflora (milky bellflower) is an upright perennial 4–6' tall and about 24" in spread. It bears white, blue or purple flowers in summer. **Var.** *alba* ('Alba') bears white flowers.

C. persicifolia (peach-leaved bellflower) is an upright perennial that grows about 36" tall and spreads about 12". It bears white, blue or purple flowers from early summer to mid-summer.

C. portenschlagiana (Dalmatian bellflower) is a low, spreading, mounding perennial 6" tall and 20–24" in spread. It bears light or deep blue to violet blue flowers from mid- to late summer.

C. poscharskyana (Serbian bellflower) is a trailing perennial that likes to wend its way through other plants. It grows 6–12" tall, spreads 24–36" and bears light violet blue flowers in summer and early fall.

Problems & Pests

Minor problems with vine weevils, spider mites, aphids, powdery mildew, slugs, rust and fungal leaf spot are possible.

C. carpatica 'Bressingham White'

Over 300 species of Campanula *grow throughout the Northern Hemisphere, in habitats ranging from high, rocky crags to boggy meadows.*

C. persicifolia

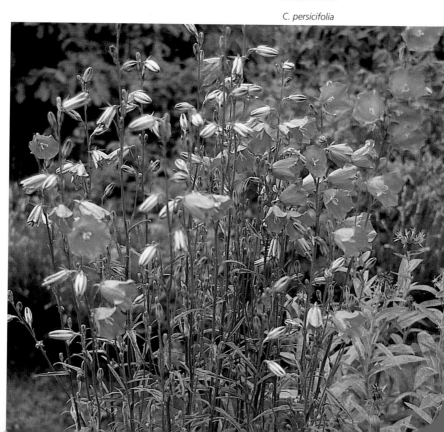

Candytuft

Iberis

Height: 6–12" **Spread:** 10–36" **Flower color:** white **Blooms:** long period in spring; sometimes again in fall **Zones:** 3–9

THE SECOND PART OF THE SCIENTIFIC NAME FOR CANDYTUFT, *sempervirens*, means 'always green.' Candytuft is a four-season plant that provides a green carpet when not in bloom. Maybe it should be called 'candy-tuff,' because it can thrive in hot, sunny locations. I planted it in a south-facing rock garden that I water only during prolonged drought. Try combining candytuft with basket-of-gold and silvermound artemisia for a perfect hot, dry garden trio.

Planting

Seeding: Direct sow in spring

Planting out: Spring

Spacing: 6–12"

Growing

Candytuft prefers **full sun**. The soil should be of **poor to average fertility, moist, well drained** and **neutral to alkaline**.

In spring, when the new buds begin to break, cut away any brown sections resulting from winter damage. Once the candytuft has finished flowering, shear it back by about one-third to promote new, compact growth. Every two or three years, shear it back by one-half to two-thirds to discourage the development of too much woody growth and to encourage abundant flowering.

Because candytuft is a subshrub with a single woody basal stem, division is not recommended. The plant is easily propagated by stem cuttings. As the stems spread outwards, they may root where they touch the ground. These rooted ends may be cut away from the central plant and replanted in new locations.

If you arrive home after dusk on a spring night, the white flowers of candytuft will welcome you with a lovely glow in the moonlight.

Tips

Use candytuft as an edging plant, in borders and rock gardens, in the crevices of rock walls and as a companion for spring-blooming bulbs.

Recommended

I. sempervirens is a spreading evergreen that grows 6–12" tall and spreads 16–36". It bears clusters of tiny white flowers in spring. '**Autumn Snow**' bears white flowers in spring and fall. '**Little Gem**' is a compact, spring-flowering plant that spreads only 10". '**Snowflake**' is a mounding plant that bears large white flowers in spring.

Problems & Pests

Occasional problems with clubroot (in wet soils), slugs, caterpillars, damping off, gray mold and fungal leaf spot are possible.

Cardinal Flower
Lobelia
Lobelia

Height: 2–4' **Spread:** 12–24" **Flower color:** red, pink, white, blue, purple
Blooms: summer, fall **Zones:** 3–9

THE FIRST TIME I SAW A CARDINAL FLOWER was in woods along a slowly moving stream. Cloud cover created a soft glow around the shimmering red flowers of *L. cardinalis*, and it was truly magical. I have tried to grow this flower in my garden, but I don't have the acidic, moist woodland conditions that it requires. Fortunately, some of the other lobelias are not as finicky. Great blue lobelia will easily spread if given moisture—too easily, according to some. Once thought to cure syphilis, *L. siphilitica* and other *Lobelia* species are often found in the medicinal herb garden, but these plants are very poisonous and their use is not recommended.

Planting

Seeding: Direct sow in garden or sow in cold frame in spring, when soil temperature is about 70° F

Planting out: Spring

Spacing: 12–18"

These lovely members of the bellflower family contain deadly alkaloids and have poisoned people who tried to use them in herbal medicines.

Growing

Cardinal flowers grow well in **full sun, light shade** and **partial shade**. The soil should be **fertile, slightly acidic** and **moist**. Never allow the soil to dry out completely, especially in a sunny location. Provide a light mulch over the winter to protect the plants.

Pinch plants in early summer to produce compact growth. Deadheading may encourage a second set of blooms. Divide every two to three years in fall to stimulate growth. To divide, lift the entire plant and remove the new rosettes growing at the plant base. Replant immediately.

Cardinal flowers self-seed quite easily. Because these plants live only about four or five years, self-seeding is an easy way to ensure subsequent generations of plants. If you deadhead, allow at least a few spent flower spikes to remain to spread their seeds. Don't worry too much about leaving spikes, though, because the lower flowers on a spike are likely to set seed before the top flowers have finished opening.

L. cardinalis

L. siphilitica

Tips

These plants are best used in streamside or pond-side plantings or in bog gardens.

Cardinal flowers may require a more acidic soil than other plants growing along a pondside. They may be planted in a container of peat-based potting soil and sunk into the ground at the edge of the pond.

Recommended

L. cardinalis (cardinal flower) forms an erect clump of bronze-green leaves. It grows 2–4' tall and spreads 12–24", bearing spikes of bright red flowers from summer to fall. 'Alba' has white flowers and is not as cold hardy as the species.

L. 'La Fresco' bears jewel-toned, plum purple flowers.

L. 'Queen Victoria' forms a clump of reddish stems with maroon foliage and scarlet flowers. It grows about 36" tall and spreads 12".

L. cardinalis (this page)

L. siphilitica (great blue lobelia, blue lobelia) forms an erect clump with bright green foliage. It grows 2–4' tall and spreads 12–18". Spikes of deep blue flowers are produced from mid-summer to fall. **Var.** *alba* has white flowers.

L. x *speciosa* (hybrid lobelia) is the hardiest, most vigorous of the cardinal flowers. **'Compliment'** is a seed series that has dark green foliage and red or blue-purple flowers. **'Rose Beacon'** has deep, rose-colored flowers. **'Ruby Slippers'** is a vigorous plant with garnet red flowers.

L. **'Wildwood Splendor'** is a vigorous plant bearing deep purple flowers.

Problems & Pests

Rare problems with slugs, rust, smut and leaf spot can occur.

L. cardinalis with *Argyranthemum*

L. cardinalis cultivar

Lobelia *was named after the Flemish physician and botanist Mathias de l'Obel (1538–1616).*

Catmint

Nepeta

Height: 10–36" **Spread:** 18–36" **Flower color:** blue, purple, white, pink
Blooms: spring, summer, occasionally again in fall **Zones:** 3–8

CATMINT IS MY CATS' FAVORITE PLANT. THEY NIBBLE IT AND ROLL around in it, and then settle down for a good catnap. It makes a pleasant herbal tea for humans, too. Though I've never felt like taking a nap after drinking it, it does have a calming effect. Catmint flowers profusely in late spring, when it is covered with bees (which, as long as they are feeding, will not be interested in you). If you deadhead the plants, you will be rewarded with another decent bloom in summer. Depending on the weather, sporadic flowering will continue into fall.

It is no mystery where the name 'catmint' comes from—cats love it! Dried leaves stuffed into cloth toys will amuse your kitty for hours.

Planting

Seeding: Most popular hybrids and cultivars are sterile and cannot be grown from seed

Planting out: Spring

Spacing: 18–24"

Growing

Catmints grow well in **full sun** or **partial shade**. The soil should be of **average fertility** and **well drained**. The growth tends to be floppy in too rich a soil.

Pinch tips in June to delay flowering and make the plants more compact. Once the plants are almost finished blooming, you may cut them back by one-third to one-half to encourage new growth and more blooms in late summer or fall. Divide in spring or fall when the plants begin to look overgrown and dense.

Tips

Catmints can be used to edge borders and pathways. They work well in herb gardens and with

N. x faassenii (this page)

The genus name Nepeta *may refer to an Etruscan town where* N. cataria *once grew in abundance.*

roses in cottage gardens. Taller varieties make lovely additions to perennial beds, and dwarf types can be used in rock gardens.

Think twice before growing *N. cataria* (catnip), as cats are heavily attracted to this plant and may wander into your garden to enjoy it. Cats do like the other catmints as well, but not to quite the same extent.

Recommended

N. '**Blue Beauty**' ('Souvenir d'André Chaudron') forms an upright, spreading clump. It grows 18–36" tall and spreads about 18". The gray-green foliage is fragrant and the large flowers are dark purple-blue.

N. x *faassenii* forms a clump of upright and spreading stems. It grows 18–36" tall, with an equal spread, and bears spikes of blue or purple flowers. This hybrid and its cultivars are sterile and cannot be grown from seed. '**Dawn to Dusk**' has pink flowers. '**Dropmore**' has gray-green foliage and light purple flowers. '**Snowflake**' is

N. x *faassenii*

N. x *faassenii* 'Walker's Low'

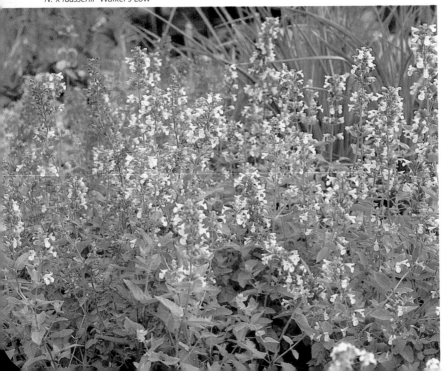

low growing, compact and spreading, with white flowers. It grows 12–24" tall and spreads about 18". **'Walker's Low'** has gray-green foliage and bears lavender blue flowers. It grows about 10" in height.

N. **'Six Hills Giant'** is a large, vigorous plant about 36" tall and about 24" in spread. It bears large, showy spikes of deep lavender blue flowers.

Catmints have long been cultivated for their reputed medicinal and culinary qualities.

Problems & Pests

These plants are pest free, except for an occasional bout of leaf spot or a visit from a neighborhood cat.

N. 'Six Hills Giant'

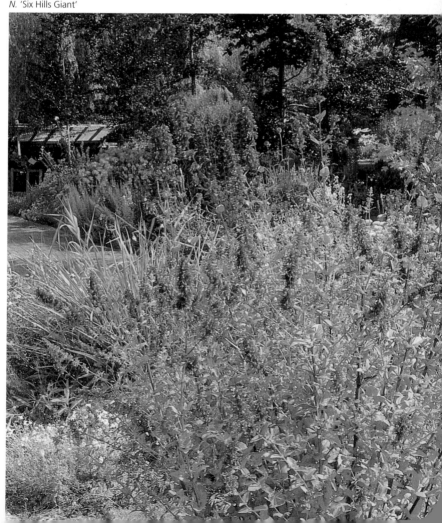

Chrysanthemum

Fall Garden Mum, Hybrid Garden Mum

Chrysanthemum

Height: 12–36" **Spread:** 2–4' or more **Flower color:** orange, yellow, pink, red, purple **Blooms:** late summer and fall **Zones:** 5–9

THE COLORS OF AUTUMN ARE REFLECTED IN THE FLOWERS OF chrysanthemums. There are so many choices that it is often easier to select the color you want, instead of looking for a particular cultivar. A common complaint is that garden mums do not overwinter. The key is to plant them as soon as you can buy them. Chrysanthemums are often planted in early to mid-fall, too late to allow their roots to develop. You may find that your mums heave themselves out of the soil in response to Ohio's famous fall and early-winter freeze-thaw cycles. If this happens, gently push the plants back into the soil and mulch around the crowns once the ground is cold.

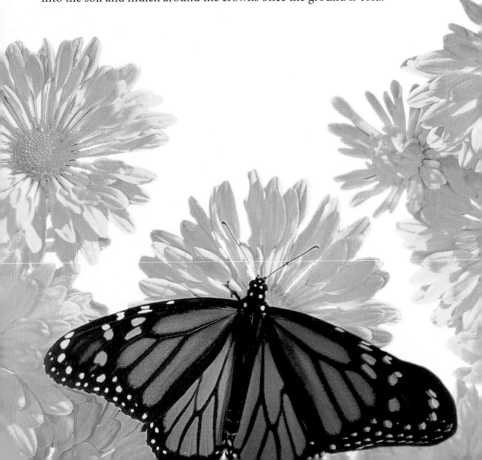

Planting

Seeding: Not recommended

Planting out: Spring, summer or fall

Spacing: 18–24"

Growing

Chrysanthemums grow best in **full sun**. The soil should be **fertile, moist** and **well drained**. The earlier you can plant chrysanthemums, the better. Early planting improves their chances of surviving the winter.

Pinch plants back in early summer to encourage bushy growth. In late fall or early winter, you can dead-head the spent blooms, but leave the stems intact to protect the crowns of the plants. Divide in spring or fall every two years to keep plants vigorous and to prevent them from thinning out in the center.

'Raquel'

'Christine'
'Stacy'

Tips

These plants provide a blaze of color in the late-season garden, often flowering until the first hard frost. Dot or group them in borders, use them as specimen plants near the house or grow them in large planters. Some gardeners purchase chrysanthemums as flowering plants in late summer and put them in the spots where summer annuals have faded.

Recommended

C. 'Mei-Kyo' is a vigorous grower that blooms in mid- to late October. The flowers are a deep pink. Be sure to pinch back the stems to prevent the need to stake. Plants grow to 24–30" tall and spread as far as you will let them.

C. 'Morden' series was developed in Canada and is reliably hardy to Zone 4. Plants come in a wide variety of colors and grow about 24" tall.

C. 'My Favorite' series is a new introduction and is heralded as a truly perennial mum and a prolific flower producer. The plants grow to about 24" tall and spread about 4'. 'Autumn Red' has red flowers.

C. 'Prophet' series is popular and commonly available. Plants grow about 24" tall and spread about 24–36". Flowers come in all colors. 'Christine' has deep salmon pink double flowers with yellow centers. 'Raquel' has bright red double flowers with yellow centers. 'Stacy' has yellow-centered flowers with pink petals that have white bases.

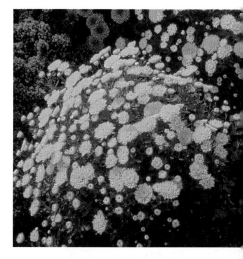

C. **Rubellum Group** cultivars grow to 24–30" in height and spread. '**Clara Curtis**' has soft pink flowers. '**Mary Stoker**' is a vigorous grower with butter yellow flowers.

Problems & Pests

Aphids can be a true menace to these plants. Insecticidal soap can be used to treat the problem, but it should be washed off within an hour because it discolors the foliage when the sun hits it. Also watch for spider mites, whiteflies, leaf miners, leaf spot, powdery mildew, rust, aster yellows, blight, borers and rot, though these problems are not as common.

Although the name Chrysanthemum *comes from the Greek and means 'golden flower,' these plants now come in a wide range of bright colors.*

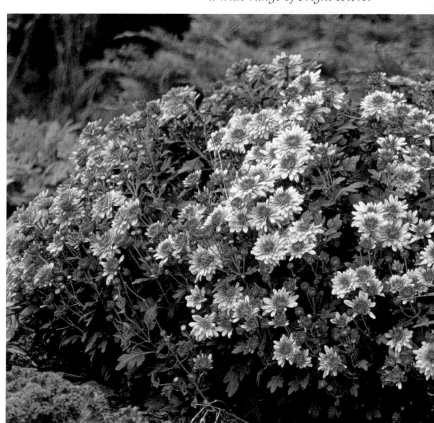

Clematis
Clematis

Height: 18"–16' **Spread:** 2–4' **Flower color:** blue, purple, pink, yellow, red, white **Blooms:** early to late summer, fall **Zones:** 3–8

SO MANY CLEMATIS, SO LITTLE TIME! IT IS IMPOSSIBLE TO CHOOSE just one favorite, and the list of recommended species and cultivars below is only a starting point. It is possible to have clematis in bloom all season, from the early, but fussy, alpine clematis to the fall-blooming, rambling virgin's bower. The pruning recommendations for the vining clematis can be daunting, but start with just one or two types and ease yourself into the maintenance of these beauties. Consider combining clematis with conifers and shrubs. Imagine a deep purple Jackman clematis threading its way through a blue spruce, or the butter yellow virgin's bower winding its way through a rose whose bloom is past.

Planting

Seeding: Indoors or in a cold frame, in late summer or fall

Planting out: Spring or fall

Spacing: 2–4'

Growing

Clematis prefer **full sun** but tolerate partial shade. The soil should be **fertile, humus rich, moist** and **well drained**. These plants are quite cold hardy but will fare best when protected from winter wind. The rootball of vining clematis should be planted about 2" beneath the surface of the soil.

The semi-woody, vine-type clematis need to be pruned. Those that bloom in early summer on last year's growth, such as alpine clematis, should be thinned after the vine blooms by pruning lateral branches back to three or four nodes. Mid- to late-season varieties that bloom on the current year's growth, such as Jackman clematis, 'Comtesse de Bouchard' and 'Ramona,' should be pruned back to 12" early in spring before new growth appears. Large mid-season varieties that bloom on year-old wood and then again on new growth, such as 'Nelly Moser,' 'The President' and 'Duchess of Edinburgh,' should be thinned occasionally after the vine ceases its first round of blooms.

Combine two clematis varieties that bloom at the same time to provide a mix of tone and texture.

C. recta

C. x jackmanii (above)

Division of vining clematis is difficult and not recommended, but herbaceous clematis may be carefully divided in early spring. Propagate vining clematis by taking stem cuttings in summer.

Tips

Clematis are attractive for most of the growing season. They are useful in borders and as specimen plants. Vining clematis need a structure such as a trellis, railing, fence or arbor to support them while they climb. They can also be allowed to grow over shrubs, up trees and as groundcovers.

Clematis like their heads in the sun and their roots in the shade. Shade the roots with a mulch or groundcover. Do not shade with a flat rock, a common practice in the past, because the rock will absorb heat and defeat the purpose of shading the roots.

Recommended

C. alpina (alpine clematis) is a vining spring and early-summer bloomer that grows up to 10' tall. The bell-like flowers are blue with white centers.

C. 'Comtesse de Bouchard' is a vining mid- to late-summer bloomer that bears mauve pink flowers. It grows about 10' tall.

C. 'Duchess of Edinburgh' is a vining clematis that blooms in early summer and bears white double flowers. It grows about 10' tall.

C. 'Gravetye Beauty' is a vining late-season bloomer about 8' tall. Its small, bright red flowers bloom on new growth.

C. heracleifolia (tube clematis) is a herbaceous plant. It grows up to 36" tall and 4' wide. The tube-shaped flowers are purple-blue and appear in summer. **Var.** *davidiana* has fragrant, larger flowers. Cut these plants back to the ground in early spring. Pinch plants when they are 15" tall to promote upright growth.

C. integrifolia (solitary clematis) grows 18–36" tall and bears flared, bell-shaped, purple flowers in summer. This herbaceous plant tends to grow

C. integrifolia (center & below)

upwards to a point, then falls to the ground and sprawls, spreading to about 4'. Stake in spring to help keep this colorful character upright.

C. x *jackmanii* (Jackman clematis) is a common vining clematis that blooms in mid- to late summer. The twining vines of this hybrid grow about 10' tall. Large, purple flowers appear on side shoots from the previous season and on new growth for most of the summer.

C. 'Nelly Moser' is a vining early-summer bloomer that grows about 10' tall. This popular cultivar bears pale mauve pink flowers with a darker pink stripe down the center of each petal.

C. 'The President' is a vining early-summer bloomer that bears dark purple flowers. It grows about 15' tall.

C. tangutica (center)

C. 'Ramona' is a vining mid-summer bloomer that bears pale purple-blue flowers and grows about 10' tall.

C. recta (ground clematis) is a bit more upright than the other two herbaceous species. It reaches 4' in height and only 24" in width. The fragrant white flowers are borne in dense clusters in mid-summer to fall. 'Purpurea' has red-tinged leaves and white flowers. Cut these plants back after flowering for a flush of new growth.

C. tangutica (virgin's bower) is a vining late-season bloomer that climbs 16' or more. Its great capacity for spreading makes it a good choice on a chain-link fence, where it will fill in thickly and create a privacy screen. The nodding yellow flowers are followed by distinctive fuzzy seedheads that persist into winter.

C. x jackmanii cultivar (below)

Problems & Pests

Problems with scale insects, whiteflies, aphids, wilt, powdery mildew, rust, leaf spot and stem canker can occur. To avoid wilt, keep mulch from touching the stem, and use clean, sharp pruning tools that leave no ragged cuts. Protect the fragile stems of new plants from injury; a bruised or damaged stem is an entry point for disease.

Columbine

Aquilegia

Height: 9–36" **Spread:** 12–18" **Flower color:** red, yellow, pink, purple, blue, white; color of spurs often differs from that of petals **Blooms:** spring, summer
Zones: 2–9

MY FIRST EXPOSURE TO OUR WILD COLUMBINE (*A. CANADENSIS*) came during a hike along a ridge. Above us a solitary plant hung on the face of a wall of shale that was wet from a trickling spring. The orange and yellow flowers contrasted sharply with the dark gray shale. When you see a plant in its natural setting, you can't help understanding its cultural needs. All columbines like excellent drainage, moist roots, morning sun and shaded afternoons. Try growing them with other partial-shade, moisture-loving plants, such as heucheras, lungworts and dead nettles.

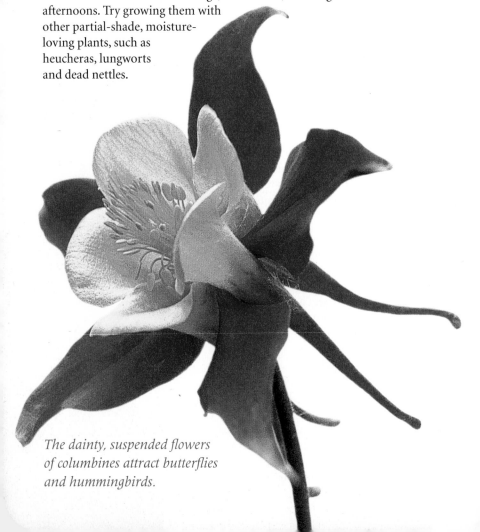

The dainty, suspended flowers of columbines attract butterflies and hummingbirds.

Planting

Seeding: Direct sow in fall or spring

Planting out: Spring

Spacing: 18"

Growing

Columbines grow well in **partial shade**. They prefer soil that is **fertile, moist** and **well drained,** but they adapt to most soil conditions. Division is not required but can be done to propagate desirable plants. The divided plants may take a while to recover because they dislike having their roots disturbed.

'McKana Giants'

Tips

Use columbines in rock gardens, formal or casual borders and naturalized or woodland gardens.

Columbines self-seed but are in no way invasive. Each year a few new seedlings may turn up near the parent plant and can be transplanted. If you have a variety of columbines planted near each other you may even wind up with a new hybrid, because these plants readily cross-breed. A wide variety of flower colors is the most likely and interesting result. Because many columbines grown in gardens are hybrids, the new seedlings may not be identical to the parent. They may revert to one of the original parent species.

A. canadensis

'McKana Giants' (above & center)

A. x hybrida (below)

Recommended

A. canadensis (wild columbine, Canada columbine) is native to Ohio and most of eastern North America and is common in woodlands and fields. It grows up to 24" tall, spreads about 12" and bears yellow flowers with red spurs.

A. x *hybrida* (A. x *cultorum;* hybrid columbine) forms mounds of delicate foliage and has exceptional flowers. Many hybrids have been developed with showy flowers in a wide range of colors. When the parentage of a columbine is uncertain, it is grouped under this name. **'Biedermeier'** is a compact variety, growing 9–12" tall with white, purple or pink flowers. **'Double Pleat'** (Double Pleat Hybrids) includes plants that grow 30–32" tall and bear double flowers in combinations of blue and white or pink and white.

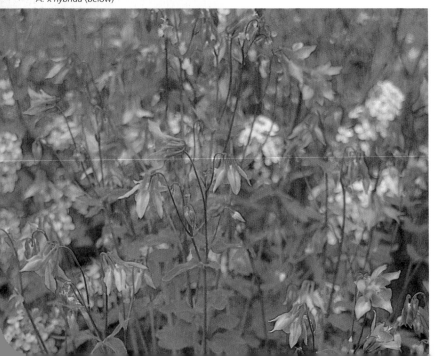

'**Dragonfly**' (Dragonfly Hybrids) includes compact plants up to 24" tall and 12" in spread, with a wide range of flower colors. '**McKana Giants**' (McKana Hybrids) are popular and bear flowers in yellow, pink, red, purple, mauve and white. They grow up to 36" tall.

A. vulgaris (European columbine, common columbine) grows about 36" tall and spreads 18". This species has been used to develop many hybrids and cultivars with flowers in a variety of colors. '**Nora Barlow**' is a popular cultivar with double flowers in white, pink and green-tinged red.

Problems & Pests

Mildew and rust can be troublesome during dry weather. Other problems include leaf miners, fungal leaf spot, aphids and caterpillars. If the foliage becomes ragged from leaf miner attack, simply cut it back and burn it. Do not put infected leaves into the compost pile, or the leaf miner larvae will overwinter and emerge as adult flies to infect next year's columbines.

Columbines are short-lived perennials that seed freely, establishing themselves in unexpected, and often charming, locations. If you wish to keep a particular form, you must preserve it carefully through frequent division or root cuttings.

'McKana Giants'

A. vulgaris 'Nora Barlow'

Coreopsis
Tickseed
Coreopsis

Height: 6–36" **Spread:** 12–24" **Flower color:** yellow, pink or orange
Blooms: early to late summer **Zones:** 3–9

TOLERANT IS ONE WAY TO DESCRIBE COREOPSIS; TOUGH WOULD be another. Three plants of *C. verticillata* 'Zagreb' insist on reappearing in my garden every year through the thick carpet of a spreading cotoneaster. They bloom happily for most of the summer even though the garden is not irrigated, and even during a drought. *C. grandiflora* and *C. verticillata* will bloom continuously through the growing season if deadheaded and if watered during extended dry periods. Unfortunately, the trade-off for the intense bloom seems to be a shortened life span. For a longer-lived coreopsis, plant *C. auriculata* 'Nana'—but you will have only one main flush of blooms in late spring and sporadic blooming thereafter.

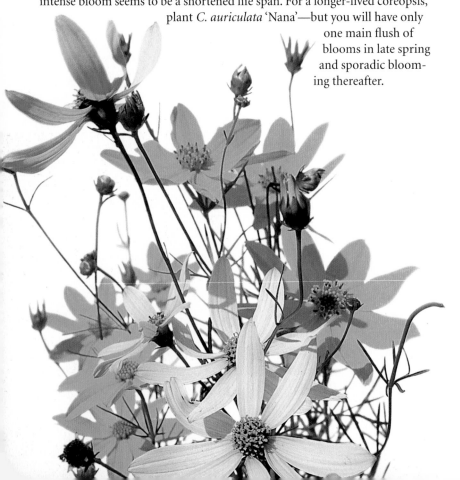

Planting

Seeding: Direct sow in spring. Seeds may be sown indoors in winter, but soil must be kept fairly cool, at 55°–61° F, in order for seeds to germinate.

Planting out: Spring

Spacing: 12–18"

Growing

Grow coreopsis in **full sun**. The soil should be **average, sandy, light** and **well drained**. Plants can develop crown rot in moist, cool locations with heavy soil. Overly fertile soil causes long, floppy growth.

Deadhead daily to keep plants in constant summer bloom. Use scissors to snip out tall stems. Shear plants by one-half in late spring for more compact growth. Frequent division may be required to keep plants vigorous and prolong their lives.

C. grandiflora cultivar

Mass plant coreopsis to fill in a dry, exposed bank where nothing else will grow, and you will enjoy the bright, sunny flowers all summer long.

C. verticillata 'Moonbeam'

C. verticillata
C. grandiflora

Tips

Coreopsis are versatile plants, useful in formal and informal borders and in meadow plantings or cottage gardens. They look best in groups. The low-growing *C. auriculata* is well suited to rock gardens or fronts of borders.

C. grandiflora self-seeds readily but is easy to remove from areas where it isn't wanted.

Recommended

C. auriculata (mouse-eared tickseed) grows 12–24" tall and will steadily creep outwards without becoming invasive. '**Nana**' grows 6–9" tall and bears orange-yellow flowers in late spring.

C. grandiflora (large-flowered coreopsis, tickseed) forms a clump of foliage and bears bright golden yellow flowers over a long period in mid- and late summer. It grows 18–36" tall and spreads 12–18". This species and its cultivars are often grown as annuals because bearing so many flowers leaves them with little energy for surviving the winter. '**Early Sunrise**' is a compact plant that grows 18–24" tall. It bears double yellow flowers and can be started from seed. '**Mayfield Giant**' bears large, bright yellow flowers on plants up to 36" tall.

C. rosea (pink tickseed) is an unusual species with pink flowers. It grows 24" tall and 12" wide. This species is more shade and water tolerant than the other species but is not as vigorous.

C. verticillata (thread-leaf coreopsis) is a mound-forming plant with attractive, finely divided foliage. It grows 24–32" tall and spreads 18". **'Golden Showers'** has large, golden yellow flowers and ferny foliage. **'Moonbeam'** forms a compact mound of delicate foliage. The flowers are a light, creamy yellow. **'Zagreb'** is an upright plant that produces golden blooms over a long period of time.

Problems & Pests

Occasional problems with slugs, bacterial and fungal leaf spot, gray mold, aster yellows, powdery mildew, downy mildew and crown rot are possible.

C. grandiflora 'Early Sunrise'

C. rosea

Cornflower
Mountain Bluet, Perennial Bachelor's Button
Centaurea

Height: 12–24" **Spread:** 12–24" or more **Flower color:** blue, purple, pink, white **Blooms:** late spring to mid-summer **Zones:** 3–8

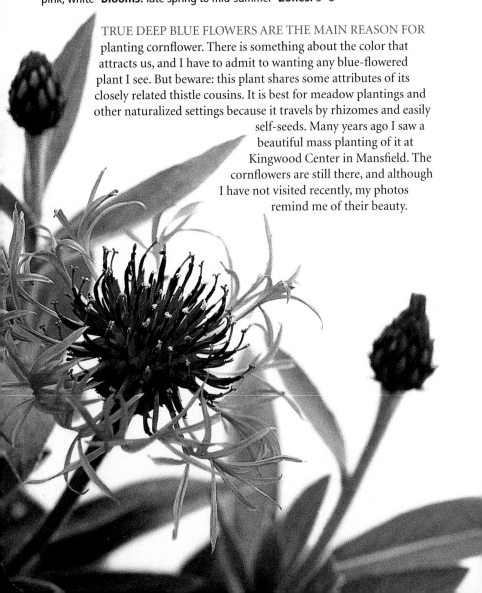

TRUE DEEP BLUE FLOWERS ARE THE MAIN REASON FOR planting cornflower. There is something about the color that attracts us, and I have to admit to wanting any blue-flowered plant I see. But beware: this plant shares some attributes of its closely related thistle cousins. It is best for meadow plantings and other naturalized settings because it travels by rhizomes and easily self-seeds. Many years ago I saw a beautiful mass planting of it at Kingwood Center in Mansfield. The cornflowers are still there, and although I have not visited recently, my photos remind me of their beauty.

Planting

Seeding: Direct sow in late summer; protect seedlings first winter

Planting out: Spring

Spacing: 24"

Growing

Cornflower grows well in **full sun** and **light shade**. The soil should be of **poor or average fertility, moist** and **well drained**. In a rich soil, plants may develop straggly, floppy growth and become invasive. Divide in spring or late summer every two or three years.

Thin the new shoots by about one-third in spring to increase air circulation through the plant. Deadhead promptly to prolong blooming and prevent self-sowing.

Tips

Cornflower makes an attractive addition to borders, informal or natural gardens and large rock gardens. Use a bed-edging material or bottomless flowerpot to surround the plant and limit its spread.

Recommended

C. montana is a mounding or sprawling plant that bears bright cobalt blue flowers from late spring until mid-summer. Plants may self-seed. 'Alba' bears white flowers. 'Carnea' ('Rosea') bears pink flowers.

Problems & Pests

Rare problems with downy or powdery mildew, rust or mold can occur.

For more flowers in late summer, cut plants right back as soon as blooming stops.

Corydalis
Corydalis

Height: 8–18" **Spread:** 8–12" or more **Flower color:** yellow, cream, blue
Blooms: spring, summer **Zones:** 5–7

IN ENGLAND, CORYDALIS GROWS BEAUTIFULLY IN ROCK AND brick walls. Try as I might, I haven't been able to achieve that effect, but even so these plants are growing nicely for me. They have been maligned in some texts as rampant self-seeders, but they haven't been invasive in my garden. The soft gray-green foliage and yellow or cream blossoms of *C. lutea* or *C. ochroleuca* blend well with any other plant. Blue corydalis *(C. flexuosa)* is charming, but its Himalayan origins don't work well with Ohio's hot, humid summers. Hope springs eternal, though, and many Ohio gardeners try to find the right spot in the garden for this blue beauty.

Planting

Seeding: Direct sow fresh seed in early fall; germination can be erratic

Planting out: Spring

Spacing: 12"

Growing

Corydalis plants grow well in **light or partial shade** with morning sun. The soil should be of **average to rich fertility, humus rich** and **well drained.**

Plants will die back in the hottest part of summer. Trim the faded foliage, and new leaves will sprout as the weather cools in late summer and fall. These plants self-seed and can be propagated by transplanting the tiny seedlings. Division can be done in spring or early summer, but corydalis resent having their roots disturbed.

Tips

Corydalis are admired for their delicate flowers and attractive, ferny foliage. Use them in woodland or rock gardens, in borders, on rock walls and along paths. Let them naturalize in unused or underused areas.

Recommended

C. flexuosa (blue corydalis) is an erect plant with blue spring flowers. It grows 12" tall and spreads 8" or more. Keep this plant well watered during hot weather.

C. lutea (yellow corydalis) is a mound-forming perennial that bears yellow flowers from late spring often to early fall. It grows 12–18" tall and spreads 12" or more. This one is the hardiest species; it is

C. flexuosa

also the most vigorous and can become invasive. Most gardeners don't mind the ferny-leaved plants turning up here and there.

C. ochroleuca (white corydalis) bears cream to white flowers in late spring and summer and is very similar to *C. lutea* in habit. It grows about 12" tall, with an equal spread.

Problems & Pests

Rare problems with downy mildew and rust are possible.

C. lutea

Crocosmia
Crocosmia

Height: 18"–4' **Spread:** 12–18" **Flower color:** red, orange, yellow
Blooms: mid- to late summer **Zones:** 5–9

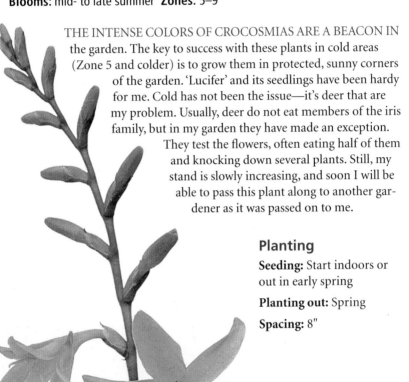

THE INTENSE COLORS OF CROCOSMIAS ARE A BEACON IN the garden. The key to success with these plants in cold areas (Zone 5 and colder) is to grow them in protected, sunny corners of the garden. 'Lucifer' and its seedlings have been hardy for me. Cold has not been the issue—it's deer that are my problem. Usually, deer do not eat members of the iris family, but in my garden they have made an exception. They test the flowers, often eating half of them and knocking down several plants. Still, my stand is slowly increasing, and soon I will be able to pass this plant along to another gardener as it was passed on to me.

Planting

Seeding: Start indoors or out in early spring

Planting out: Spring

Spacing: 8"

Some people still know crocosmias by the older name montbretia. The newer name comes from the Greek words krokos, *'saffron,' and* osme, *'smell,' referring to the saffron-like scent of the dried flowers when placed in water.*

Growing

Crocosmias prefer **full sun**. The soil should be of **average fertility, humus rich, moist** and **well drained**. Plant in a protected area and provide a good mulch of shredded leaves or other organic matter in fall to protect the roots from fluctuating winter temperatures. Divide in spring before growth starts, every two or three years, when the clump is becoming dense. Overgrown clumps produce fewer flowers.

Tips

These attractive and unusual plants create a striking display when planted in groups in a herbaceous or mixed border. They look good when planted next to a pond, where the brightly colored flowers can be reflected in the water.

Recommended

C. x *crocosmiflora* is a spreading plant with long, strap-like leaves. It grows 18–36" tall and the clump spreads about 12". One-sided spikes of red, orange or yellow flowers are borne in mid- and late summer. 'Citronella' ('Golden Fleece') bears bright yellow flowers.

C. 'Lucifer' is the hardiest of the bunch and bears bright scarlet red flowers. It grows 3–4' tall, with a spread of about 18".

Problems & Pests

Occasional trouble with spider mites can occur. Hose the mites off as soon as they appear.

If your garden is too cold in winter for crocosmias to survive, don't despair. The corms can be dug up in fall and stored in slightly damp sawdust or peat moss in a cool, dark place over the winter. Check on them regularly. When they start to sprout, pot them and move them to a well-lit but cool room until they can be planted out.

C. 'Lucifer' with ornamental grasses

Cupid's Dart

Catananche

Height: 18–36" **Spread:** 12" **Flower color:** blue, purple, white
Blooms: mid-summer to fall **Zones:** 3–8

THIS UNASSUMING, DELICATE-LOOKING PLANT DOESN'T LOOK like an arrow, so how did it come by its common name? Historically it was used in love potions, and today it is still used in bouquets as a symbol of love. In the garden, cupid's dart adds movement; its dainty blue flowers sway on long stems in the slightest breeze. This is a plant for drier locations, especially in winter. Place it in a cottage garden, where it will combine beautifully with the annual California poppy and the many summer-blooming daisies.

Planting

Seeding: Direct sow in mid- to late spring when soil temperature is about 70° F

Planting out: Spring

Spacing: 12"

Growing

Cupid's dart prefers **full sun** but tolerates partial shade. The soil should be **sandy, humus rich** and **well drained.** Cupid's dart dislikes wet soil and is very drought tolerant. Find a spot where the ground is well drained and dries out quickly in spring. Divide every year or so to keep the plant vigorous.

This fast-growing perennial will flower the first year from seed. It can be grown as an annual if your soil becomes too wet over the winter for this plant to survive.

Tips

Use cupid's dart in borders, in mass plantings, on dry banks and in cottage gardens, rock gardens and planters.

Recommended

C. caerulea is a clump-forming perennial with narrow, grass-like foliage. Blue or purple-blue flowers are borne from mid-summer to frost. **'Bicolor'** has white flowers with purple centers.

Problems & Pests

Powdery mildew can occur but is unlikely to be a serious problem.

'Bicolor'

The cut flowers of cupid's dart look lovely in fresh or dried arrangements.

C. caerulea & 'Bicolor' with *Limnanthes* & *Gilia*

Daylily
Hemerocallis

Height: 1–4' **Spread:** 2–4' or more **Flower color:** every color except blue and pure white **Blooms:** summer **Zones:** 2–9

HOW CAN A SIMPLE SIX-PETALED FLOWER MANAGE TO INCITE such fascination and passion? I continue to ask myself this question as I buy a fragrant yellow daylily or an intense red daylily or a green spider form. And then there are the miniatures that fit anywhere in the garden. Few gardens are without at least one daylily, even if it is only the orange 'ditch lily' *(H. fulva)*. Daylilies combine well with so many plants. Even out of bloom, the long strap-like leaves create a backdrop for later bloomers. Ohio boasts active daylily clubs that are part of the larger American Hemerocallis Society. In central Ohio, several breeders have introduced many cultivars to daylily lovers. I own a few myself, including 'Pardon Me,' 'Hyperion' and 'Little Grapette.'

Planting

Seeding: Not recommended; hybrids and cultivars don't come true to type

Planting out: Spring

Spacing: 1–4'

Growing

Daylilies grow in any light from **full sun to full shade.** The deeper the shade, the fewer flowers will be produced. The soil should be **fertile, moist** and **well drained,** but these plants adapt to most conditions and are hard to kill once established. Feed your daylilies in spring and mid-summer to produce the best display of blooms. Divide every two to three years to keep plants vigorous and to propagate them. They can, however, be left indefinitely without dividing.

Tips

Plant daylilies alone, or group them in borders, on banks and in ditches

Derived from the Greek words for day, hemera, *and beauty,* kallos, *the genus name, like the common name, indicates that each lovely bloom lasts for only one day.*

to control erosion. They can be naturalized in woodland or meadow gardens. Small varieties are nice in planters.

Deadhead small varieties to keep them blooming as long as possible. Be careful when deadheading purple-flowered daylilies, because the sap can stain fingers and clothes.

Recommended

You can find an almost infinite number of forms, sizes and colors in a range of species, cultivars and hybrids. See your local garden center or daylily grower to find out what's available and most suitable for your garden. Several commonly available and attractive daylilies are listed here.

H. citrina (citron daylily, lemon lily) grows up to 4' tall and spreads about 24". It bears very fragrant, yellow flowers that open in the evening.

H. fulva (tawny daylily, orange daylily) is a large, often invasive plant. It is not native but

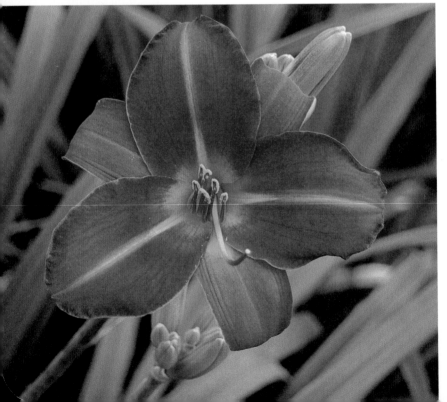

has naturalized in most of eastern North America. It grows 3–4' tall, can spread 2–4' or more and bears orange flowers for a long period in mid- and late summer. This plant is often seen growing in ditches alongside roads.

H. '**Happy Returns**' bears yellow flowers for most of the summer. It grows about 16" tall.

H. '**Hyperion**' has fragrant yellow flowers and grows about 36" tall and wide.

H. '**Little Grapette**' has small purple flowers and grows 12" tall and wide.

H. '**Pardon Me**' has bright red flowers with greenish throats. It grows 18" tall and wide.

H. '**Stella d'Oro**' is a repeat bloomer. The bright, golden apricot flowers are borne on modest-sized 12" plants.

Problems & Pests

Generally these plants are pest free. Rare problems with rust, *Hemerocallis* gall midge, aphids, spider mites, thrips and slugs are possible.

H. fulva cultivar

More than 12,000 daylily varieties have been developed, and hundreds more are added yearly.

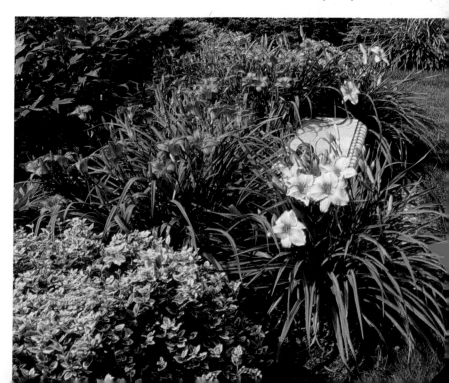

Dead Nettle

Lamium, Spotted Dead Nettle, Yellow Archangel

Lamium

Height: 4–24" **Spread:** indefinite **Flower color:** white, pink, yellow, mauve; plant also grown for foliage **Blooms:** spring, summer **Zones:** 3–8

DEAD NETTLES ARE AMONG MY FAVORITE GROUNDCOVERS, BUT it is difficult to sell a plant with such a dismal common name. The association with death and stinging plants is unfortunate, but dead nettles are such good garden performers that they rise above the name. Once established they are relatively drought tolerant, but they prefer to receive a good drink when our summer heats up. In mild winters, they are evergreen and provide that much-needed green fix in January. Plant dead nettles under columbines and other spring ephemerals to provide a summer and fall carpet, and to hide holes left by plants that go dormant in summer.

Planting

Seeding: Not recommended; cultivars don't come true to type

Planting out: Spring

Spacing: 12–24"

Growing

Dead nettles prefer **partial to light shade.** They tolerate full sun but may become leggy. The soil should be of **average fertility, humus rich, moist** and **well drained.** The more fertile the soil, the more vigorously the plants will grow. These plants are drought tolerant when grown in the shade but can develop bare patches if the soil is allowed to dry out for extended periods. Divide and replant in fall if bare spots become unsightly.

Dead nettles remain more compact if sheared back after flowering. If they remain green over winter, shear back in early spring.

L. maculatum cultivar

Dead nettles are so named because their leaves resemble those of stinging nettle but have no sting.

L. galeobdolon 'Florentinum'

Tips

These plants make useful groundcovers for woodland or shade gardens or for under shrubs in a border, where the dead nettles will help keep weeds down.

Keep in mind that dead nettles can overwhelm less vigorous plants. If your dead nettles become invasive, pull some of them up, making sure to remove the fleshy roots.

Recommended

L. galeobdolon (*Lamiastrum galeobdolon;* yellow archangel) can be quite invasive, though the cultivars are less so. It grows 12–24" tall and spreads indefinitely. The flowers are yellow and bloom in spring to early summer. **'Florentinum'** ('Variegatum') has silver foliage with green margins. **'Hermann's Pride'** is a clump former instead of a runner. The leaves are silver between the veins. **'Silver Angel'** is a prostrate cultivar with silvery foliage.

L. galeobdolon 'Florentinum' (this page)

L. maculatum (spotted dead nettle) is the most commonly grown dead nettle. This low-growing, spreading species grows 8" tall and at least 36" wide. The green leaves often have white or silvery markings. White, pink or mauve flowers are borne in spring and early summer. '**Aureum**' has gold or yellow foliage with white-striped centers. Its flowers are pink. '**Beacon Silver**' has green-edged, silver foliage and pink flowers. '**Beedham's White**' has yellow to gold foliage with white flowers. '**Chequers**' has green leaves with silver stripes down the centers. The flowers are mauve. '**Orchid Frost**' has silvery foliage with green margins. It bears deep pink flowers on 4–6" stems. '**White Nancy**' bears white flowers and its silver leaves have green margins.

Problems & Pests

Rare problems with slugs, powdery mildew, downy mildew and leaf spot are possible.

L. maculatum 'Beacon Silver'

L. maculatum cultivar with *Verbena*

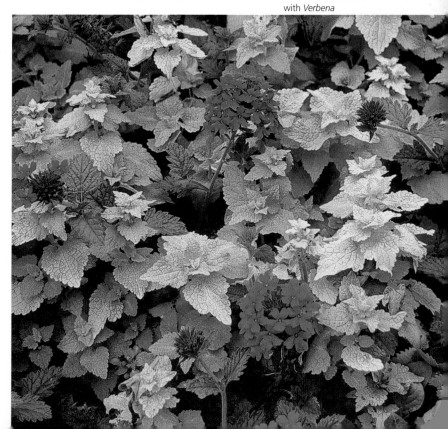

Dwarf Plumbago
Plumbago, Leadwort
Ceratostigma

Height: 10–18" **Spread:** 12–18" **Flower color:** deep blue
Blooms: late summer **Zones:** 5–9

A CLUE TO DWARF PLUMBAGO'S RHIZOMATOUS HABIT WAS CLEAR
to me when I purchased my first—and only—plant. Small plantlets were
growing out of the drainage holes at the bottom of the pot. My 'single' plant
has spread nicely at the front edge of a partly shaded bed. Dwarf plumbago is
tough, especially when it is not situated in a western exposure. During a
recent seven-week dry spell, I watered it only twice. For the early part of the
season, this groundcover's leaves are a soft, almost lime green. In summer it
produces deep, true blue flowers that are cradled in red calyces (the sepals).
Later in fall the leaves turn a beautiful burnished red. Plant dwarf plumbago
under a tree that changes to scarlet in fall for an eye-catching combination.

Planting

Seeding: Not recommended

Planting out: Spring or fall

Spacing: 12"

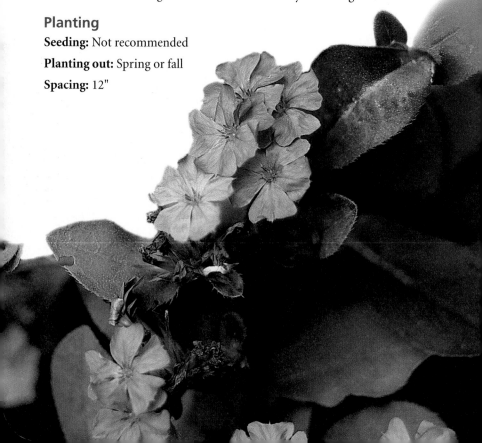

Growing

Grow dwarf plumbago in **full sun** or **partial shade**—plants will not bloom in full shade. The soil should be **average or rich** and **well drained**. This quick-growing plant is moderately drought tolerant once established and makes an excellent, tough groundcover. A mulch should be used to provide protection in winter. Divide dwarf plumbago in spring.

Dwarf plumbago may not die back completely in winter, and any growth that has been killed or damaged in winter should be removed in spring. Any unsightly or irregular growth may be removed in fall. Cuttings may be started from new growth in early summer.

'Plumbago' comes from plumbum, *Latin for 'lead,' referring to a traditional belief that some species could cure lead poisoning.*

Tips

This plant is useful on exposed banks where mowing is impossible or undesirable. Dwarf plumbago also makes a wonderful addition to a rock garden. It creeps happily between the rocks of a stone wall.

Be careful not to disturb the planting site in early spring because the foliage emerges late.

Recommended

C. plumbaginoides (Plumbago larpentiae) is a low, mounding, spreading plant. It bears bright blue flowers in late summer. The foliage turns an attractive bronzy red in fall.

Problems & Pests

Powdery mildew causes occasional problems that are preventable with good drainage.

Euphorbia
Cushion Spurge
Euphorbia

Height: 12–24" **Spread:** 12–24" **Flower color:** yellow, green, orange; plant also grown for foliage **Blooms:** spring to mid-summer **Zones:** 4–9

NEXT TO CACTI, EUPHORBIAS ARE THE BEST DROUGHT-TOLERANT plants for Ohio gardens. Their leaves can be gray to dark green and leathery, or small and numerous. Both leaf types are adaptations to hot, dry conditions and poor soils. Watch out, though: some euphorbias can be invasive, especially in fertile soil, and can take over the garden in two to three years. Right now, my favorite is *E. amygdaloides* var. *robbiae*. It is a shade-tolerant, drought-tolerant evergreen that looks great when the rest of the garden is wilting. Like many other euphorbias, it does spread, but its rhizomes are large and close to the surface and therefore easy to pull up. Try this plant in your worst dry shade site, and you won't be disappointed.

Planting

Seeding: Start seed in cold frame in spring; use fresh seed for best germination

Planting out: Spring or fall

Spacing: 18"

Growing

Euphorbias grow well in **full sun** and **light shade**. The soil should be of **average fertility, moist, humus rich** and **well drained**. These plants are drought tolerant and can be invasive in a too-fertile soil. They do not tolerate wet conditions.

You can propagate euphorbias by stem cuttings; they may also self-seed in the garden. Division is rarely required. These plants dislike being disturbed once established.

Tips

Use euphorbias in a mixed or herbaceous border, rock garden or lightly shaded woodland garden.

If you are cutting the stems for propagation, dip the cut ends into hot water before planting to stop the sticky white sap from running.

E. polychroma

E. dulcis 'Chameleon'

E. polychroma (this page)

Don't confuse these euphorbias with the highly invasive leafy spurge *(E. esula)*. Leafy spurge is a noxious weed and is rarely sold in garden centers, but it is common at perennial exchanges and should be strenuously avoided.

Recommended

E. amygdaloides var. *robbiae* is a shade-tolerant and very drought-tolerant euphorbia. It grows about 24" tall and spreads about 12". The deep green, glossy leaves are evergreen to semi-evergreen in Zone 5 winters. This variety is excellent for the difficult dry shade garden.

E. dulcis is a compact, upright plant about 12" tall, with an equal spread. The spring flowers and bracts are yellow-green. The dark bronze-green leaves turn red and orange in fall. 'Chameleon' has purple-red foliage that turns darker purple in fall. It bears clusters of chartreuse flowers. This cultivar and the species will self-seed.

E. polychroma (*E. epithimoides;* cushion spurge) is a mounding, clump-forming plant 12–24" tall and 18–24" in spread. The inconspicuous flowers are surrounded by long-lasting yellow bracts. The foliage turns shades of purple, red or orange in fall. There are several cultivars, though the species is more commonly available. **'Candy'** has yellow bracts and flowers, and the leaves and stems are tinged with purple. **'Emerald Jade'** is a compact plant that grows to 14" in height. The bracts are yellow and the flowers are bright green.

You may wish to wear gloves when handling these plants; some people find the milky sap irritates their skin. Many euphorbias are also toxic if ingested.

Problems & Pests

Aphids, spider mites and nematodes are possible problems, along with root rot in poorly drained, wet soil.

E. polychroma

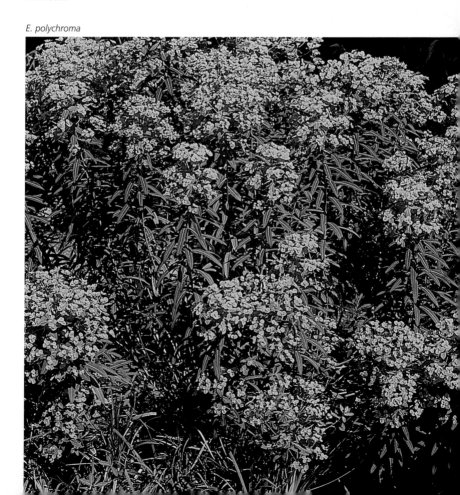

False Solomon's Seal

Smilacina

Height: 36" **Spread:** 2–4' **Flower color:** white
Blooms: mid- to late spring **Zones:** 3–9

A NATIVE SPECIES OF NORTH AMERICAN WOODLANDS, FALSE
Solomon's seal is easily recognized by its beautiful white plumes of flowers.
In summer, the flowers develop into small red berries that weigh the tips of
the stems nearly to the ground. This plant is often confused with Solomon's
seal *(Polygonatum)*, but Solomon's seal's bell-like flowers dangle from the
stem in pairs, rather than clustering in a plume at the tip. Combine false
Solomon's seal with other native, spring-blooming woodland plants, such as
bloodroot *(Sanguinaria canadensis)*, wild columbine *(Aquilegia canadensis)*,
wild ginger *(Asarum canadense)* and Virginia bluebell *(Mertensia virginica)*.
A bonus: false Solomon's seal is usually untouched by browsing deer.

Planting

Seeding: Not recommended

Planting out: Spring or fall

Spacing: 24"

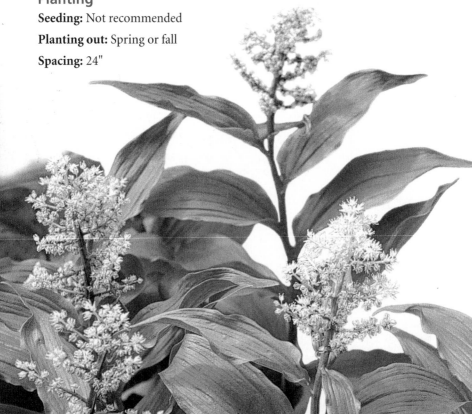

Growing

False Solomon's seal grows well in **light or full shade**. The soil should be of **average fertility, humus rich, acidic, moist** and **well drained**. Add peat moss to the soil when planting, and mulch with shredded oak leaves or pine needles to provide the acidic, humus-rich conditions this plant enjoys. Divide in spring.

Tips

Use false Solomon's seal in an open woodland or natural garden. In a shaded border it can be combined with hostas and other shade-loving perennials.

Recommended

S. racemosa (Maianthemum racemosum) forms a spreading clump of upright, arching stems. White, plume-like flowers appear in spring, followed by berries that ripen in late summer and fall.

Problems & Pests

Rust and leaf spot are possible but rarely serious problems.

The berries of this plant develop in an unusual way. The unripe green berries develop little red spots that eventually cover the entire fruit.

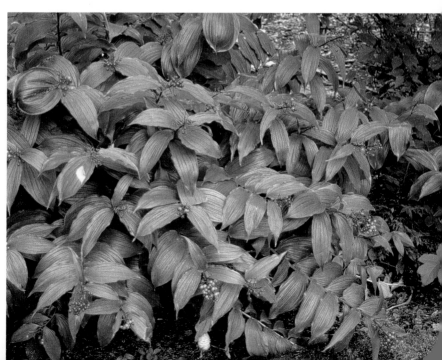

Foamflower

Tiarella

Height: 4–12" **Spread:** 12–24" **Flower color:** white, pink
Blooms: spring, sometimes to early summer **Zones:** 3–8

FOAMFLOWERS ARE ATTRACTIVE WHETHER IN OR OUT OF BLOOM
While the native *T. cordifolia* is lovely, consider also the modern cultivars,
which have been selected for attractive leaf colors and patterns. The creamy
flowers are a bonus, rising above the leaves like elongated bottlebrushes.
Combine foamflowers with other moisture-loving shade plants, such as
Jacob's ladder, bugbane *(Cimicifuga),* goat's beard and the hostas. The foamflower genus, *Tiarella,* is closely related to *Heuchera*—so closely that they
will cross to form the intergeneric hybrid *Heucherella.* The hybrid cultivars
seem to combine the best foliage and flowers of the two genera.

Planting

Seeding: Start seed in cold frame in spring

Planting out: Spring

Spacing: 6–24"

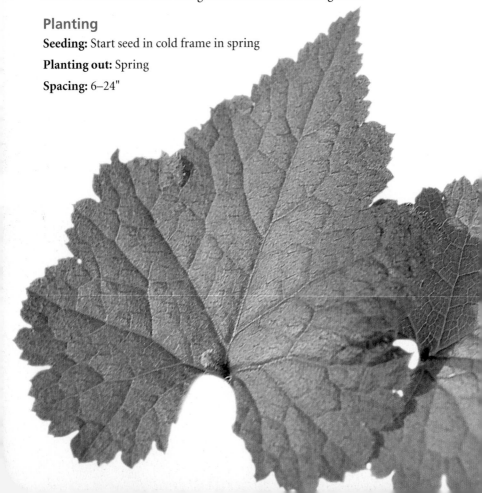

Growing

Foamflowers prefer **partial, light or full shade** without afternoon sun. The soil should be **humus rich, moist** and **slightly acidic.** These plants adapt to most soils.

Divide in spring. Deadhead to encourage re-blooming. If the foliage fades or rusts in summer, cut it partway to the ground. New growth will emerge.

Tips

Foamflowers are excellent groundcovers for shaded and woodland gardens. They can be included in shaded borders and left to naturalize in wild gardens.

These plants spread by underground stems, which are easily pulled up to stop excessive spread.

Recommended

T. cordifolia is a low-growing, spreading plant that bears spikes of foamy-looking, white flowers. This species is native to Ohio and eastern North America. It is attractive enough to be grown for its foliage alone, and cultivars with interesting variegation are becoming available. 'Oakleaf' forms a dense clump of dark green leaves and bears pink flowers. Its foliage turns red in fall.

T. '**Maple Leaf**' is a clump-forming hybrid with bronze green, maple-like leaves and pink-flushed flowers.

Problems & Pests

Rust and slugs are possible problems.

T. 'Maple Leaf'

T. cordifolia 'Oakleaf'

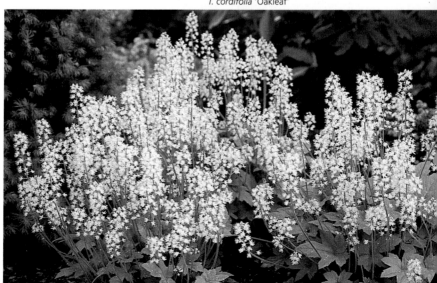

Foxglove
Digitalis

Height: 2–5' **Spread:** 12–24" **Flower color:** pink, purple, yellow, maroon, red, white **Blooms:** late spring, summer **Zones:** 3–8

TWO OLD COMMON NAMES FOR FOXGLOVE ARE FAIRY THIMBLES and fairy bells. Legend has it that fairies sleep in the pendent bells, and you must *never* disturb a fairy when he or she is asleep. At least this is what we tell children so they will avoid touching or eating any part of these plants. They contain digitoxin, a very strong heart stimulator. At times they have been mistaken for comfrey and made into a tea, with fatal results. Plant foxgloves out of easy reach, and enjoy the strong vertical accent they add to the garden. They make a perfect foil for the daisy family members that are so common in the summer landscape.

Planting

Seeding: Direct sow or start in cold frame in early spring. Seeds need light in order to germinate. Flowering is unlikely the first year.

Planting out: Spring

Spacing: 12–24"

Foxgloves are extremely poisonous; simply touching one of these plants has been known to cause rashes, headaches and nausea.

Growing

Foxgloves grow well in **partial or light shade**. The soil should be **fertile, humus rich and moist**. Purple and strawberry foxgloves prefer an acidic soil, while yellow and rusty foxgloves prefer an alkaline soil, but these plants adapt to most soils that are neither too wet nor too dry. Division is unnecessary for purple foxglove because this plant will not live long enough to be divided. It continues to occupy your garden by virtue of its ability to self-seed. Yellow, strawberry and rusty foxgloves can be divided in spring or fall.

You may wish to deadhead foxgloves once they have finished flowering, but it is a good idea to leave some of the spikes of purple foxglove in place to self-seed. Remember to wear gloves when handling these toxic plants.

The hybrid varieties become less vigorous with time and self-sown seedlings may not come true to type. Sprinkle new seed in your foxglove bed each spring to ensure a steady show from the lovely flowers.

D. purpurea (this page)

D. purpurea 'Alba' (above)

Tips

Foxgloves are must-haves for the cottage garden or for people interested in heritage plants. They make excellent vertical accents along the back of a border. They also make interesting additions to woodland gardens.

Some staking may be required if the plants are in a windy location. Remove the tallest spike and the side shoots will bloom on shorter stalks that may not need staking.

Recommended

D. ferruginea (rusty foxglove) is a biennial or perennial that spreads about 12". This plant forms a basal rosette of leaves and produces 3–4' spikes of reddish orange flowers. It self-seeds easily.

D. lutea (yellow foxglove, small yellow foxglove) is a true perennial, unlike purple foxglove and its varieties, which are generally biennials. *D. lutea* is a clump-forming plant that grows 24" tall and spreads about 12". It bears spikes of yellow flowers in summer.

D. x *mertonensis* (strawberry foxglove) is also a true perennial. It forms a clump of foliage with flower-bearing stems 3–4' tall. The spring and early-summer flowers are rose pink.

D. purpurea (purple foxglove) forms a basal rosette of foliage from which tall flowering spikes emerge, growing 2–5' tall and spreading 24". The flowers bloom in early summer and come in a wide range of colors. The insides of the flowers are often spotted with contrasting colors. If purple foxglove is not winter hardy in your garden, it can be grown as an annual from purchased plants. 'Alba' bears white flowers. 'Apricot' bears apricot pink flowers. **Excelsior Hybrids**, available in many colors, bear dense spikes of flowers. **Foxy Hybrids**, which also come in a range of colors, are considered dwarf by foxglove standards but easily reach 36" in height. They bloom in their first year and often need to be replaced each year.

D. purpurea (this page)

Problems & Pests

Anthracnose, fungal leaf spot, powdery mildew, root and stem rot, aphids, Japanese beetles and mealybugs are possible problems for foxgloves.

The heart medication digitalis is made from extracts of foxglove. For over 200 years, D. purpurea *has been used for treating heart failure.*

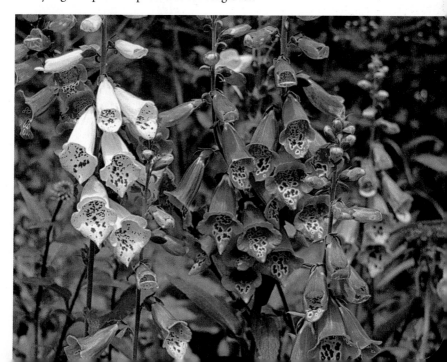

Gaura

Gaura

Height: 2–5' **Spread:** 24–36" **Flower color:** white, pink
Blooms: late spring, summer, early fall **Zones:** 5–8

THE AIRY GAURA IS THE PERFECT SEE-THROUGH PLANT. ITS LONG
stems and delicate flowers wave gently in the wind and add movement to the
garden with the slightest breeze. *G. lindheimeri*, which comes to us from
Texas and Louisiana, is a tough customer once it has established its long taproot. Finally, here is a plant that will tolerate our hot, humid summers. But
do not place it where it will have wet feet in winter. As with so many perennials that are described as cold intolerant, it's not the cold weather but the
wet soils that do it in.

Planting

Seeding: Start seed in spring or early summer
when soil temperature is 65°–75° F

Planting out: Spring

Spacing: 18–24"

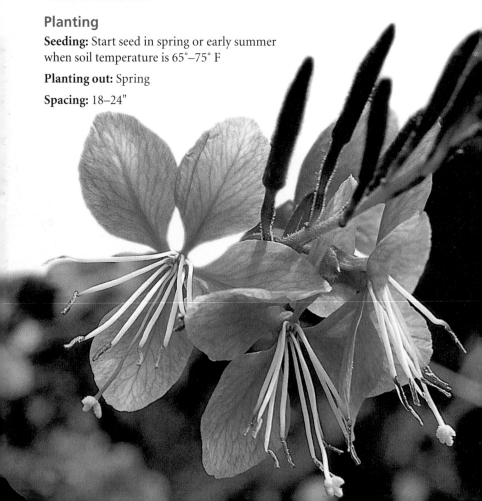

Growing

Gaura prefers **full sun** but tolerates partial shade. The soil should be **fertile, moist** and **well drained**. Gaura is drought tolerant once established. Plants dislike sitting in wet soil over the winter, so amend your soil to improve the drainage if needed. Clumps rarely need dividing and resent having their roots disturbed. Most plants self-seed, and the new seedlings can be carefully transplanted if desired.

Tips

Gaura makes a wonderful addition to mixed borders. Its airy habit softens the effect of brightly colored flowers. It bears only a few flowers at a time, but if the faded flower spikes are removed it will keep flowering all summer. Plant gaura behind low, bushy plants, such as hardy geraniums, cornflowers or asters, to display the delicate, floating flowers to best advantage.

Recommended

G. lindheimeri (white gaura, Lindheimer's beeblossom) forms a large, bushy clump 3–5' tall and 24–36" in spread. Spikes of small white or pinkish flowers are borne on long slender stems all summer. 'Corrie's Gold' has a more compact habit, 24–36" tall. It has yellow-variegated foliage and its white flowers are tinged pink. 'Siskiyou Pink' bears bright pink flowers. 'Whirling Butterflies' is a long-flowering, compact cultivar that grows 24–36" tall. The white flowers are borne from late spring to early fall. This cultivar will not self-seed.

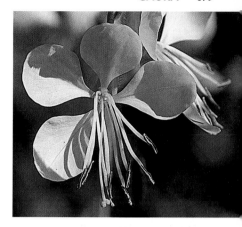

Problems & Pests

Rare problems with rust, fungal leaf spot, downy mildew and powdery mildew can occur.

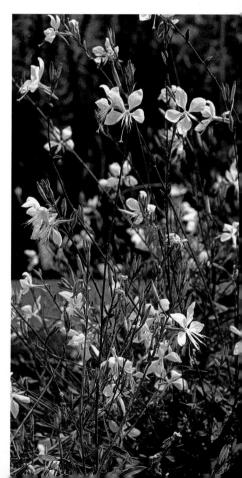

Globe Thistle
Small Globe Thistle
Echinops

Height: 2–4' **Spread:** 24" **Flower color:** blue, purple
Blooms: late summer **Zones:** 3–8

I HAVE BEEN ASKED WHY I LET WEEDY thistles grow in my garden, and I get looks of disbelief as I explain that globe thistle is not a weed, it's a perennial. If one defines a weed as a plant that grows in the wrong place, then my globe thistle is not a weed as long as I remove errant seedlings to keep it growing where I want it. Unfortunately, the leaves of globe thistle do look a lot like those of the weedy Canada thistle. The flowerhead, however, is very different. Picture a round globe of silvery blue flowers as a subtle accent to other summer-blooming perennials, such as garden phlox and gas plant *(Dictamnus)*.

Planting

Seeding: Direct sow in spring

Planting out: Spring or fall

Spacing: 18–24"

*This plant is a good choice
for gardeners who need a large,
low-maintenance specimen
to fill an unused corner.*

Growing

Globe thistle prefers **full sun** but tolerates partial shade. The soil should be of **poor to average fertility** and **well drained**. Divide in spring when the clump appears dense or overgrown, becomes less vigorous or begins to show dead areas. Wear gloves and long sleeves to protect yourself from the prickles when dividing.

Deadheading prevents self-seeding. Cutting back to the basal foliage after flowering may result in a second round of blooms.

Tips

Globe thistle is a striking plant for the back or center of the border and for neglected areas of the garden that often miss watering.

Recommended

E. ritro forms a compact clump of spiny foliage with round clusters of purple or blue flowers. **'Vietch's Blue'** has smaller but more abundant flowers.

Problems & Pests

Globe thistle rarely has any problems, but aphids can show up from time to time.

Goat's Beard

Aruncus

Height: 6"–6' **Spread:** 1–6' **Flower color:** cream, white
Blooms: early summer, mid-summer **Zones:** 3–7

GIANT GOAT'S BEARD *(A. DIOICUS)* IS THE KING OR QUEEN OF THE shade garden, depending on which sex it is. Goat's beard is one of the few herbaceous perennials that is dioecious: it has only male or female flowers on each plant. Given optimal conditions, giant goat's beard can grow to 6' tall and wide, so it is often used as a specimen. Most people do not have the space to include more than one or two of these giants in the garden. If you like the fern-like foliage but have limited space, consider the more diminutive *A. dioicus* cultivars or the dwarf Korean goat's beard *(A. aethusifolius)*. Goat's beards are sometimes confused with the rather similar astilbes (p. 86), which thrive in similar conditions and make good companion plants.

Planting

Seeding: Use fresh seed and keep soil moist and conditions humid; soil temperature should be 70°–75° F

Planting out: Spring or fall

Spacing: 18"–6'

Growing

These plants prefer **partial to full shade**. If planted in deep shade, they bear fewer blooms. They will tolerate some full sun as long as the soil is kept evenly moist and they are protected from the afternoon sun. The soil should be **rich** and **moist,** with plenty of **humus** mixed in.

A. dioicus (this page)

Divide in spring or fall, though goat's beard plants may be difficult to divide because they develop a thick root mass. Use a sharp knife to cut the root mass into pieces. An axe may be required for large plants with very dense root masses. Fortunately, these plants will remain happy in the same location for a long time.

Goat's beards self-seed if flowers are left in place, but deadheading maintains an attractive appearance and encourages a longer blooming period. If you want to start some new plants from seed, allow the seedheads to ripen before removing them. You will need to have both male and female plants in order to produce seeds that will sprout. Don't save male flower clusters—they will not produce seeds.

Tips

These plants look very natural growing at the sunny entrance or edge of a woodland garden, in a native plant garden or in a large island planting. They may also be used in a border or alongside a stream or pond.

Recommended

A. aethusifolius (dwarf Korean goat's beard) forms a low-growing, compact mound. It grows 6–16" tall and spreads up to 12". Branched spikes of loosely held, cream flowers are produced in early summer. This plant looks similar to astilbe and is sometimes sold by that name.

A. dioicus (giant goat's beard, common goat's beard) forms a large, bushy, shrub-like perennial 3–6' tall, with an equal spread. Large plumes of cream white flowers are borne

A. dioicus

from early to mid-summer. There are several cultivars, though some can be hard to find. **Var.** *astilbioides* is a dwarf variety that grows only 24" tall. **'Kneiffii'** is a dainty cultivar with finely divided leaves and arching stems with nodding plumes. It grows about 36" tall and spreads 18". **'Zweiweltkind'** ('Child of Two Worlds') is a compact plant with drooping, white flowers.

Problems & Pests
Occasional problems with fly larvae and tarnished plant bugs are possible.

Male goat's beard plants have full, fuzzy flowers; female plants have more pendulous flowers.

A. dioicus

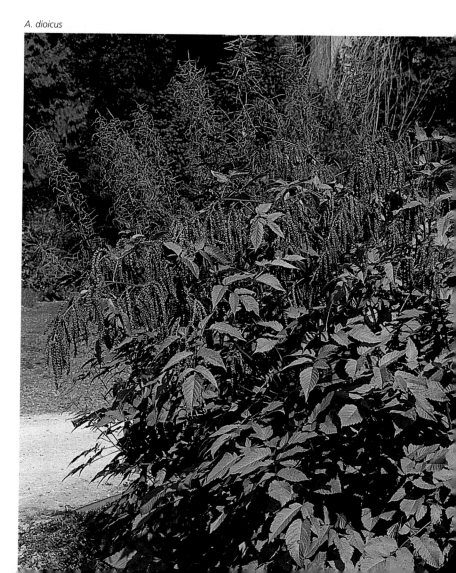

Golden Marguerite
Marguerite Daisy, Marshall Chamomile
Anthemis

Height: 8–36" **Spread:** 24–36" **Flower color:** yellow, orange, cream, white
Blooms: summer **Zones:** 3–7

GOLDEN MARGUERITES ROAM AROUND MY GARDEN. THEIR golden blooms and gray-green leaves blend beautifully with most other plants. These perennials tend to be short-lived, but they self-seed easily. I suppose I could divide the mature plants to help them live longer, but why bother when a seedling is happy to take its place? Golden Marguerites are undemanding and freely flower through most of the summer. They mix contentedly with other non-fussy perennials, such as thyme, butterfly weed, perennial salvia and sea holly.

Planting
Seeding: Direct sow in spring

Planting out: Spring

Spacing: 18–24"

Growing
Golden Marguerites prefer **full sun**. The soil should be of **average fertility** and **well drained**. These plants are drought tolerant. The clumps tend to die out in the middle and should be divided every two or three years in spring or fall.

Flowering tends to occur in waves. Deadhead to encourage continuous flowering all summer. If the plants begin to look thin, cut them back hard to promote new growth and flowers. These plants are avid self-seeders, so deadhead if you don't want new plants popping up all over.

To avoid the need for staking, cut plants back in May or group several of them together so they can support each other. Otherwise, when the plants are young, insert twiggy branches around them as future supports.

Tips

Golden Marguerites form attractive clumps that blend wonderfully into a cottage-style garden. Their drought tolerance makes them ideal choices for rock gardens and for exposed slopes.

Recommended

A. marshalliana (Marshall chamomile) is a low, mounding plant up to 18" tall. Its finely divided leaves are covered in long, silvery hairs. Bright golden yellow flowers are borne in summer.

A. tinctoria (golden Marguerite, Marguerite daisy) forms a mounded clump of foliage that is completely covered in bright or pale yellow, daisy-like flowers in summer. '**Beauty of Grallach**' has deep orange-yellow flowers. '**E.C. Buxton**' has flowers with creamy yellow petals and yellow centers. '**Grallach Gold**' has bright golden yellow flowers. '**Kelwayi**' bears rich yellow blossoms up to 2" in diameter.

'**Moonlight**' has large, pale yellow flowers. '**Sauce Hollandaise**' flowers have pale, creamy petals and bright yellow centers.

Problems & Pests

Golden Marguerites may occasionally have problems with aphids and with fungal problems such as powdery or downy mildew.

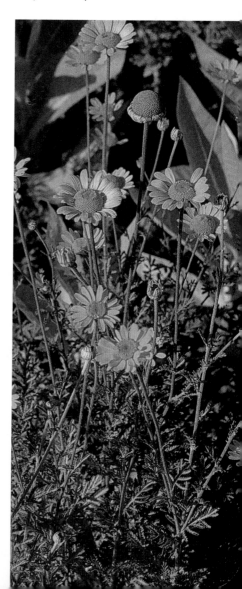

Goldenrod

Solidago

Height: 2–4' **Spread:** 18" **Flower color:** yellow
Blooms: mid-summer through fall **Zones:** 2–8

LIKE OUR ASTERS, THE GOLDENRODS HAD TO GO OVERSEAS TO
get respect. Goldenrods are beautiful prairie plants, and if you travel in late
summer you will see their cheerful yellow blooms in fields and along roads
with our native asters and grasses. Most of the garden-worthy goldenrods are
of hybrid origin because several of the species are quite weedy. I mistakenly
let *S. canadensis*, which can grow 6' tall, into my garden, and I have been
pulling out rhizomes and seedlings for three years. In another area, 'Crown
of Rays' is behaving itself nicely.

Planting

Seeding: Not recommended; desirable cultivars do not come true to type
from seed

Planting out: Spring or fall

Spacing: 12"

Growing

Goldenrods prefer **full sun** but tolerate partial shade. The soil should be of **poor to average fertility, light** and **well drained**. Too fertile a soil will result in lush, invasive growth but few flowers. Divide in spring or fall when needed to control growth and keep plants vigorous.

Tips

Goldenrods are good plants for late-season color. They look at home in a large border, cottage garden or wild-flower garden. Don't plant them near less vigorous plants because the goldenrods can quickly over-whelm them.

Goldenrods have long been unjustly accused as the cause of hay fever. These plants, with their very noticeable yellow flowers, bloom at the same time as the actual, less showy culprit—ragweed.

Recommended

S. **hybrids** have been developed for their improved habit and flowering over the common wild goldenrods. Plants form a clump of strong stems with narrow leaves. They generally grow about 24–36" tall and spread about 18". Plume-like clusters of yellow flowers are produced from mid-summer to fall. 'Crown of Rays' holds its flower clusters in horizontal spikes. 'Golden Shower' bears flowers in horizontal or drooping plumes. This is a taller cultivar that reaches 3–4'.

Problems & Pests

Goldenrods seldom have major problems, though stem galls, leaf spot, rust and powdery mildew may occur from time to time.

Hardy Geranium
Cranesbill Geranium
Geranium

Height: 4–36" **Spread:** 12–36" **Flower color:** white, red, pink, purple, blue
Blooms: spring, summer, fall **Zones:** 3–8

WHEN PRESSED TO NAME MY FAVORITE PLANT (AN IMPOSSIBLE task), I tend to gravitate toward the hardy geraniums. Many have striking incised foliage that provides a wonderful backdrop for other plants. Quite a few have leaves that turn scarlet in fall. Some have scented foliage. And last but not least, many have deeply colored flowers in red to blue jewel tones. Hardy geraniums tend to have one major bloom time and then bloom sporadically over the rest of the season. One of my favorites is bigroot geranium (*G. macrorrhizum*). It tolerates a wide range of conditions, and on warm days it releases a wonderful citrus-like scent.

Planting
Seeding: Species are easy to start from seed in early fall or spring; cultivars and hybrids may not come true to type

Planting out: Spring or fall

Spacing: 12–24"

Growing

Hardy geraniums grow well in **full sun, partial shade** and **light shade**. Some tolerate heavier shade. These plants dislike hot weather. Soil of **average fertility** and **good drainage** is preferred, but most conditions are tolerated except water-logged soil. *G. renardii* needs a poor, well-drained soil to grow well.

Divide in spring. Shear back spent blooms for a second set of flowers. If the foliage looks tatty in late summer, prune it back to rejuvenate.

Tips

These long-flowering plants are great in the border, filling in the spaces between shrubs and other larger plants and keeping the weeds down. They can be included in rock gardens and woodland gardens and mass planted as groundcovers.

Recommended

G. 'Brookside' is a clump-forming, drought-tolerant geranium with finely cut leaves. It grows 12–18" tall and spreads about 24". The deep blue

G. pratense
G. sanguineum

G. sanguineum var. striatum

Hardy geraniums are often called cranesbills because the distinctive seed capsule resembles a crane's long bill.

G. x oxonianum

to violet blue flowers appear in summer. (Zones 3–8)

G. cinereum (grayleaf geranium) forms a basal rosette of gray-green foliage 4–6" tall and about 12" in spread. It produces small clusters of white or pink-veined flowers in early summer. It is often grown in rock gardens and other well-drained spots. 'Ballerina' has silvery foliage and pink flowers darkly veined in purple. (Zones 5–8)

G. 'Johnson's Blue' forms a spreading mat of foliage 12–18" tall and about 30" wide. It bears bright blue flowers over a long period in summer. (Zones 3–8)

G. macrorrhizum (bigroot geranium, scented cranesbill) forms a spreading mound of fragrant foliage. It grows 12–20" tall and spreads 16–24". This plant is quite drought tolerant. Flowers in various shades of pink are borne in spring and early summer. 'Album' bears white flowers in summer on compact plants. 'Bevan's Variety' bears magenta flowers. (Zones 3–8)

G. x oxonianum is a vigorous, mound-forming plant with attractive evergreen foliage; it bears pink flowers from spring to fall. It grows up to 30" tall and spreads about 24". 'A.T. Johnson' bears many silvery pink flowers. 'Wargrave Pink' is a vigorous cultivar that grows 24" tall, spreads about 36" and bears salmon pink flowers. (Zones 3–8)

G. pratense (meadow cranesbill) forms an upright clump 24–36" tall and about 24" in spread. Many white, blue or light purple flowers are borne for a short period in early summer. This species self-seeds freely. 'Mrs. Kendall Clarke' bears rose pink flowers with blue-gray veins. 'Plenum Violaceum' bears purple double flowers for a longer period than the species because it sets no seed. (Zones 3–8)

G. renardii (Renard's geranium) forms a clump of velvety, deeply veined, crinkled foliage about 12" tall, with an equal spread. A few purple-veined white flowers appear over the summer, but the foliage is the main attraction. (Zones 3–8)

G. sanguineum (bloodred cranesbill, bloody cranesbill) forms a dense, mounding clump 6–12" tall and 12–24" in spread. Bright magenta flowers are borne mostly in early summer and sporadically until fall. '**Album**' has white flowers and a more open habit than other cultivars. '**Alpenglow**' has bright rosy red flowers and dense foliage. '**Elsbeth**' has light pink flowers with dark pink veins. The foliage turns bright red in fall. '**Shepherd's Warning**' is a dwarf plant to 6" tall, with rosy pink flowers. Var. *striatum* is heat and drought tolerant. It has pale pink blooms with blood red veins. (Zones 3–8)

Problems & Pests

Rare problems with leaf spot and rust can occur.

G. sanguineum cultivar

G. pratense 'Plenum Violaceum'

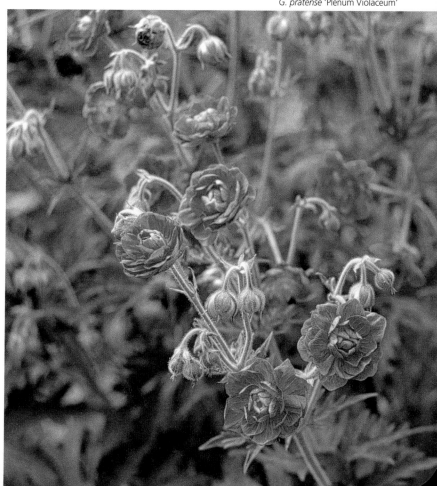

Helen's Flower
Sneezeweed
Helenium

Height: 30"–6' **Spread:** 18–36" **Flower color:** red, orange, yellow, brown, maroon, bicolored **Blooms:** late summer and fall **Zones:** 3–9

AT FIRST YOU MIGHT THINK HELEN'S FLOWER IS JUST ANOTHER daisy, but it has a charm all its own. The center is raised and brightly hued, often contrasting with the sunset-colored petals. This plant does have a downside. If the summer is hot and the ground is dry, it suffers from 'naked leg' syndrome: in an effort to put on a good flower display, it sacrifices its lower leaves. Make sure to plant Helen's flower where this potentially embarrassing habit will be hidden. Baptisias, irises and daylilies make good companions because their foliage will conceal any leggy growth.

Planting

Seeding: Start seed indoors or out in spring; cultivars do not come true to type

Planting out: Spring or fall

Spacing: 18–36"

Growing

Helen's flower grows best in **full sun**. The soil should be **fertile, moist** and **well drained**. Be sure to water well in summer. Divide every two or three years to keep clumps from becoming overgrown and dying out in the middle. Deadheading helps prolong blooming.

Some support may be needed to hold mature stems upright. A peony hoop, shortened tomato cage or twiggy branches inserted into the soil in early spring will hold up the stems as they grow and will be hidden by the foliage as it matures. Pinch growth back in early summer to encourage lower, bushier growth that is less likely to need support.

Tips

Helen's flower adds bright color to the border in late summer and fall. It looks at home in an informal cottage or meadow garden. It will also work well near a pond or other water feature, where it will get regular water.

No part of this plant should be eaten because it can cause stomach upset. Sensitive individuals may get a rash or other skin irritation from contact with the leaves. Use gloves when handling.

Recommended

H. autumnale (common sneezeweed) forms an upright clump of stems and narrow foliage up to 6' tall. It bears yellow, red, brown, orange, maroon or bicolored, daisy-like flowers. **'Bruno'** bears mahogany flowers on compact plants 30"–4' tall, not quite the height of the species. **'Kugelsonne'** bears golden yellow flowers with golden centers on plants 3–4' tall. **'Moerheim Beauty'** bears flowers with rusty red petals and deep brown centers. It also grows 3–4' tall.

Problems & Pests

Powdery mildew can cause problems during dry spells.

The name Helenium *honors Helen of Troy. 'Sneezeweed' reflects the former use of this plant as a substitute for snuff.*

Hens and Chicks
Houseleek
Sempervivum

Height: 3–6" **Spread:** 12" to indefinite **Flower color:** red, yellow, white, purple; plant grown mainly for foliage **Blooms:** summer **Zones:** 3–8

THE GENUS NAME *SEMPERVIVUM* MEANS 'ALWAYS LIVING,' WHICH is appropriate for these constantly regenerating plants. The little plantlets are simple to pass along. Just separate a 'chick' and you have the start of a whole colony of plants. And for those who may think hens and chicks are boring, please take a look at the many striking cultivars and hybrids available in garden centers and from specialty catalogs. Semps, as these plants are nicknamed, are easy to grow. They need little care other than a very well-drained medium and a light sprinkle of water during extended dry periods. Many of my plants are growing in hypertufa troughs and on rocks in the rock garden.

Planting

Seeding: Not recommended; remove and replant young rosettes to propagate

Planting out: Spring

Spacing: 10–12"

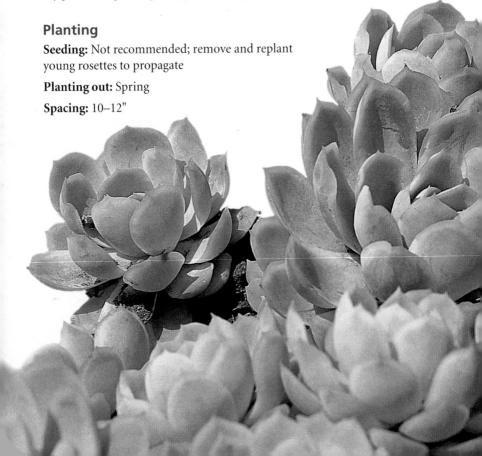

Growing

Grow hens and chicks in **full sun** or **partial shade**. The soil should be of **poor to average fertility** and very **well drained**. Add fine gravel or grit to the soil to provide adequate drainage. Once a plant blooms, it dies. When you deadhead the faded flower, pull up the soft parent plant as well to provide space for the new daughter rosettes that sprout up, seemingly by magic. Divide by removing these new rosettes and rooting them.

Tips

These plants make excellent additions to rock gardens and rock walls, where they will grow even right on the rocks.

Recommended

S. arachnoideum (cobweb house-leek) is identical to *S. tectorum* except that the tips of the leaves are entwined with hairy fibers, giving the appearance of cobwebs. This plant may need protection during wet weather.

S. tectorum is one of the most commonly grown hens and chicks. It forms a low-growing mat of fleshy-leaved rosettes, each about 6–10" across. Small new rosettes are quickly produced and grow and multiply to fill almost any space. Flowers may be produced in summer but are not as common in colder climates. 'Atropurpureum' has dark reddish purple leaves. 'Limelight' has yellow-green, pink-tipped foliage. 'Pacific Hawk' has dark red leaves that are edged with silvery hairs.

Problems & Pests

These plants are generally pest free, although rust and root rot can occur in wet conditions.

The juice from the leaves can be applied to burns, insect bites and other skin irritations.

S. tectorum

Heuchera
Coralbells, Alumroot
Heuchera

Height: 6"–4' **Spread:** 6–18" **Flower color:** red, pink, white, purple; plant also grown for foliage **Blooms:** spring, summer **Zones:** 3–9

FROM SOFT GREENS TO MIDNIGHT PURPLES AND SILVERY, DAPPLED maroons, heucheras offer a variety of foliage options for the part-shade perennial garden. They have become indispensable to the gardener looking for lower-maintenance perennials that blend beautifully with hostas, ferns and our many native wildflowers. Heuchera leaves expand over the season and effectively cover the holes left by spring ephemerals, such as trillium and the early-blooming bulbs. For those who must have flowers there are heucheras that oblige. *H.* x *brizioides* 'Raspberry Regal' boasts both beautiful flowers and handsome foliage.

Planting
Seeding: Species, but not cultivars, may be started from seed in spring in a cold frame

Planting out: Spring

Spacing: 12–18"

Cut flowers of Heuchera *(hew-ker-uh) species can be used in arrangements.*

Growing

Heucheras grow best in **light or partial shade.** The foliage colors can bleach out in full sun, and plants become leggy in full shade. The soil should be of **average to rich fertility, humus rich, neutral to alkaline, moist** and **well drained.** Good air circulation is essential.

Deadhead to prolong the bloom. Every two or three years, heucheras should be dug up to remove the oldest, woodiest roots and stems. Plants may be divided at this time, if desired, then replanted with the crown at or just above soil level. Cultivars may be propagated by division in spring or fall.

Tips

Use heucheras as edging plants, in clusters in woodland gardens or as groundcovers in low-traffic areas. Combine different foliage types for an interesting display.

Heucheras have a strange habit of pushing themselves up out of the soil because of their shallow root systems. Mulch in fall if the plants begin heaving from the ground.

H. micrantha cultivars (this page)

These delicate woodland plants will enhance your garden with their bright colors, attractive foliage and airy sprays of flowers.

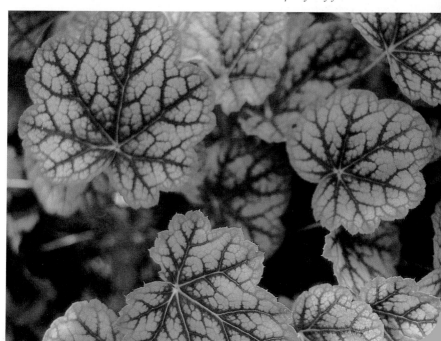

Recommended

Most of the cultivars listed are hybrids developed from crosses between the various species. They are grouped with one of their acknowledged parents in the following list. There are many more beautiful cultivars available than can be listed here.

H. americana is native to the central and eastern U.S. This plant forms a mound about 18" tall and 12" in spread. Its heart-shaped foliage is marbled and bronze-veined when it is young and matures to deep green. Cultivars have been developed for their attractive and variable foliage. **'Chocolate Veil'** has dark chocolaty purple leaves with silvery patches between the veins. Its flowers are greenish purple. **'Pewter Veil'** has silvery purple leaves with dark gray veins. Its flowers are white flushed with pink.

H. x *brizioides* is a group of mound-forming hybrids developed for their attractive flowers. They grow 12–30" tall and spread 12–18". **'Firefly'** has fragrant, bright pinkish red flowers. **'June Bride'** has large, white flowers. **'Raspberry Regal'** is a larger plant, growing up to 4' tall. The foliage is strongly marbled and the flowers are bright red.

H. micrantha is a mounding, clump-forming plant up to 36" tall. The foliage is gray-green and the flowers are white. The cultivars are more commonly grown. **Bressingham Hybrids** are compact and can be started from seed. The flowers are pink or red. **'Chocolate Ruffles'** has ruffled, glossy brown foliage with purple undersides, giving the leaves a bronzed look. **Var.** *diversifolia* **'Palace Purple'** is a well-known cultivar, and it was one of the first

H. micrantha var. *diversifolia* 'Palace Purple'

heucheras grown for its interesting foliage. This compact plant grows 18–20" tall and has deep purple foliage and white blooms. It can be started from seed, but only some of the seedlings will be true to type. '**Pewter Moon**' has light pink flowers and silvery leaves with bronzy purple veins.

H. sanguinea is the hardiest species. It forms a low mat of foliage and reaches 6–18" in height, with an equal spread. The dark green foliage is marbled with silver. Red, pink or white flowers are borne in summer. '**Coral Cloud**' has pinkish red flowers and glossy, crinkled leaves. '**Frosty**' has red flowers and silver-variegated foliage. '**Northern Fire**' has red flowers and leaves mottled with silver. '**White Cloud**' has silver-mottled leaves and bears white flowers in late spring.

H. americana 'Pewter Veil'

Problems & Pests

Healthy heucheras have very few problems. In stressed situations, they can be afflicted with foliar nematodes, powdery mildew, rust or leaf spot.

The genus name Heuchera *honors* Johann Heinrich von Heucher *(1677–1747), a German professor of medicine and an amateur botanist.*

H. x brizioides 'Firefly'

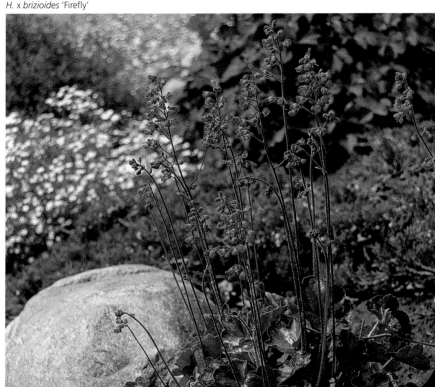

Hosta
Plantain Lily
Hosta

Height: 2–36" **Spread:** 5"–6' **Flower color:** white or purple; plants grown mainly for foliage **Blooms:** summer, early fall **Zones:** 3–8

IT WOULD BE DIFFICULT TO FIND A SHADE GARDEN THAT DID NOT contain at least one hosta. You have choices ranging from the bold-leaved 'Elegans' and 'Sum and Substance' to the tiny teardrop-leaved 'Baby Bunting' and 'Pandora's Box.' Ohio is a veritable hotbed of hosta hybridization and introduction efforts. One beautiful public garden to visit is Van Wade's garden at the Wade and Gatton Nurseries in Bellville. The hosta collection is impressive enough, but Van Wade has included many other plants that combine beautifully with his hostas: gorgeous Rodgersflowers *(Rodgersia)*, ligularias, martagon lilies and ferns. And, while you're there, don't forget to visit the daylily and ornamental grass collections.

Hostas are considered by some gardeners to be the ultimate in shade plants. They are available in a wide variety of leaf shapes, colors and textures.

Planting

Seeding: Direct sow or start in cold frame in spring. Young plants can take three or more years to reach flowering size.

Planting out: Spring

Spacing: 1–4'

Growing

Hostas prefer **light or partial shade** but will grow in full shade. Morning sun is preferable to afternoon sun in partial shade situations. The soil should ideally be **fertile, moist** and **well drained,** but most soils are tolerated. Hostas are fairly drought tolerant, especially if given a mulch to help retain moisture.

Division is not required but can be done every few years in spring or summer to propagate new plants.

Tips

Hostas make wonderful woodland plants, looking very attractive when combined with ferns and other fine-textured plants. Hostas are also good plants for a mixed border, particularly when used to hide the ugly, leggy lower stems and branches of some shrubs. The dense growth and thick, shade-providing leaves of hostas make them useful for suppressing weeds.

Although hostas are commonly grown as foliage plants, they are becoming more appreciated for the

Once established, these hardy plants need little attention. Water them occasionally and keep them mulched with a rich organic layer.

H. fortunei 'Gold Standard'

spikes of lily-like flowers, some of which are fragrant and make lovely cut flowers. Some gardeners, however, find that the flower color clashes with the leaves, which are the main decorative feature of the plant. If you don't like the look of the flowers, feel free to remove them before they open—it will not harm the plant.

Recommended

Hostas have been subjected to a great deal of crossbreeding and hybridizing, resulting in hundreds of cultivars. The exact parentage of many is uncertain. The cultivars below have been grouped with a generally accepted parent species.

H. fortunei (Fortune's hosta) is the parent of many hybrids and cultivars. It has broad, dark green foliage and bears lavender purple flowers in mid-summer. It quickly forms a dense clump 12–24" tall and 24–36" in spread. 'Albomarginata' has variable cream or white margins on the leaves. 'Aureomarginata' has yellow-margined leaves and is more tolerant of sun than many cultivars. 'Francee' is often listed without a parent species. It has puckered, dark green leaves with a narrow white margin. 'Gold Standard' is also often listed without a species. The bright yellow leaves have a narrow green margin.

H. plantaginea (fragrant hosta) has glossy, bright green leaves with distinctive veins; it grows 18–30" tall, spreads to about 36" and bears large, white, fragrant flowers in late summer. 'Aphrodite' has white double flowers. 'Honeybells' has sweetly fragrant, light purple flowers. 'Royal Standard' is durable and low growing. It reaches only 4–8" in height and spreads up to 36". The dark green leaves are deeply veined, and the flowers are light purple.

H. sieboldiana (Siebold's hosta) forms a large, impressive clump of blue-green foliage. It grows about 36" tall and spreads up to 4'. The early-summer flowers are a light grayish purple that fades to white. 'Blue Angel' has wavy, blue-green foliage and white flowers. '**Elegans**' (var. *elegans*) has deeply puckered, blue-gray foliage and light purple flowers. It was first introduced to gardens in 1905 and is still popular today. '**Frances Williams**' ('Yellow Edge') has puckered blue-green leaves with yellow-green margins. '**Great Expectations**' has pale yellow or cream leaves with wide, irregular, blue-green margins. '**Sum and Substance**' has immense gold-green leaves and may spread to 6'. This cultivar resists slugs.

H. sieboldii (seersucker hosta) grows 12–30" tall and spreads about 20–24". It has undulating, narrow green leaves with white margins. In late summer and early fall it bears light purple flowers with darker purple veins. '**Alba**' has light green leaves with undulating margins and white flowers. '**Kabitan**' has narrow, bright yellow foliage with undulating green margins. This compact cultivar grows about 8" tall and spreads 12".

H. tokudama grows slowly into a groundcovering clump 12–16" tall and 18–24" in spread. It has blue, heart-shaped, puckered leaves and produces white flowers in early to mid-summer. The species is not often available commercially, but it has been used as a parent plant in various hybridization programs. Some of the dwarf and miniature hostas are thought to have this species in their heritage. '**Baby Bunting**' is a popular cultivar that grows 6–10" tall and spreads 12–18". It has dark green to slightly bluish green leaves and bears light purple flowers in early to mid-summer. '**Pandora's Box**' is a sport of 'Baby Bunting' and is one of the tiniest available hostas, growing only 2–4" tall and spreading 5–10". The tiny leaves are creamy white with irregular green to blue-green margins.

Problems & Pests

Slugs, snails, leaf spot, crown rot and chewing insects such as black vine weevils are all possible problems for hostas. Varieties with thick leaves tend to be more slug resistant.

H. fortunei 'Francee' (above)

Dwarf cultivar (below)

Iris

Iris

Height: 4"–4' **Spread:** 6"–4' **Flower color:** many shades of pink, red, purple, blue, white, brown, yellow **Blooms:** spring, summer, sometimes fall **Zones:** 3–10

IRISES ARE STEEPED IN HISTORY AND LORE. THE *FLEUR-DE-LIS*, which represents an iris flower, has been a symbol of French culture at least since the reign of King Louis XIV. To the ancient Greeks, *Iris* referred both to rainbows and to the goddess who used the rainbow as a bridge when she carried messages from Zeus to the mortal world. And, indeed, many say the range in flower color of bearded irises approximates that of a rainbow. Unfortunately, bearded irises are susceptible to the iris borer, so they can increase your maintenance load. Fortunately, there are many other beautiful irises. Flowers of the Siberian and Japanese irises can look like crushed velvet in the garden. The netted iris is one of the early bulbs that tell us spring has really arrived.

Planting

Seeding: Not recommended; germination is erratic and hybrids and cultivars may not come true to type

Planting out: Late summer or early fall

Spacing: 2"–4'

Growing

Irises prefer **full sun** but tolerate very light or dappled shade. The soil should be **average to fertile** and **well drained.** Japanese iris and Siberian iris prefer a moist but still well-drained soil.

Divide in late summer or early fall. Bearded iris and variegated iris must be divided yearly to maintain good condition. When dividing bearded iris rhizomes, replant with the flat side of the foliage fan facing the garden. Dust the toe-shaped rhizome with a powder cleanser before planting to help prevent soft rot.

Iris hybrid

The wall of a 3500-year-old Egyptian temple features an iris, making this plant one of the oldest cultivated ornamentals.

I. germanica

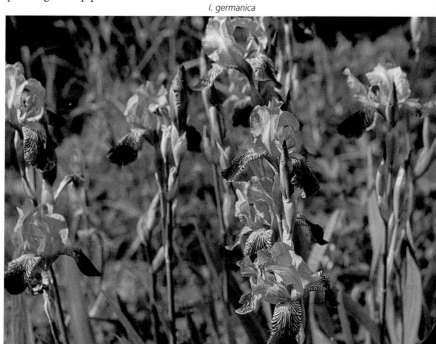

Deadhead irises to keep them tidy. Cut back the foliage of Siberian iris in spring.

Tips

All irises are popular border plants, but Japanese iris and Siberian iris are also useful alongside a stream or pond, and dwarf cultivars make attractive additions to rock gardens.

It is a good idea to wash your hands after handling irises because they can cause severe internal irritation if ingested. You may not want to plant them close to places where children like to play.

Recommended

I. ensata (*I. kaempferi;* Japanese iris) is a water-loving species. It grows up to 36" tall and spreads about 18". White, blue, purple or pink flowers are produced from early to mid-summer. This species rarely needs dividing, and it resists iris borers.

I. **hybrids** (bearded iris) have flowers in all colors. *I. germanica* is the parent of many cultivars and hybrids, which vary in height and width from 6" to 4'. Flowering periods range from mid-spring to mid-summer and some cultivars flower again in fall.

I. pallida (variegated iris, sweet iris) is rarely grown, but its variegated cultivars are a popular addition to the perennial garden. Light purple flowers are borne on plants that grow about 24" tall and spread 12". **'Argentea Variegata'** has foliage with cream and green stripes. **'Variegata'** ('Aurea Variegata') has foliage with gold and green stripes.

I. reticulata (netted iris) forms a small clump 4–10" tall. This iris bears flowers in various shades of blue and purple. The plants grow from bulbs and can be left undisturbed. Bulbs sometimes divide naturally, and plants may not flower again until the bulbs mature.

I. sibirica

I. sibirica (Siberian iris) is more resistant to iris borers than other species. It grows 2–4' tall and 36" wide and flowers in early summer. Many cultivars are available in various shades, mostly purple, blue and white. Plants take a year or two to recover after dividing.

Problems & Pests

Irises have several problems that can be prevented or mitigated through close observation. Iris borers are a potentially lethal pest. They burrow their way down the leaf until they reach the root, where they continue eating until there is no root left. The tunnels they make in the leaves are easy to spot, and if infected leaves are removed and destroyed or the borers squished within the leaf, the pests will never reach the roots.

Leaf spot is another problem that can be controlled by removing and destroying infected leaves. Be sure to give irises the correct growing conditions. Too much moisture for some species will allow rot diseases to settle in and kill the plants. Plant rhizomes high in the soil to deter root rot. Slugs, snails and aphids may also cause some trouble.

Powdered iris root, called orris, smells like violets and can be added to perfumes and potpourris as a fixative.

I. germanica

Iris hybrid

Jacob's Ladder

Polemonium

Height: 8–36" **Spread:** 8–16" **Flower color:** purple, white, blue
Blooms: late spring, summer **Zones:** 3–7

GARDENING IS A LABOR OF LOVE AND FAITH. WE OFTEN KILL A
plant but try it again because we are so attracted to it. With creeping Jacob's
ladder *(P. reptans)*, the third time was the charm for me. It probably didn't
help that I first planted it in a drier area. And the second time we had a very
long dry spell. Now it is happily creeping and self-seeding in soil amended
with mushroom compost. Its taller cousin *P. caeruleum* looks lovely in the
middle of a partially shaded border. The cultivar 'Brise d'Anjou' is stunning
in the shade, but I have not been able to carry it over the winter despite three
attempts.

*The leaflets of the foliage are
organized in a neat, dense,
ladder-like formation, giving
these plants their common name.*

Planting

Seeding: Start seed in spring or fall. Keep soil temperature at about 70° F. Seed can take up to a month to germinate.

Planting out: Spring

Spacing: About 12"

Growing

Jacob's ladder species grow best in **partial shade** or very **light shade**. The soil should be **fertile, humus rich, moist** and **well drained.** Deadhead regularly to prolong blooming. These plants self-seed readily. Division is rarely required but should be done in late summer if desired.

Tips

Include Jacob's ladder plants in borders and woodland gardens. *P. caeruleum* can be used as a tall focal point in planters. *P. reptans* can be used in rock gardens and as an edging along paths.

Recommended

P. caeruleum is the commonly grown Jacob's ladder. This plant grows 18–36" tall and spreads about 12". It forms a dense clump of basal foliage, with leafy upright stems that are topped with clusters of purple flowers. **Var.** *album* has white flowers. '**Apricot Delight**' produces many mauve flowers with apricot pink centers. '**Brise d'Anjou**' has cream white leaflet margins. It does not bear as many flowers as the species and is difficult to overwinter in Ohio. If you try to grow it, site it in the shade.

P. reptans (creeping Jacob's ladder) is a very hardy, mounding perennial 8–16" tall, with an equal spread. It bears small blue or lilac flowers in late spring and early summer.

Problems & Pests

Powdery mildew, leaf spot and rust are occasional problems.

P. caeruleum

P. caeruleum 'Brise d'Anjou'

Joe-Pye Weed
Boneset, Snakeroot
Eupatorium

Height: 2–7' **Spread:** 18"–4' **Flower color:** white, purple, blue, pink
Blooms: late summer, fall **Zones:** 3–9

YOU JUST CAN'T ALWAYS GO BY WHAT IT SAYS ON THE TAG.
The *E. maculatum* 'Gateway' I bought seven years ago was supposed to grow
4–5' tall and 3' wide. It is now 6–7' tall and 7–8' wide! I'm waiting to see
who will win: Joe-Pye weed, ironweed *(Vernonia)* or black-eyed Susan
(*Rudbeckia nidita* 'Herbstsonne'), which are all planted in the same area.
Boneset *(E. rugosum)* is most often seen in large native colonies in moist,
open woodland areas east of the Mississippi. Mother Nature combines it
with blue lobelia and false sunflowers.
One of its cultivars, 'Chocolate,'
is a good foliage plant for the
middle of the border. Its
bronzy leaves are especially
effective in spring.

Planting
Seeding: Start seed indoors in late
winter or early spring; soil temperature should be 59°–68° F

Planting out: Spring

Spacing: 18–36"

*The flowers attract butterflies to
the garden and can be used in
fresh arrangements.*

Growing

Joe-Pye weeds prefer **full sun** but tolerate **partial shade**. The soil should be **fertile** and **moist**. Wet soils are tolerated. Divide plants in spring when clumps become overgrown. Don't put off dividing if space is a problem, because dividing over-sized clumps is a tough job.

Pruning growth back in May encourages branching and lower, denser growth, but it can delay flowering.

Tips

These plants can be used in a moist border or near a pond or other water feature. The tall types are ideal in the back of a border or center of a bed where they will create a backdrop for lower-growing plants. *E. coelestinum* might seem a tad weedy for a formal border, but it makes a fantastic addition to a native planting.

It may take a couple of seasons for these plants to mature, so don't crowd them.

Recommended

E. coelestinum (*Conoclinium coelestinum;* hardy ageratum, blue boneset, mistflower) is a bushy, upright plant that grows 24–36" tall and spreads 18–36". From late summer until frost it bears clusters of flossy, light blue to lavender flowers. '**Album**' bears white flowers.

E. maculatum is a huge plant 5–7' tall and 3–4' in spread. In late summer it bears clusters of purple flowers and is difficult to tell apart from the closely related *E. purpureum.*

'**Gateway**' is slightly shorter, usually growing up to 6' tall. The large flower clusters are rose pink and the plant's stems are reddish.

E. rugosum (*Ageratina altissima;* boneset, white snakeroot) forms a bushy, mounding clump of foliage. It grows 3–4' tall, or taller, and spreads 24–36". Clusters of white flowers appear in late summer and early fall. '**Chocolate**' grows 2–3' tall. This self-seeding cultivar has dark bronzy purple leaves that mature to dark green.

Problems & Pests

These plants may have occasional problems with powdery mildew, fungal leaf spot, rust, aphids, whiteflies and leaf miners.

E. rugosum

Jupiter's Beard
Red Valerian
Centranthus

Height: 24–36" **Spread:** 12–24" **Flower color:** red, pink, white
Blooms: summer **Zones:** 4–8

JUPITER'S BEARD WAS PART OF MY FIRST BUTTERFLY AREA, AND
I planted it far too close to a butterflybush *(Buddleia davidii)*. Eventually the
Jupiter's beard was overtaken, but not before it attracted its share of butterflies and bees. This plant is lovely in a mass, which it will create by itself if
allowed to self-seed. The red of the flowers has a different quality than that
of most reds. It is a blue red with a touch of white, so you might call it pink,
or maybe not. Combine Jupiter's beard with spiky blue speedwells, perennial
salvia (*Salvia* x *sylvestris* 'May Night') and white Shasta daisy.

Planting

Seeding: Start seed in spring indoors
or in a cold frame

Planting out: Spring or fall

Spacing: 12–18"

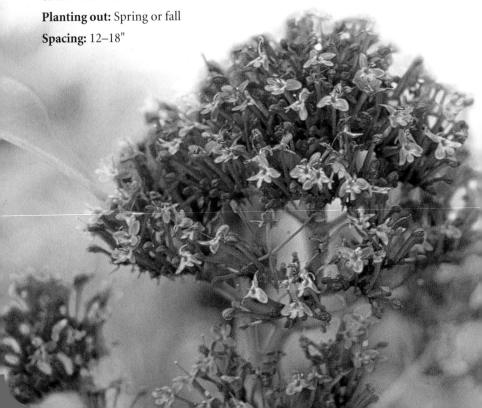

Growing

Jupiter's beard grows best in **full sun**. The soil should be of **average fertility, neutral to alkaline** and **well drained**. Too rich a soil or too much fertilizer will encourage floppy, disease-prone growth. Division is rarely required but can be done in spring or fall to propagate desirable plants. Deadheading will extend the blooming season and prevent excessive self-seeding.

If flowering slows during the summer months, cut the plant back by up to half to encourage new growth and more flowering. Cut the plant back in fall, leaving the basal foliage in place, to give it time to harden off before winter.

Tips

Jupiter's beard can be included in borders. It looks particularly impressive when left to self-seed into an unused corner of the garden, where it will form a sea of bright red flowers. The blossoms are popular for fresh arrangements.

Recommended

C. ruber forms a bushy, upright plant. It bears large clusters of red, pink or white flowers on and off over the whole summer. Deadheading will encourage sporadic blooming through the fall, but extending the bloom too long will shorten the life of the plant. For white flowers try **var. *albus*.**

Var. *albus*

Jupiter's beard is rarely plagued by any pests or diseases.

Lady's Mantle
Alchemilla

Height: 3–18" **Spread:** 20–24" **Flower color:** yellow, green
Blooms: early summer to early fall **Zones:** 3–7

FEW OTHER PERENNIALS ARE AS CAPTIVATING AS LADY'S MANTLE
dappled with morning dew. The finely hairy leaves capture water, creating
pearly drops that cling to the edges of the leaves. Alchemists in the Middle
Ages thought the dew captured in the center of the leaf could change lead
into gold. We know that belief was an impossible dream, but these plants do
have an air of magic. Place a Lady's mantle at the front of the garden to feature its airy mass of chartreuse flowers. Once the flowers fade, remove them
and let the foliage take over the show. Hardy geranium (*Geranium* 'Brookside'), foxgloves, turtleheads *(Chelone)* and spotted dead nettle (*Lamium
maculatum* 'Beedham's White') are all good
companions.

*The airy flowers make a
fabulous filler for fresh
and dried flower
arrangements.*

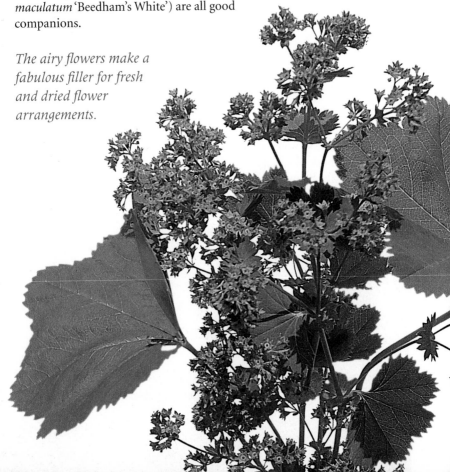

Planting

Seeding: Direct sow fresh seed or start in containers in fall or spring; transplant while seedlings are small

Planting out: Spring

Spacing: 24"

Growing

Lady's mantle plants prefer **light or partial shade,** with protection from the afternoon sun. They dislike hot locations, and excessive sun will scorch the leaves. The soil should be **fertile, humus rich, moist** and **well drained.** These plants are drought resistant once established.

Division is rarely required but can be done in spring before flowering starts or in fall once flowering is complete. If more plants are desired, move some of the self-seeded plants that are bound to show up to where you want them.

A. alpina
A. mollis

A. *mollis* (this page)

Deadhead to keep the plants tidy and prevent excessive re-seeding. For *A. mollis,* deadheading may encourage a second flush of flowers in late summer or fall.

Tips

Lady's mantles are ideal for grouping under trees in woodland gardens and along border edges, where they soften the bright colors of other plants. A wonderful location is alongside a pathway that winds through a lightly wooded area. They are also attractive in containers.

If your Lady's mantle begins to look tired and heat stressed during summer, rejuvenate it in one of two ways. Trim the whole plant back, encouraging new foliage to fill in, or remove the dead leaves and then trim the plant back once new foliage has started to fill in. Leave plants intact over the winter, then clean them up in spring.

Recommended

A. alpina (alpine Lady's mantle) is a diminutive, low-growing plant that reaches 3–5" in height and up to 20" in spread. Soft white hairs on the backs of the leaves give the appearance of a silvery margin around each leaf. Clusters of tiny, yellow flowers are borne in summer. This species is an excellent trough plant in combination with miniature hostas.

A. mollis (common Lady's mantle) is the most frequently grown species. It grows 8–18" tall and spreads up to about 24". Plants form a mound of soft, rounded foliage, above which are held sprays of frothy-looking, yellowish green flowers in early summer.

Problems & Pests

Lady's mantles rarely suffer from any problems, though fungi may be troublesome during warm, wet summers. These plants are deer resistant.

The young leaves of these plants have a mildly bitter flavor and can be added to salads and dips. The leaves have also been boiled to make a green dye for wool.

A. mollis

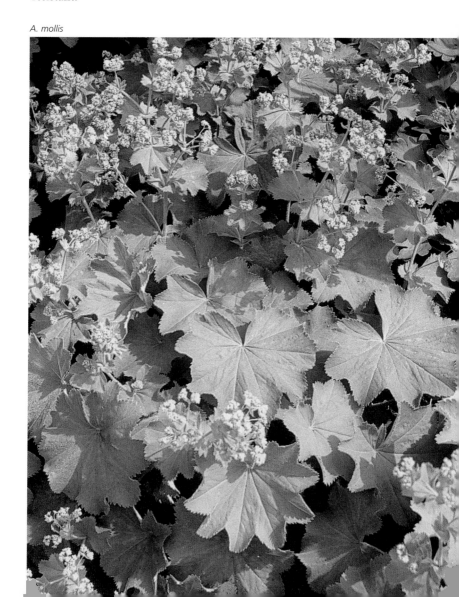

Lamb's Ears
Woolly Betony
Stachys

Height: 6–18" **Spread:** 18–24" **Flower color:** pink, purple
Blooms: summer **Zones:** 3–8

THE SOFT, FUZZY LEAVES OF LAMB'S EARS ARE CHILD
magnets. In the herb garden at Inniswood Metro Gardens in
Westerville, children constantly pat this plant. Fortunately,
it is a benevolent species that, in the not-so-distant past,
was used to bandage small wounds. Many plants in the
mint family contain antibacterial and antifungal
compounds, so lamb's ears not only feels soft but
may actually encourage healing. Lamb's ears can
ramble, but its root system is very shallow, and
plants are easily removed from places they aren't
wanted. A very attractive cultivar is 'Big Ears.' It seldom blooms, which may explain how it can look so
good all season long: it spends its energy on leaves
rather than on flowers and seeds.

Planting
Seeding: Direct sow or start in containers in
cold frame in spring

Planting out: Spring

Spacing: 18–24"

*Cut the flowerheads
when they are in bud or after
they bloom, and hang them
to dry for use in dried-
flower arrangements.*

Growing

Lamb's ears grows best in **full sun**. The soil should be of **poor or average fertility** and **well drained**. The leaves can rot in humid weather if the soil is poorly drained. Divide in spring.

Remove spent flower spikes to keep plants looking neat. Select a flowerless cultivar if you don't want to deadhead. Cut back diseased or damaged foliage; new foliage will sprout when the weather cools down.

Tips

Lamb's ears makes a great groundcover in a new garden where the soil has not yet been amended. It can be used to edge borders and pathways, providing a soft, silvery backdrop for more vibrant colors in the border. For a silvery accent, plant a small group of lamb's ears in a border.

Leaves can look tatty by the middle of summer. The more of this plant you use, the more you will have to clean up. Plant only as much as you can tend, or plant in an out-of-the-way spot where the stressed foliage will not be noticeable.

Recommended

S. byzantina (S. lanata) forms a mat of thick, woolly rosettes of leaves. Pinkish purple flowers are borne all summer. **'Big Ears'** ('Helen von Stein') has greenish silver leaves that are twice as big as those of the species. **'Silver Carpet'** has silvery white, fuzzy foliage. These cultivars rarely produce flowers.

Problems & Pests

Fungal leaf problems including rot, powdery mildew, rust and leaf spot are rare but can occur in hot, humid weather.

S. byzantina
'Big Ears'

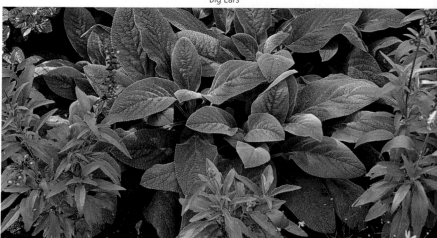

Lavender
English Lavender, Lavandin
Lavandula

Height: 8–36" **Spread:** up to 4' **Flower color:** purple, pink, blue
Blooms: mid-summer to fall **Zones:** 5–9

IF I COULD HAVE ONLY ONE GARDEN plant with me on a deserted island, it would be lavender. Its history of use in medicines and perfumes dates back to the Roman Empire. Today it is still used in many toiletry and household products for its sharp, clean scent and its antibacterial and antifungal properties. Its essential oil can relax yet energize the nervous system. Lavender is also a key ingredient in the *herbes de Provence* mixture of French cuisine, in which it imparts an unusual but pleasant flavor. All parts of the lavender plant are aromatic, and the flowers are my favorite shade of violet blue. The foliage is 'evergray.' In winter, the lavandins (*L.* x *intermedia* cultivars) are especially attractive.

Planting

Seeding: Start in fall or spring in a cold frame; plants don't always come true to type

Planting out: Spring

Spacing: 12–24"

Lavender was one of the plants that the pilgrims took to America on the Mayflower.

Growing

Lavenders grow best in **full sun**. The soil should be **average to fertile** and **alkaline,** and it *must* be **well drained**. Once established, these plants are heat and drought tolerant. *L.* x *intermedia* can be sensitive to winter cold and should be sited out of winter winds.

Lavender plants are woody and cannot be divided, but 3–4" cuttings can be taken in early spring and late summer when the vegetative growth flushes after flowering. The cuttings can be started in damp sand, and each should have a heel attached. (A heel cutting has a small strip of woody growth at the base.)

Deadhead to encourage a second bloom. Growth can be trimmed

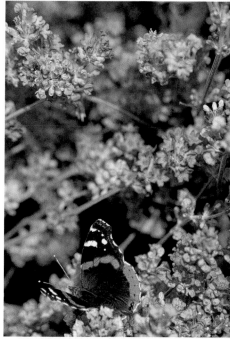

L. angustifolia 'Hidcote'

L. angustifolia

L. angustifolia 'Jean Davis' (above)

back in late spring and summer after it blooms. Never cut into old woody growth because lavenders do not form new shoots from old wood. Frequent trimming keeps plants from becoming too woody. Allow new buds to emerge in spring before cutting to show you how far back you can cut. Always leave at least one of these new buds in place when cutting a branch back. Avoid heavy pruning after August to give plants time to harden off for winter.

In colder areas, lavenders should be covered with mulch and, if possible, a good layer of snow. Gardeners in cold areas may have to replace plants every few years if too much growth is killed back in winter. The key to ensuring the survival of lavenders in winter is to provide good drainage. Often, 'winter' kill results from wet feet, not from cold.

Tips

Lavenders are wonderful, aromatic edging plants and can be used to form a low hedge. Good companions for these deer-resistant plants include other drought-tolerant specimens, such as pinks, thyme, lamb's ears, sedum and goldenrod.

To dry the flowers, cut them when they show full color but before they open completely.

Recommended

L. angustifolia (English lavender) is an aromatic, bushy subshrub that is often treated as a perennial. It grows up to about 24" tall, with an equal spread. From mid-summer to fall, it bears spikes of small flowers in varied shades of violet blue. '**Hidcote**' ('Hidcote Blue') bears spikes of deep violet blue flowers and grows 18–24" tall. '**Jean Davis**' is a compact cultivar with spikes of pale pink flowers. It grows 12–14" tall. '**Lady**' can be grown from seed and will flower the first summer. It grows 8–10" tall and bears pale violet flowers. '**Munstead**' is a compact plant that grows to about 18" tall and up to 24" wide. Its flowers are lavender blue.

L. x *intermedia* (lavandin) is a natural hybrid between English lavender and spike lavender *(L. latifolia).* It grows to 36" tall, with an equal spread. The flowers are held on long spikes. '**Grosso**' has larger flowers of lavender. '**Provence**' is heavily scented and has light lavender flowers.

Problems & Pests

As is the case with many aromatic plants, pest problems are few. Keep an eye open for root rot and fungal leaf spot, particularly during wet winters and springs when the soil may stay wet for extended periods.

The scent of lavender is considered relaxing and soothing and is often used in aromatherapy. Dry a few sprigs for use in scented sachets and pillows or in the bath.

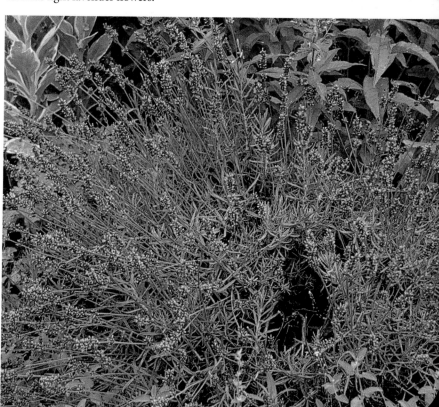

Lenten Rose
Christmas Rose, Hellebore
Helleborus

Height: 12–18" **Spread:** 12–18" **Flower color:** white, green, pink, purple, yellow **Blooms:** late winter, mid-spring **Zones:** 4–9

LENTEN ROSES ARE AMONG THE EARLIEST HARBINGERS OF SPRING. Their bloom often coincides with the beginning of Lent, and they are still blooming by Easter. In my protected back garden, the leaves can stay green all winter, and it's where I go to see some green in January. To make the blossoms stand out, prune off the old leaves in late winter. If you have a more naturalized garden, and you practice 'in-place composting,' you can let the old leaves stay to be covered by the new foliage. But if last year's leaves are diseased, remove them to prevent the spread of disease. The texture of these plants provides a nice contrast to hostas and astilbes.

Planting
Seeding: Not recommended; seed is very slow to germinate and time to flowering size is long

Planting out: Spring or late summer

Spacing: 12–18"

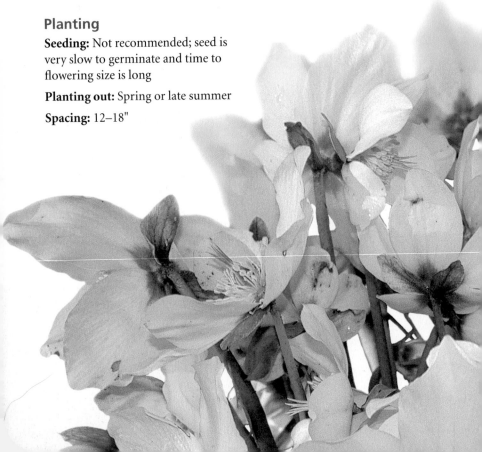

Growing

Lenten roses prefer **light, dappled shade** in a **sheltered** site, but they accept some direct sun if the soil is moist. The soil should be **fertile, moist, humus rich, neutral to alkaline** and **well drained**. Divide in spring, after flowering, or whenever plants are becoming crowded. These plants self-seed and the seedlings are variable.

H. niger

Protect plants with mulch in winter if they are in an exposed location, though in a mild winter the leaves will be evergreen and the flowers might poke up through the snow in early February.

Tips

Use these plants in a sheltered border or rock garden, or naturalize in a woodland garden.

All parts of *Helleborus* species are toxic, and the leaf edges are very sharp, so wear long sleeves and gloves when planting or dividing.

Recommended

H. x *hybridus* plants grow about 18" in height and spread. They are very attractive and may be deciduous or evergreen. Plants bloom in late winter to spring in a wide range of flower colors, including white, purple, yellow, green and pink. Trends in breeding include deeper-colored flowers, picotees (with differently colored petal margins), doubles and spotted flowers.

H. niger (Christmas rose) is a clump-forming evergreen that is picky about its growing conditions. It grows 12" tall, spreads 18" and bears crystal white flowers in late winter to early spring.

H. orientalis (Lenten rose) is a clump-forming evergreen perennial. It grows 12–18" tall, with an equal spread. In mid-spring it bears white to greenish flowers that fade to pink.

Problems & Pests

Problems may be caused by aphids, crown rot and leaf spot, and by slugs when the leaves are young.

H. orientalis

Lily-of-the-Valley

Convallaria

Height: 6–12" **Spread:** indefinite **Flower color:** white, pink
Blooms: spring **Zones:** 2–7

THE DAINTY BELLS OF LILY-OF-THE-VALLEY POSSESS A HEADY
scent. The flowers are sometimes hidden within the folded leaves, and it isn't
until you walk by and detect the sweet perfume wafting past that you think
to look for them. Lily-of-the-valley used to be a common addition to wedding bouquets because it is a symbol of purity. Many of those old-fashioned
wedding flowers, sadly, have been passed over in favor of more ostentatious,
longer-lasting blooms. Ah, nostalgia . . .

Planting

Seeding: Not recommended; easy to propagate by division

Planting out: Spring or fall

Spacing: About 12" (plants spread quickly to fill an area)

Growing

Lily-of-the-valley grows well in any light from **full sun** to **full shade.** The soil should ideally be of **average fertility, humus rich** and **moist,** but almost any soil conditions are tolerated. This plant is drought resistant.

Division is rarely required but can be done whenever you need plants for another area or to donate to someone else's garden. The pairs of leaves grow from small pips, or eyes, that form along the spreading rhizome. Divide a length of root into pieces, leaving at least one pip on each piece.

Var. *rosea*

European legend claims the origin of lily-of-the-valley to be either the tears the Virgin Mary shed at the cross or the tears Mary Magdalene shed at Christ's tomb.

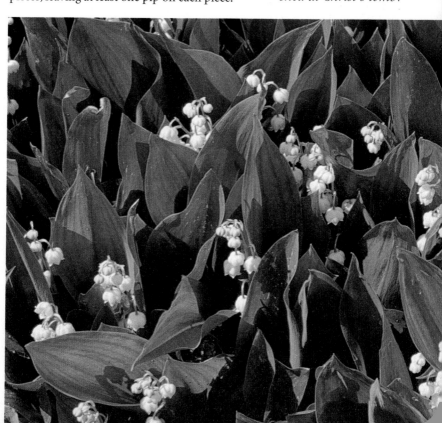

Tips

This versatile groundcover can be grown in a variety of locations. It is a good plant to naturalize in woodland gardens, perhaps bordering a pathway or beneath shade trees where little else will grow. It also makes a good groundcover in a shrub border, where its dense growth and fairly shallow roots will keep the weeds down but won't interfere with the shrubs' roots.

Lily-of-the-valley can be quite invasive. It is a good idea not to grow it with plants that are less vigorous and likely to be overwhelmed, such as alpine plants in a shady rock garden. Give lily-of-the-valley plenty of space to grow and let it go. Avoid planting it in a place where you may later spend all your time trying to get rid of it.

Lily-of-the-valley is currently being researched for its possible usefulness in treating heart disease. Like foxglove, it contains compounds that can affect heart rate and rhythm. These same medicinal qualities make lily-of-the-valley potentially very toxic, and no part of it should be eaten.

This plant is well known for the delightful fragrance of its flowers. In fall, dig up a few roots and plant them in pots. Keep the pots in a sheltered spot outdoors, such as a window well, or in a cold frame or unheated porch, for the winter. Check the pot periodically to make sure it hasn't dried out completely; if it has, water enough to moisten the soil. In early spring bring the pots indoors. The plants will sprout and flower early, and you can enjoy the delicious scent.

Recommended

C. majalis forms a mat of foliage. It grows 6–10" tall and will spread indefinitely. In spring it produces

Var. *rosea*

small arching stems lined with fragrant, white, bell-shaped flowers. **'Albostriata'** and **'Aureovariegata'** have leaves that are white-striped and yellow-striped, respectively. These cultivars tend to be less vigorous than the species but are not as easy to find. **'Flore Pleno'** has white double flowers and also tends to be less invasive than the species. **'Fortin's Giant'** has larger leaves and flowers than the species and can grow up to 12" tall. **Var. *rosea*** ('Rosea') has light pink or pink-veined flowers; it is less vigorous than the species.

Problems & Pests
Occasional problems with molds and stem rot can occur.

Lungwort
Pulmonaria

Height: 8–24" **Spread:** 8–36" **Flower color:** blue, red, pink, white, purple **Blooms:** spring **Zones:** 3–8

BLOOMS IN EARLY SPRING ARE A NICE TOUCH, BUT THE LEAVES are the real stars of lungworts. The name comes from the appearance of the leaves. According to the Doctrine of Signatures, which guided medieval herbalists, the way a plant looked indicated the part of the body it would heal. The herbalists saw a representation of a diseased lung and decided that common lungwort would cure respiratory ailments. Curiously enough, the plant does have chemical compounds that alleviate some respiratory disorders. Lungworts look lovely in combination with other shade lovers. Their bold leaves provide a dappled contrast for astilbes, common bleeding heart, Lenten roses and Japanese anemone.

Planting

Seeding: Start seed in containers outdoors in spring; plants don't consistently come true to type

Planting out: Spring or fall

Spacing: 12–18"

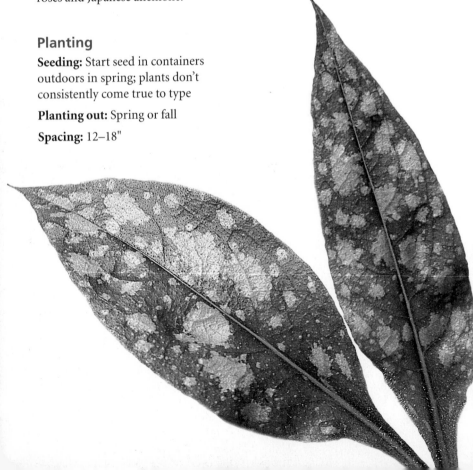

Growing

Lungworts prefer **partial to full shade**. The soil should be **fertile, humus rich, moist** and **well drained**. Rot can occur in very wet soil.

Divide in early summer after flowering or in fall. Provide the newly planted divisions with lots of water to help them re-establish.

Shear plants back lightly after flowering to deadhead and show off the fabulous foliage and to keep the plants tidy.

P. longifolia

Tips

Lungworts make useful and attractive groundcovers for shady borders, woodland gardens and pond and stream edges.

These plants have more than 20 common names. Many are biblical references, such as Abraham, Isaac and Jacob, Adam and Eve, Children of Israel and Virgin Mary.

P. saccharata

Recommended

P. angustifolia (blue lungwort) forms a mounded clump of foliage. The leaves have no spots. This plant grows 8–12" tall and spreads 18–24". Clusters of bright blue flowers, held above the foliage, are borne from early to late spring.

P. longifolia (long-leaved lungwort) forms a dense clump of long, narrow, white-spotted green leaves. It grows 8–12" tall, spreads 8–24" and bears clusters of blue flowers in spring or even earlier, as the foliage emerges.

P. officinalis (common lungwort, spotted dog) forms a loose clump of evergreen foliage, spotted with white. It grows 10–12" tall and spreads about 18". The spring flowers open pink and mature to blue. This species was once grown for its

P. saccharata

P. longifolia

reputed medicinal properties, but it is now valued for its ornamental qualities. **'Cambridge Blue'** bears many blue flowers. **'Sissinghurst White'** has pink buds that open to white flowers. The leaves are heavily spotted with white.

P. rubra (red lungwort) forms a loose clump of unspotted, softly hairy leaves. It grows 12–24" tall and spreads 24–36". Bright red flowers appear in early spring. This species tends to be less drought tolerant than other lungworts and often transfers this trait to its hybrids. **'Redstart'** has pinkish red flowers.

P. saccharata (Bethlehem sage) forms a compact clump of large, white-spotted, evergreen leaves. It grows 12–18" tall, with a spread of about 24". The spring flowers may be purple, red or white. This species has given rise to many cultivars and hybrids. **'Berries and Cream'** has foliage heavily spotted with silver and bears raspberry red flowers. **'Janet Fisk'** is very heavily spotted and appears almost silvery in the garden. Its pink flowers mature to blue. **'Mrs. Moon'** has pink buds that open to a light purple-blue. The leaves are dappled with silvery white spots. **'Pink Dawn'** has dark pink flowers that age to purple. **'Spilled Milk'** is a compact plant that has pink flowers and leaves splotched with silvery green.

Problems & Pests

These plants are generally problem free but may become susceptible to powdery mildew if the soil dries out for extended periods. Remove and destroy damaged leaves.

Pulmonaria species (usually P. officinalis) are traditional culinary and medicinal herbs. The young leaves may be added to soups and stews to flavor and thicken the broth. When dried, the spotted leaves also make an attractive addition to potpourri.

P. saccharata

Lychnis
Maltese Cross, Rose Campion
Lychnis

Height: 2–4' **Spread:** 12–18" **Flower color:** magenta, white, scarlet, red, orange **Blooms:** summer **Zones:** 3–8

THERE ARE MORE THAN 100 SPECIES OF *LYCHNIS*, OCCURRING primarily in Europe and Asia. Only a few are considered garden-worthy. Rose campion *(L. coronaria)* was my first lychnis. By chance I planted it in a small, well-drained nook in my rock garden. It thrived and left behind some seedlings to carry on its legacy. They pop up where they will with flowers of soft to bright pink. To raise the temperature in the garden, plant Maltese cross *(L. chalcedonica)*, with its intense red-orange flowers. Some gardeners say they won't have orange in their garden because it's too garish, but be bold and give it a chance. Use blue balloon flower or peach-leaved bellflower to tame Maltese cross's heat.

Planting
Seeding: Start seeds indoors in late spring; soil temperature should be 68°–70° F

Planting out: Spring

Spacing: 12–18"

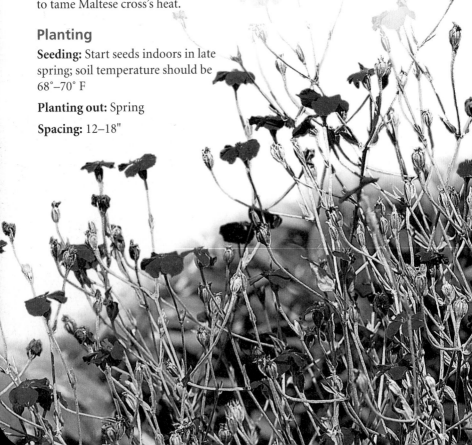

Growing

Lychnis plants grow well in **full sun** but enjoy some afternoon shade to protect them from excessive heat. The soil should be **well drained** and of **average fertility**. These plants do not tolerate heavy soils; if you garden in clay, use raised beds or amend the planting space with organic matter and gypsum to loosen the soil. Division can be done in spring, though lychnis plants may not live long enough to need it.

Although these plants are short-lived and should almost be treated as annuals or biennials, in light or gravelly soils they re-seed prolifically. Basal cuttings can also be taken to propagate the plants.

Tips

Lychnis make beautiful, carefree additions to a border, cottage garden, rock garden or naturalized garden.

The taller species may need some support, particularly in a windy location. Peony supports or twiggy branches pushed into the soil are best and are less noticeable than stakes.

Recommended

L. chalcedonica (Maltese cross) is a stiff, upright plant growing 3–4' tall and 12–18" wide. The scarlet flowers are borne in clusters in early to mid-summer. Some support may be required to keep this plant standing upright. 'Alba' has white flowers.

L. coronaria (rose campion) forms an upright mass of silvery gray leaves and branching stems 24–36" tall and about 18" wide. It tends to be a biennial, forming a basal rosette of gray leaves in its first year, then flowering, setting seed and dying in its second year. In late summer the plant is dotted with magenta pink flowers, which are very striking against the silvery foliage. 'Alba' has white flowers. 'Angel's Blush' features white flowers with reddish pink centers. 'Atrosanguinea' has red flowers.

Lychnis species are rarely affected by pests or diseases.

L. chalcedonica

L. coronaria with Phlox

Mallow

Malva

Height: 8"–4' **Spread:** 12–24" **Flower color:** purple, pink, white, blue
Blooms: summer, fall **Zones:** 4–9

I INADVERTENTLY SHARED A MALLOW WITH my neighbor when it self-seeded into his English ivy from my adjacent border. Being a rather free-spirited cottage-garden plant, it looked somewhat out of place in his well-manicured groundcover bed. Related to hollyhocks, mallows confer an old-fashioned look on the garden. These plants have long taproots and are very drought tolerant. Other than removing unwanted seedlings, not much maintenance is required. A favorite of mine is *M. sylvestris* 'Zebrina,' with its striking, purple-veined flowers that nicely echo the color of *Liatris*.

Some mallows are called 'cheese' or 'cheese plant' because the round, flattened fruits resemble wheels of cheese.

Planting

Seeding: Sow indoors in spring or direct sow in early summer

Planting out: Spring, summer

Spacing: 12–24"

Growing

Mallows grow well in **full sun** or **partial shade**. The soil should be of **average fertility, moist** and **well drained**. These plants are drought tolerant.

Mallows do not need dividing. Propagate by basal cuttings taken in spring. These plants also self-seed readily.

In rich soils mallows may require staking. Cutting plants back by about half in late May will encourage more compact, bushy growth but will delay flowering by a couple of weeks. Transplant or thin out seedlings if they are too crowded.

M. sylvestris 'Zebrina'

Some types of mallow are reputed to have a calming effect when ingested. They were used in the Middle Ages as antidotes for aphrodisiacs and love potions.

M. alcea 'Fastigiata'

M. *sylvestris* 'Primley Blue' (this page)

When rubbed against the skin, mallow leaves are said to relieve the sting of nettles.

Tips

Use mallows in a mixed border or in a wildflower or cottage garden. Deadhead to keep the plants blooming until October. Mallows also make good cut flowers.

Recommended

M. alcea (hollyhock mallow) is a loose, upright, branching plant 2–4' tall and 18–24" in spread. It bears pink flowers with notched petals all summer. 'Fastigiata' has a neat, upright form. If deadheaded, it continues to produce flowers well into fall.

M. moschata (musk mallow) is a bushy, upright plant with musk-scented leaves. It grows about 36" tall, spreads about 24" and bears pale pink or white flowers all summer. 'Pirouette' ('Alba') bears pure white flowers.

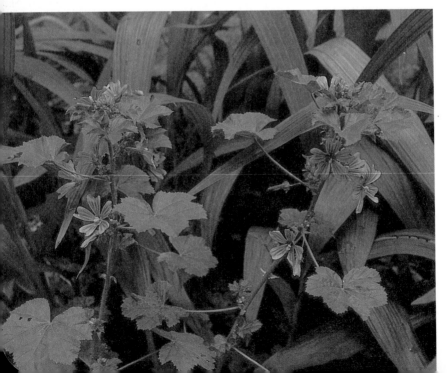

M. sylvestris (cheeses) may be upright or spreading in habit. Plants of this species grow 1–4' tall and spread about 12–24". The pink flowers have darker veins and are produced all summer. Many cultivars are available. **'Bibor Felho'** has an upright form and rose purple flowers with darker purple veins. **'Braveheart,'** also an upright cultivar, has light purple-pink flowers with dark purple veins. **'Primley Blue'** is a prostrate cultivar, growing only about 8" tall. It has pale purple-blue flowers. **'Zebrina'** is an upright grower that bears pale pink or white flowers with purple veins.

Problems & Pests

Problems with rust, leaf spot, Japanese beetles and spider mites can occur occasionally.

M. sylvestris 'Bibor Felho'
M. moschata

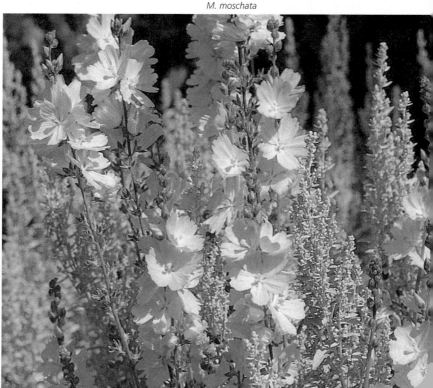

Meadow Rue

Thalictrum

Height: 2–6' **Spread:** 12–36" **Flower color:** pink, purple, yellow, white
Blooms: summer, fall **Zones:** 3–8

MANY OF THE MEADOW RUES HAVE LEAVES THAT ARE SIMILAR
to those of columbines. One species, *T. aquilegifolium*, looks almost exactly
like a columbine—until its purple puffball blooms appear. These curious
flowers are missing petals and achieve the fluffy look by producing a mass of
stamens surrounded by a row of sepals. The blooms set the genus *Thalictrum*
apart from other species in the buttercup family, although this family does
have its share of flowers with unusual shapes. A few of the meadow rues can
be massive. The later-blooming 'Lavender Mist' sends flowers up as high as
5–6' on slender stems.

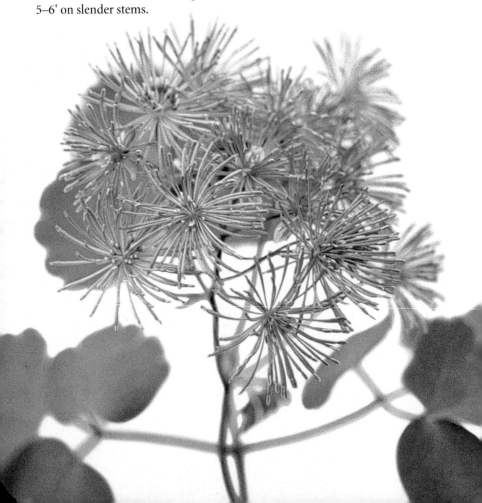

Planting

Seeding: Direct sow in fall or start indoors in early spring; soil temperature should be 70° F

Planting out: Spring

Spacing: 12–24"

Growing

Meadow rues prefer **light or partial shade** but tolerate full sun with moist soil. The soil should be **humus rich, moist** and **well drained**. These plants rarely need to be divided. In fact, meadow rues dislike being disturbed, and plants may take a while to re-establish once they have been divided. If necessary for propagation, divide in spring as the foliage begins to develop.

Tips

In the middle or at the back of a border, meadow rues make a soft backdrop for bolder plants and flowers and are beautiful when naturalized in an open woodland or meadow garden.

These plants often do not emerge until quite late in spring. Mark the location where they are planted so that you do not inadvertently disturb

T. rochebruneanum 'Lavender Mist'

Meadow rue flowers are generally petal-less. The unique flowers consist of showy sepals and stamens.

T. aquilegifolium

T. delvayi
'Hewitt's Double' (this page)

the roots if you are cultivating their bed before they begin to grow.

Do not place individual plants too close together because their airy stems can become tangled. Consider giving the taller meadow rues some support if they are in an exposed location—a good wind may topple them.

Recommended

*T. **aquilegifolium*** (columbine meadow rue) forms an upright mound 24–36" tall, with an equal spread. Fluffy purple flowers are borne in early summer. The leaves are similar in appearance to those of columbines. '**Thundercloud**' ('Purple Cloud') has dark purple flowers. '**White Cloud**' has white flowers.

T. delvayi (Yunnan meadow rue) forms a clump of narrow stems that usually need staking. It grows 4–5' tall and spreads about 24". It bears fluffy purple or white flowers from mid-summer to fall. '**Album**' has white flowers. '**Hewitt's Double**' is a popular cultivar that produces many tiny, purple, pompom-like flowers.

T. rochebruneanum '**Lavender Mist**' (lavender mist meadow rue) forms a narrow, upright clump 3–6' tall and 12–24" in spread. The late-summer blooms are lavender purple and have numerous distinctive yellow stamens.

Although the common name suggests sadness, the genus name Thalictrum *is related to a Greek word that means 'abundance' or 'good cheer.'*

Problems & Pests

Infrequent problems with powdery mildew, rust, smut and leaf spot can occur.

T. aquilegifolium

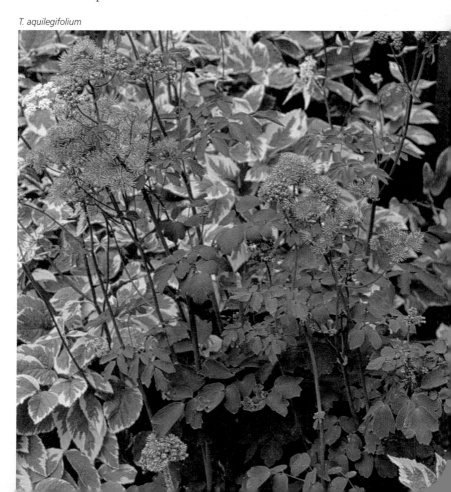

Meadowsweet
Queen-of-the-Prairie
Filipendula

Height: 2–8' **Spread:** 18"–4' **Flower color:** white, cream, pink, red
Blooms: late spring, summer, fall **Zones:** 3–8

THE QUEEN-OF-THE-PRAIRIE *(F. RUBRA)* THAT RESIDES IN MY
garden is a pass-along plant from a dear friend. At times it doesn't bloom
because my garden tends to be on the drier side, but the plant holds on and
rewards me with beautiful, deep pink masses of flowers in wetter seasons.
Native to our 'edge of the woods' moist meadows, the statuesque queen-
of-the-prairie mixes well with asters, Joe-Pye weed and ironweed *(Vernonia)*
in the back of the perennial bed. The more modest queen-of-the-meadow
(F. ulmaria) mixes well with shorter plants in the middle of the bed. Look
for the striking golden cultivar 'Aurea' to brighten up a shady area.

Planting

Seeding: Germination can be erratic; start seed in cold frame in fall and keep soil evenly moist

Planting out: Spring

Spacing: 18–36"

Growing

Meadowsweets prefer **partial or light shade.** Full sun is tolerated if the soil remains sufficiently moist. The soil should be **fertile, deep, humus rich** and **moist,** except in the case of *F. vulgaris,* which prefers dry soil.

Divide in spring or fall. You may need a sharp knife to divide these plants, because they grow thick, tough roots. Meadowsweets tend to self-seed, and if dividing these perennials seems daunting, transplanting the seedlings could be an easier way to get new plants. Deadhead meadowsweets if desired, but the faded seedheads are quite attractive when left in place.

The flowers of F. ulmaria *were often used to flavor ales and mead in medieval times, giving rise to the name meadowsweet, from the Anglo-Saxon word* medesweete.

F. ulmaria cultivar

F. ulmaria

F. rubra

Tips

Most meadowsweets are excellent plants for bog gardens or wet sites. Grow them alongside streams or in moist meadows. Meadowsweets may also be grown in the back of a border, as long as they are kept well watered. Grow *F. vulgaris* if you can't provide the moisture the other species need.

The flowers of *F. ulmaria,* once used to flavor mead and ale, are now becoming popular as a flavoring for vinegars and jams. They may also be used to make a pleasant wine, which is made in much the same way as dandelion wine.

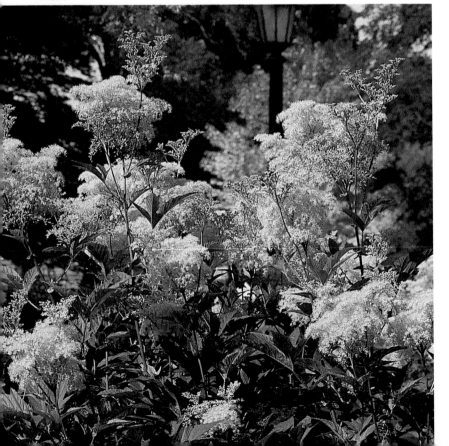

Recommended

F. purpurea (Japanese meadow-sweet) forms a clump of stems and large, deeply lobed foliage. It grows up to 4' tall and spreads about 24". Pinkish red flowers fade to pink in late summer. 'Elegans' has fragrant white flowers. The spent flower-heads develop an attractive red tint.

F. rubra (queen-of-the-prairie) forms a large, spreading clump 6–8' tall and 4' in spread. It bears clusters of fragrant pink flowers from early to mid-summer. 'Venusta' bears very showy pink flowers that fade to light pink in fall.

F. ulmaria (queen-of-the-meadow) grows 24–36" tall and 24" wide. It bears cream white flowers in large clusters. 'Aurea' has yellow foliage that matures to light green as the summer progresses. 'Flore Pleno' has double flowers.

F. vulgaris (dropwort, meadow-sweet) is a low-growing species up to 24" tall and 18" wide. 'Flore Pleno' has white double flowers. 'Rosea' has pink flowers.

Problems & Pests

Powdery mildew, rust and leaf spot can be troublesome.

In the 16th century it was customary to strew rushes and herbs to insulate the floor underfoot, freshen the air and combat infections. Meadowsweet was the herb Queen Elizabeth I preferred for these purposes.

F. ulmaria

Monkshood
Aconitum

Height: 3–6' **Spread:** 12–18" **Flower color:** purple, blue, white
Blooms: mid- to late summer **Zones:** 3–8

BEAUTIFUL BUT DEADLY ARE THESE late-blooming perennials. The curious helmet-shaped flowers invite closer inspection, but be careful when touching any monkshood. Some people may experience an uncomfortable tingling or numbing sensation, especially on warm days when the skin's pores are more open. *A. napellus* was once used externally as a therapeutic rub for rheumatism. It was also apparently used as a tincture, but this use makes me shudder because even a small amount taken internally can be fatal. Place this dangerous beauty in inaccessible areas away from pathways, such as in the middle or back of beds. Its blue flowers look lovely in combination with white mugwort (*Artemisia lactiflora* 'Guizho') and bronze fennel (*Foeniculum vulgare* 'Rubrum').

Aconitum *may come from the Greek* akoniton, *meaning 'dart.' The ancient Chinese and the Arabs used the juice of monkshood to poison arrow tips. Europeans used it to poison wolves.*

Planting

Seeding: Germination may be irregular. Seeds direct sown in spring may bloom the following summer; seeds sown later will not likely bloom until the third year.

Planting out: Spring; bare-rooted tubers may be planted in fall

Spacing: 18"

Growing

Monkshoods grow best in **light or partial shade**. These plants will grow in any **moist** soil but prefer to be in a **rich** soil with lots of **organic matter** worked in.

Monkshoods prefer not to be divided, as they may be slow to re-establish. If division is desired to increase the number of plants, it should be done in late fall after blooming or in early spring. When dividing or transplanting monkshoods, the crown should never be planted at a depth lower than where it was previously growing. Burying the crown any deeper will cause it to rot and the plant to die.

Tall monkshoods may need to be staked. Peony hoops or tomato cages inserted around young plants will be hidden as the plants fill in.

Tips

Monkshood plants are perfect for cool, boggy locations along streams or next to ponds. They make tall, elegant additions to woodland gardens in combination with lower-growing plants. Do not plant monkshoods near tree roots because these plants cannot compete with trees.

A. x cammarum 'Bicolor'

The upper petals of monkshood flowers are fused, making an enclosure that looks like the cowl worn by medieval monks.

A. napellus

Monkshoods, like their cousins the delphiniums, prefer conditions on the cool side. They will do poorly when the weather gets hot, particularly if conditions do not cool down at night. Mulch the roots to keep them cool; keep plants well watered; and trim back faded foliage in summer to encourage new growth to fill in when cooler fall weather arrives. Be careful not to cut back too hard or the plant will fail to flower.

Recommended

A. x *cammarum* (Cammarum hybrids) is a group that contains several of the more popular hybrid cultivars. **'Bicolor'** (bicolor monkshood) bears blue and white, helmet-shaped flowers. The flower spikes are often branched. **'Bressingham Spire'** bears dark purple-blue flowers on strong spikes. It grows up to 36" tall but needs no staking.

A. napellus

A. x *cammarum* 'Bicolor'

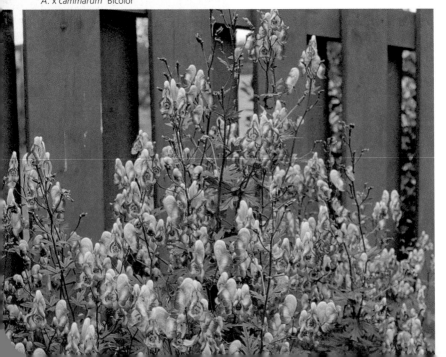

A. charmichaelii (azure monkshood) forms a low mound of basal leaves from which the flower spikes emerge. The foliage generally grows to about 24" in height, but the plant can grow 6' tall when in flower. Purple or blue flowers are borne a week or so later than those of other species. **'Arendsii'** bears dark blue flowers on strong spikes that need no staking.

A. napellus (common monkshood) is an erect plant that forms a basal mound of finely divided foliage. It grows 3–5' tall, spreads 12–18" and bears dark purple-blue flowers.

A. napellus (this page)

Always take care to avoid getting the juice from monkshood plants in open wounds or in your mouth or eyes.

Problems & Pests

Problems with aphids, root rot, stem rot, powdery mildew, downy mildew, wilt and rust can occur.

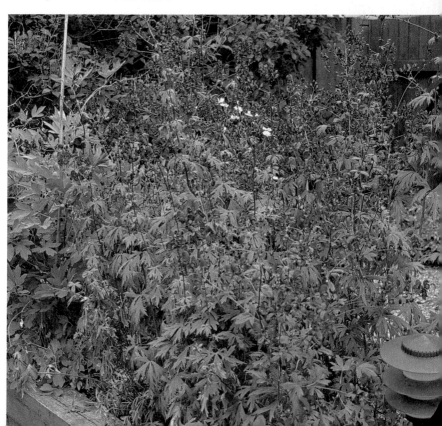

Obedient Plant
False Dragonhead
Physostegia

Height: 1–4' **Spread:** 12–24" **Flower color:** pink, purple, white
Blooms: mid-summer to fall **Zones:** 2–9

WE ARE FASCINATED WITH plants that 'do' something unexpected. If you look down on the flower spike of an obedient plant, you will notice that the flowers line up to form a cross. But each flower can be rearranged in any number of positions. After a short time the flowers move, very slowly, back to their original spots. Perhaps this perennial should be renamed 'obedient flower,' because the *plant* is not very obedient when it comes to staying in one place. It grows vigorously by rhizomes and has a tendency to run over more well-mannered plants. Use it in a naturalized setting where it can roam. Try the cultivar 'Summer Snow' if you like the plant but don't wish to divide it every two years or so.

Planting

Seeding: Direct sow in early fall or in spring with soil temperature 70°–75° F. Protect fall-started seedlings from winter cold the first year.

Planting out: Spring or fall

Spacing: 12–24"

Growing

Obedient plant prefers **full sun** but tolerates partial or light shade. Its native habitat is moist meadows in eastern and central North America. Therefore, the soil should be **moist** and of **average to high fertility**. In a fertile soil these plants are more vigorous and may need staking. Choose a compact cultivar to avoid staking.

This plant can become invasive. Growing it in a slightly drier site can slow the spread. Divide in early to mid-spring, once ground can be worked, every two years or so to curtail invasiveness.

Tips

Use obedient plant in borders, cottage gardens, informal borders and naturalistic gardens. The flowers can be cut for use in fresh arrangements.

Recommended

P. virginiana has a spreading root system from which upright stems sprout. It grows 2–4' tall and spreads 24" or more. **'Crown of Snow'** ('Snow Crown') has white flowers. **'Pink Bouquet'** bears bright pink flowers. **'Summer Snow'** is a more compact, less invasive plant with white flowers. **'Variegata'** is a desirable variegated specimen with cream-margined leaves and bright pink flowers. **'Vivid'** bears bright purple-pink flowers. This compact plant grows 12–24" tall and spreads 12".

Problems & Pests

Rare problems with rust and slugs are possible.

'Variegata'

P. virginiana

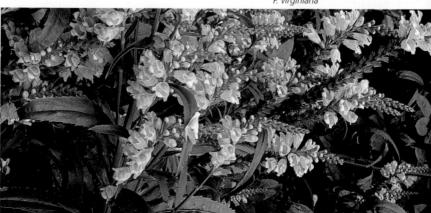

Oriental Poppy

Papaver

Height: 18"–4' **Spread:** 18–36" **Flower color:** red, orange, pink, white; often with black blotches in center of flower **Blooms:** spring, early summer **Zones:** 3–7

BOLD YET GRACEFUL, ORIENTAL POPPY NEVER FAILS TO CATCH my eye. The papery petals flutter in the slightest breeze, and they are soon replaced by ornamental seedpods. Then, all too quickly, the plant disappears and enters summer dormancy as the temperature begins to rise. Most *Papaver* species tend to have ephemeral natures, but their beauty makes up for their lack of longevity. Oriental poppy combines well with the cool blues of baptisias and hardy geranium (*Geranium* 'Brookside') and the soft yellows of *Coreopsis verticillata* 'Moonbeam.'

Planting

Seeding: Direct sow in spring or fall

Planting out: Spring

Spacing: 24"

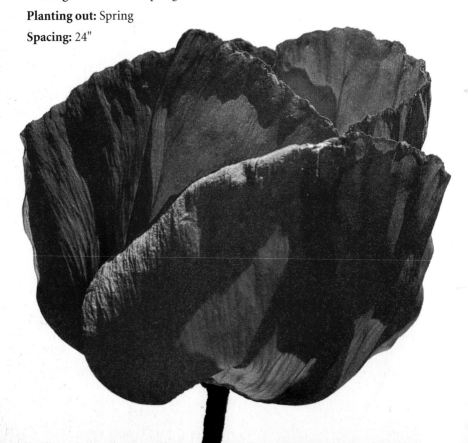

Growing

Grow Oriental poppy in **full sun**. The soil should be **average to fertile** and must be **well drained**.

Plants die back after flowering and send up fresh new growth in late summer. This growth should be left in place for winter insulation. Division is rarely needed but may be done in fall once new rosettes begin to form. Oriental poppy can also be propagated by root cuttings taken from dormant plants in mid- to late summer.

Tips

Small groups of Oriental poppy look attractive in an early-summer border, although they may leave a bare spot during the dormant period in summer. Baby's breath and catmints make good companions and will fill in any blank spaces.

Use of poppy seeds in cooking and baking can be traced as far back as the ancient Egyptians.

Recommended

P. orientale forms an upright, oval clump 18"–4' tall and 24–36" wide. Red, scarlet, pink or white flowers with prominent black stamens are borne in late spring and early summer. There are numerous cultivars. **'Allegro'** has bright scarlet red flowers. **'Carneum'** bears salmon pink flowers early in the season. **'Pizzicato'** is a dwarf cultivar, with flowers in a wide range of colors. It forms a mound 18–24" tall, with an equal spread.

Problems & Pests

Problems with powdery mildew, leaf smut, gray mold, root rot and damping off are possible but rare in well-drained soil.

Pasqueflower
Pulsatilla

Height: 4–12" **Spread:** 8–12" **Flower color:** purple, blue, red, white
Blooms: early to mid-spring **Zones:** 3–7

I'M NOT SURE WHICH IS MORE BEAUTIFUL: PASQUEFLOWER'S
early mauve blooms or its soft, wispy seedheads. Early-spring bloomers are
all the more appreciated when the winter has been long. As the blooms fade,
the spring show is continued by pasqueflower's cousin, Grecian windflower,
which thrives in the same cultural conditions. Pasqueflower has grown happily in my sunny rock garden, but it does tend to be short-lived. As with a
number of other perennials, its reduced life span may be attributed to our
hot and humid summers. Complement pasqueflower with flowing carpets
of moss phlox and small, early-blooming bulbs.

*Pasqueflower is
rarely troubled by
pests or diseases.*

Planting

Seeding: Sow seed as soon as it is ripe (mid-summer to fall)

Planting out: Spring

Spacing: 8–12"

Growing

Pasqueflower grows well in **full sun** or **partial shade**. The soil should be **fertile** and very **well drained**. Poorly drained, wet soil can quickly kill this plant. Pasqueflower resents being disturbed. Plant it while it is very small, and don't divide it.

Propagate pasqueflower by carefully taking root cuttings in early spring. You may have to soak the soil around the plant to loosen it and get at the roots. Dig carefully to expose a root, then remove it and replant it. The 'Propagating Perennials' section in the introduction gives more information about starting root cuttings. Be sure to protect the remaining plant from spring frosts with mulch if you have taken cuttings from it.

Tips

Pasqueflower can be grown in rock gardens, woodland gardens and borders and on gravelly banks. It also works well in pots and planters but should be moved to a sheltered location for the winter. An unheated garage or porch will offer some protection from the freeze-thaw cycles and excessive moisture of winter. Make sure the pots get some light once the plants begin to grow.

Pasqueflower is harmful if eaten, and repeated handling may cause skin irritation.

Recommended

P. vulgaris (Anemone pulsatilla) forms a mound of lacy foliage. Flowers in shades of blue, purple or occasionally white are borne in early spring, before the foliage emerges. The seedheads are very fluffy and provide interest when the flowers are gone. **Var.** *alba* has white flowers. **'Rubra'** has bright purple-red flowers.

The early blooming time of many Pulsatilla *species gave rise to the common name. 'Pasque' refers to the Paschal, or Easter, season.*

Penstemon
Beard Tongue
Penstemon

Height: 9"–5' **Spread:** 6–24" **Flower color:** white, pink, purple, red, blue
Blooms: late spring, summer, fall **Zones:** 4–8, some to Zone 3

MY FIRST SIGHTING OF A PENSTEMON WAS 'SOUR GRAPES,'
a cultivar with iridescent blue to purple flowers. As I was thinking how wonderful it would look in my blue-yellow-white beds, I was informed that it wouldn't make it through an Ohio winter. Since then I have looked for the same intense color in a penstemon that will overwinter here. Many of the showier larger species and hybrids prefer warmer zones, but the native foxglove penstemon and its cultivars are hardy and worth trying. Penstemons come in all sizes, from diminutive rock garden gems to stately specimens. Combine *P. digitalis* 'Husker Red,' *Phlox paniculata* 'David' and *Heuchera americana* 'Pewter Veil' for a stunning white and maroon vignette.

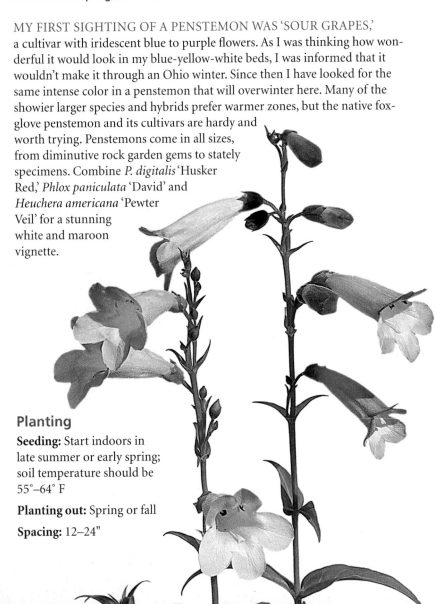

Planting

Seeding: Start indoors in late summer or early spring; soil temperature should be 55°–64° F

Planting out: Spring or fall

Spacing: 12–24"

Growing

Penstemons prefer **full sun** but tolerate some shade. The soil should be of **average to rich fertility, sandy** and **well drained**. These plants are drought tolerant and will rot in wet soil. Mulch in winter with pea gravel to protect the crowns from excessive moisture, especially the smaller species that are from the mountain regions of North America.

Divide every two or three years in spring. Pinch plants when they are 12" tall to encourage bushy growth.

Tips

Use penstemons in a mixed or herbaceous border, a cottage garden or a rock garden. These plants are also good for hummingbird gardens. *P. digitalis* 'Husker Red' makes an attractive mass planting.

Twiggy branches pushed into the ground around young penstemon plants will support them as they grow.

Recommended

P. 'Alice Hindley' bears pinkish purple flowers with white throats from mid-summer to fall. It grows 24–36" tall and spreads 12–18".

P. 'Apple Blossom' bears pink-flushed white flowers from late spring to mid-summer. This

P. 'White Bedder'

rounded perennial grows 18–24"
tall, with an equal spread.

P. barbatus (beardlip penstemon)
is an upright, rounded perennial.
It grows 18–36" tall and spreads
12–18". Red or pink flowers are
borne from early summer to early
fall. 'Alba' has white flowers. 'Elfin
Pink' is very reliable and has compact spikes of pink flowers. It grows
up to 18" tall. 'Hyacinth Mix' is a
hardy seed strain producing a mix of
pink, lilac, blue and scarlet flowers
on plants up to 12" tall. 'Praecox
Nanus' ('Nanus Rondo') is a compact, dwarf plant that grows about
half the size of the species. It bears
pink, purple or red flowers. 'Prairie
Dusk' has tall spikes of tubular, rose
purple flowers; it blooms over a long
season. *P. barbatus* and its hybrids
and cultivars are the hardiest of the
penstemons, to Zone 3.

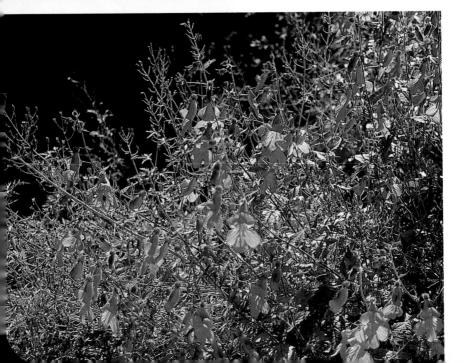

P. digitalis (foxglove penstemon, talus slope penstemon) is a very hardy, upright, semi-evergreen perennial. It grows 2–5' tall and it spreads 18–24". It bears white flowers, often veined with purple, all summer. '**Husker Red**' combines white flowers with vibrant burgundy foliage that adds season-long interest. Chosen as the 1996 Perennial Plant of the Year by the American Perennial Plant Association, this cultivar was developed for hardiness as well as good looks.

P. '**White Bedder**' grows 24–30" tall and 18" wide. Its white flowers become pink tinged as they mature. It blooms from mid-summer to mid-autumn.

Problems & Pests

Powdery mildew, rust and leaf spot can occur but are rarely serious problems.

Over 200 species of Penstemon *are native to varied habitats from mountains to open plains throughout North and South America.*

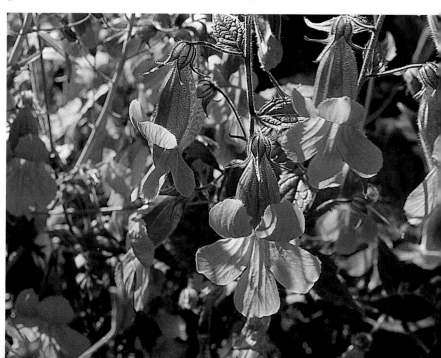

Peony
Paeonia

Height: 24–32" **Spread:** 24–32" **Flower color:** white, yellow, pink, red
Blooms: spring, early summer **Zones:** 2–7

FROM THE SIMPLE SINGLE FLOWERS TO THE EXTRAVAGANT doubles, it's easy to become mesmerized with these voluptuous plants. At first, I was nervous about planting peonies. As a young gardener I was given a division with very specific planting instructions, which if not followed exactly would result in a flowerless plant. It flowered. The key is to plant the crown of a peony no more than 2" below the soil surface, at the same level it was planted originally. One of the most incredible peony collections—with both herbaceous and tree peonies—resides at the Montréal Botanical Garden in Canada. It's a bit of a trek for an Ohioan but worth the effort. Closer to home, visit Kingwood Center in Mansfield, which displays more than 170 species, hybrids and cultivars.

Planting

Seeding: Not recommended; seeds may take two to three years to germinate and many more years to grow to flowering size

Planting out: Fall or spring

Spacing: 24–36"

Growing

Peonies prefer **full sun** but tolerate some shade. The planting site should be well prepared before the plants are introduced. Peonies like **fertile, humus-rich, moist, well-drained** soil, to which lots of compost has been added. Mulch peonies lightly with compost in spring. Too much fertilizer, particularly nitrogen, causes floppy growth and retards blooming. Division is not required, but it is usually the best way to propagate new plants and should be done in fall.

Cut back the flowers after blooming and remove any blackened leaves to prevent the spread of gray mold. Red peonies are more susceptible to disease.

Peony seed capsules

In the past, peonies were used to cure a variety of ailments. They are named after Paion, the physician to the Greek gods.

P. lactiflora cultivar

Whether you choose to clean most of your perennial garden in fall or spring, it is essential to deal with peonies in fall. To reduce the possibility of disease, clean up and discard or destroy all leaf litter before the snow falls.

Tips

These are wonderful plants that look great in a border combined with other early bloomers. They may be underplanted with bulbs and other plants that will die down by mid-summer, when the emerging foliage of peonies will hide the dying foliage of spring plants. Avoid planting peonies under trees, where they will have to compete for moisture and nutrients.

Planting depth is a very important factor in determining whether or not a peony will flower. Tubers planted too shallowly or, more commonly, too deeply will not flower. The buds or eyes on the tuber should be 1–2" below the soil surface.

Place wire tomato or peony cages around the plants in early spring to support heavy flowers. The cage will be hidden by the foliage as it grows up into the wires.

Young peony growth (above)

Recommended

Peonies may be listed as cultivars of a certain species or as interspecies hybrids. Hundreds are available.

P. lactiflora (common garden peony, Chinese peony) forms a clump of red-tinged stems and dark green foliage. It grows up to 30" tall, with an equal spread, and bears single, fragrant white or pink flowers with yellow stamens. Some popular hybrid cultivars are **'Dawn Pink'** with single, rose pink flowers; **'Duchess de Nemours'** with fragrant, white double flowers tinged yellow at the bases of the inner petals; and **'Sara Bernhardt'** with large, fragrant, pink double flowers. These cultivars may also be sold as hybrids and not listed as cultivars of this species.

P. officinalis (common peony) forms a clump of slightly hairy stems and deeply lobed foliage. It bears single red or pink flowers with yellow stamens. **'Alba Plena'** has white double flowers. **'Rubra Plena'** has red double flowers.

Problems & Pests

Peonies may have trouble with *Verticillium* wilt, ringspot virus, tip blight, stem rot, gray mold, leaf blotch, nematodes and Japanese beetles.

Peonies are slow growers and often take a couple of years to bloom, but once established they may well outlive their owners. Despite their exotic appearance, these tough perennials can survive winter temperatures as low as −40° F.

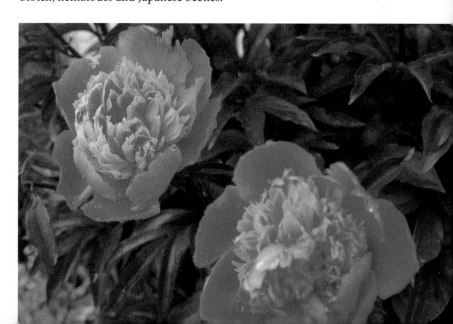

Perennial Salvia
Sage
Salvia

Height: 12–36" **Spread:** 18–36" **Flower color:** purple, blue, pink, cream
Blooms: late spring, summer, early fall **Zones:** 3–9

SALVIAS ARE LOW-CARE WORKHORSES THAT SEEM TO ENJOY OUR
hot summers. I use them throughout my gardens to tie different spaces
together. A real performer is *S. verticillata* 'Purple Rain,' which blooms
through hot weather and drought. My plants are also dealing with competition from a nearby oak, and not many plants can handle three tough conditions gracefully. *S. nemorosa* and *S.* x *sylvestris* will flower from late spring
into fall if deadheaded and kept watered during extended dry periods. Flowering may stall in very hot weather but will resume when temperatures drop.
Common sage *(S. officinalis)* is often relegated to the herb garden, but its
variegated cultivars supply wonderful foliage interest. Use them to help
bridge the lulls when other perennials take a rest from blooming.

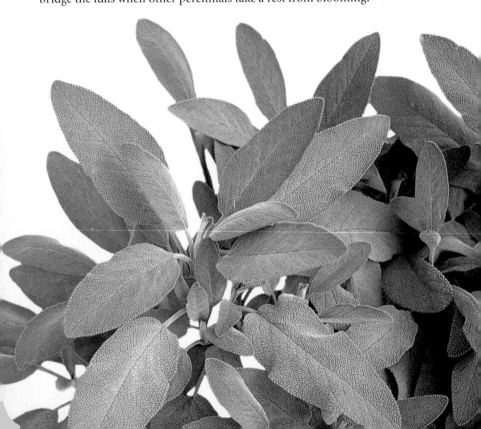

Planting

Seeding: Cultivars do not come true to type; species can be started in early spring

Planting out: Spring

Spacing: 18–24"

Growing

Salvias prefer **full sun** but tolerate light shade. The soil should be of **average fertility** and **well drained.** These plants benefit from a light mulch of compost each year. They are drought tolerant once established. Division can be done in spring, but the plants are slow to re-establish and resent having their roots disturbed. They are easily propagated by tip cuttings.

Deadhead to prolong blooming. Trim plants back in spring to encourage new growth and keep plants tidy. New shoots will sprout from old, woody growth.

S. x *sylvestris* 'May Night'

Tips

All *Salvia* species are attractive plants for the border. Taller species and cultivars add volume to the middle or back of the border, and the smaller specimens make an attractive edging or feature near the front. Perennial salvias can also be grown in mixed planters.

S. officinalis, *the common culinary sage, has aromatic foliage that is used as a flavoring in many dishes.*

S. officinalis 'Icterina'

S. *nemorosa* 'Lubeca'

Salvia *is considered the true sage, but species of* Artemisia, Perovskia *and* Pulmonaria *are often called 'sage' as well.*

S. x *sylvestris* 'May Night'

Recommended

S. nemorosa (*S.* x *superba;* perennial salvia) is a clump-forming, branching plant with gray-green leaves. It grows 18–36" tall and spreads 18–24". Spikes of blue or purple flowers are produced in summer. '**Lubeca**' bears long-lasting purple flowers. (Zones 3–7)

S. officinalis (common sage) is a woody, mounding plant with soft gray-green leaves. It grows 12–24" tall and spreads 18–36". Spikes of light purple flowers appear in early and mid-summer. '**Berggarten**' ('Bergarden') has silvery leaves about the size and shape of a quarter. '**Icterina**' ('Aurea') has yellow-margined foliage. '**Purpurea**' has purple stems. The new foliage emerges purple and matures to purple-green. '**Tricolor**' has green or purple-green foliage outlined in cream. New growth emerges pinkish purple. It is the least hardy of the variegated sages. (Zones 4–7)

S. sclarea (clary sage) is a short-lived perennial or biennial up to 36" tall and about 12" in spread. It forms a mound of large, fuzzy leaves and bears large, loose spikes of purple-bracted cream, purple, pink or blue flowers in late spring and early summer. (Zones 4–9)

S. x *sylvestris* (perennial salvia) grows 30–36" tall and about 12" in spread. It is often confused with the very similar *S. nemorosa.* Cultivars have been listed under both species at different times. **'Blue Queen'** bears dark purple-blue blossoms, **'May Night'** has deep purple blue flowers and **'Rose Queen'** bears unique rosy purple flowers. The growth of 'Rose Queen' is somewhat floppier than that of the other cultivars. (Zones 3–7)

S. verticillata **'Purple Rain'** is a low, mounding plant that grows 18" tall, with an equal spread. It bears purple blooms in late summer and early fall. The colorful bracts remain long after the flowers fade. (Zones 5–8)

Problems & Pests

Scale insects, whiteflies and root rot (in wet soils) are the most likely problems.

S. officinalis 'Tricolor'

The genus name Salvia *comes from the Latin* salvus, *'save,' referring to the medicinal properties of several species.*

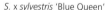

S. x *sylvestris* 'Blue Queen'

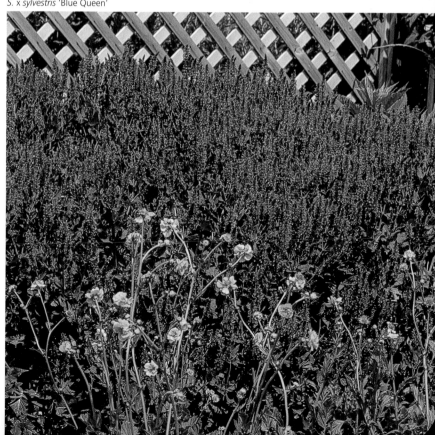

Phlox

Phlox

Height: 2"–4' **Spread:** 12–36" **Flower color:** white, orange, red, blue, purple, pink **Blooms:** spring, summer, fall **Zones:** 3–8

AMONG THE SWEETEST SMELLS OF SUMMER ARE THOSE OF GARDEN phlox and early phlox. These old-fashioned plants from Grandmother's garden never quite went out of fashion. We don't even seem to mind that the summer-blooming phloxes take a bit of care to look good, because they return our efforts in spades. In spring, moss phlox takes center stage with its waterfall of pinwheel flowers, especially when planted over the edge of a wall or combined with spring bulbs. Garden centers can't keep this plant in stock while it is in flower. When sheared after it blooms, moss phlox covers the ground with a dark green carpet that often persists into winter. I have found it extremely drought tolerant once established.

Planting

Seeding: Not recommended

Planting out: Spring

Spacing: 12–36"

Growing

P. paniculata and *P. maculata* prefer **full sun**; *P. subulata* prefers **full sun to partial shade**; *P. divaricata* 'Chatahoochee' prefers **light shade**; and *P. stolonifera* prefers **light to partial shade** but tolerates heavy shade. All like **fertile, humus-rich, moist, well-drained** soil. *P. paniculata* and *P. maculata* bloom better if fertilized and watered regularly. Divide in fall or spring.

P. stolonifera spreads out horizontally as it grows. The stems grow roots where they touch the ground, and new plants are easily obtained by detaching the rooted stems in spring or early fall. Do not prune this phlox in fall; it is an early-season bloomer and will have already formed next spring's flowers.

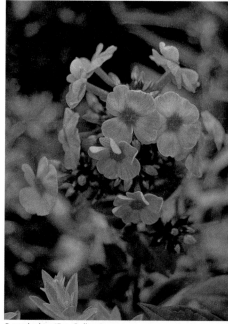

P. paniculata 'Eva Cullum'

The name Phlox *is from the Greek word for 'flame,' referring to the colorful flowers of many species.*

P. subulata

Tips

Low-growing species are useful in a rock garden or at the front of a border. Taller phloxes may be used in the middle of a border and are particularly effective if planted in groups.

To prevent mildew, make sure *P. paniculata* has good air circulation. Thin out large stands to help keep the air flowing. *P. maculata* is more resistant to powdery mildew than *P. paniculata*.

Recommended

P. divaricata 'Chatahoochee' (woodland phlox) is a low, bushy plant. It grows 6–12" tall and spreads about 12". It produces lavender blue flowers with darker purple centers for most of the summer and early fall.

P. maculata (early phlox, garden phlox, wild sweet William) forms an upright clump of hairy stems and narrow leaves that are sometimes spotted with red. It grows 24–36" tall and spreads 18–24". Pink, purple or white flowers are borne in conical clusters in the first half of summer. This species resists powdery mildew. 'Miss Lingard' bears white flowers all summer. 'Omega' bears white flowers with

P. paniculata
P. maculata

light pink centers. 'Rosalinde' bears dark pink flowers. These cultivars are taller than the species, usually 30" or more.

P. paniculata (garden phlox, summer phlox) blooms in summer and fall. The many cultivars vary greatly in size, growing 20"–4' tall and spreading 24–36". Many colors are available, often with contrasting centers. 'Bright Eyes' has light pink flowers with deeper pink centers. 'David' (sometimes listed under *P. maculata* or as *P.* 'David') was Perennial Plant of the Year for 2002. It bears white flowers and resists powdery mildew. 'Eva Cullum' bears pink flowers with red centers. 'Starfire' bears crimson red flowers.

P. stolonifera (creeping phlox) is a low, spreading plant. It grows 4–6" tall, spreads about 12" and bears flowers in shades of purple in spring. This species was Perennial Plant of the Year in 1990.

P. subulata (moss phlox, moss pink) is very low growing, only 2–6" tall, with a spread of 20". Its cultivars bloom from late spring to early summer in various colors. The foliage is evergreen. 'Candy Stripe' bears bicolored pink and white flowers.

Problems & Pests

Occasional problems with powdery mildew, stem canker, rust, leaf spot, leaf miners and caterpillars are possible.

P. subulata 'Candy Stripe'

Phloxes come in many forms, from low-growing creepers to tall, clump-forming uprights. The many species can be found in diverse climates including dry, exposed mountainsides and moist, sheltered woodlands.

P. paniculata 'David'

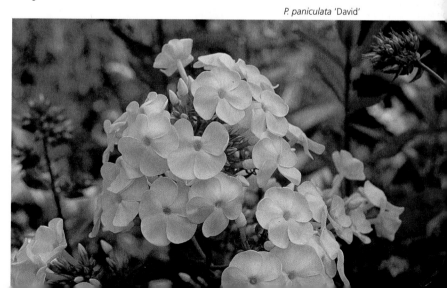

Pincushion Flower
Scabiosa

Height: 12–24" **Spread:** 24" **Flower color:** purple, blue, white, pink
Blooms: summer, fall **Zones:** 3–7

PINCUSHION FLOWERS HAVE ONE OF THE LONGEST BLOOM TIMES
of any perennial, provided the spent flowers are removed and the soil is not
allowed to dry out. Adding compost will also help maintain the profuse
bloom. In my garden, these plants tend to be rather short-lived perennials;
the reduced life span is probably the trade-off for their extended bloom season. The soft lavender blues of 'Butterfly Blue' at the front of the border and
'Fama' in the middle of the border will complement all nearby plants.

Planting
Seeding: Direct sow in
spring or summer

Planting out: Spring

Spacing: 24"

Growing

Pincushion flowers prefer **full sun** but tolerate partial shade. The soil should be **light, moderately fertile, neutral or alkaline** and **well drained**. Divide in early spring, whenever the clumps become overgrown.

Remove the flowers as they fade, to promote a longer flowering period. Cutting flowers at their peak every few days for indoor use will make this maintenance chore more enjoyable. Leave the evergreen foliage intact over the winter and remove dead and tattered leaves in spring.

Tips

These plants look best in groups of three or more in a bed or border. The blooms attract butterflies and can be used as cut flowers.

Recommended

S. caucasica forms a basal rosette of narrow leaves. Blue or lavender flowers are borne in summer on long stems up to 24" tall; the plant spreads 24" as well. '**Fama**' bears sky blue flowers with silvery white centers. '**House's Hybrids**' (Isaac House Hybrids) are slightly smaller plants with large, shaggy, blue flowers. '**Miss Wilmont**' bears white flowers.

Several hybrids have been developed from crosses between *S. caucasica* and *S. columbaria*, a smaller species. These hybrids may be listed as cultivars of either species. '**Butterfly Blue**' bears lavender blue flowers from early summer until frost. '**Butterfly Pink**' ('Pink Mist') grows about 12" tall and bears many pink blooms from summer to frost.

Problems & Pests

Pincushion flowers rarely have problems, though aphids may be troublesome.

S. caucasica (this page)

Pinks

Dianthus

Height: 2–18" **Spread:** 6–24" **Flower color:** pink, red, white, lilac
Blooms: spring, summer **Zones:** 3–9

THE MUTED COLORS OF THE WINTER GARDEN ARE EARTH TONES
mixed with gray and black. Fortunately, many species of *Dianthus* can relieve
the winter landscape with a touch of blue or green. Cheddar pinks are especially vibrant. The blue leaves of *D. gratianopolitanus* 'Firewitch' against a
fresh layer of snow makes an electric combination. During the growing season, the pinks are just as pleasing mixed with other sun-loving perennials.
After their fragrant blooms are finished, they provide a lovely carpet at the
feet of later-flowering plants. Combine pinks with English lavender, basket-
of-gold *(Aurinia)*, perennial salvias and roses. All require good drainage
throughout the year.

Planting

Seeding: Not recommended; cultivars do not come true to type from seed

Planting out: Spring

Spacing: 10–20"

Growing

Pinks prefer **full sun** but tolerate some light shade. A **well-drained, neutral or alkaline** soil is required. The most important factor in the successful cultivation of pinks is drainage—they hate to stand in water. The native habitat of many species is rocky outcroppings. Mix organic matter and sharp sand or gravel into their area of the flowerbed to encourage good drainage, if needed.

Pinks may be difficult to propagate by division. It is often easier to take cuttings in summer, once flowering has finished. Cuttings should be 1–3" long. Strip the lower leaves from the cutting. The cuttings should be kept humid, but be sure to give them some ventilation so that fungal problems do not set in. Roots should begin developing in 7–10 days.

The lovely, delicate petals of pinks can be used to decorate cakes. Be sure to remove the white part at the base of each petal before using the petals or they will be bitter.

D. plumarius

The scarlet carnation (Dianthus caryophyllus) *is Ohio's lovely state flower.*

D. deltoides

Tips

Pinks make excellent plants for rock gardens and rock walls, and for edging flower borders and walkways. They can also be used in cutting gardens and even as groundcovers.

To prolong blooming, deadhead as the flowers fade, but leave a few flowers in place to go to seed. Pinks self-seed quite easily. Seedlings may differ from the parent plants, often with new and interesting results.

Recommended

D. x *allwoodii* (Allwood pinks) are hybrids that form a compact mound and bear flowers in a wide range of colors. Cultivars generally grow 8–18" tall, with an equal spread. '**Aqua**' bears pure white double flowers. '**Doris**' bears salmon pink semi-double flowers with darker pink centers. It is popular as a cut flower. '**Laced Romeo**' bears spice-scented red flowers with cream-margined petals. '**Sweet Wivelsfield**' bears fragrant, two-toned flowers in a variety of colors.

D. deltoides (maiden pink) grows 6–12" tall and about 12" wide. The plant forms a mat of foliage and flowers in spring. This is a popular species to use in rock gardens. '**Brilliant**' ('Brilliancy,' 'Brilliance') bears dark red flowers. '**Zing Rose**' bears carmine red blooms.

D. gratianopolitanus (cheddar pink) usually grows about 6" tall but can grow up to 12" tall and 18–24" wide. This plant is long-lived and forms a very dense mat of evergreen, silver gray foliage with sweet-scented flowers borne in summer. '**Bath's Pink**' bears plentiful, light pink flowers and tolerates warm, humid conditions. It spreads up to 24". '**Firewitch**' forms a compact hummock of deep blue leaves. It grows to 6" tall and 6–10" wide and bears deep magenta single flowers. '**Petite**' is even smaller, growing 2–4" tall, with pink flowers.

D. plumarius (cottage pink) is noteworthy for its role in the development of many popular cultivars known as garden pinks. They are generally 12–18" tall and 24" wide, although smaller cultivars are available. They all flower in spring and into summer if deadheaded regularly. The flowers can be single, semi-double or fully double and are available in many colors. '**Sonata**' bears fragrant double flowers in many colors all summer. '**Spring Beauty**' bears double flowers in many colors. The petal edges are more strongly frilled than those of the species.

Problems & Pests

Providing good drainage and air circulation will keep most fungal problems away. Occasional problems with slugs, blister beetles, sow bugs and grasshoppers are possible. Rabbits seem to find the flowers tasty.

D. gratianopolitanus

Cheddar Pink is a rare and protected species in Britain. It was discovered in the 18th century by British botanist Samuel Brewer, and it became as locally famous as Cheddar cheese.

D. plumarius

Plume Poppy
Macleaya

Height: 6–10' **Spread:** 12–36"; clumps spread indefinitely
Flower color: cream **Blooms:** mid- to late summer **Zones:** 3–10

PLUME POPPY IS BOLD, NOT ONLY IN ITS VISUAL
presence, but also in its space-grabbing maneuvers. This is
not a plant for the small garden or the timid gardener. One
way to slow its spread is to plant it in a dry, low-fertility location, but you may still need to remove seedlings and side
shoots when necessary. Plume poppy is beautiful by itself
as a seasonal hedge or in combination with the larger
ornamental grasses. Two cautions: make sure anything
you plant with plume poppy is sturdy; and be prepared to remove plume poppy rhizomes that have
invaded adjacent plants.

Planting

Seeding: Start seed in cold
frame in early or mid-
spring

Planting out: Spring

Spacing: 36"

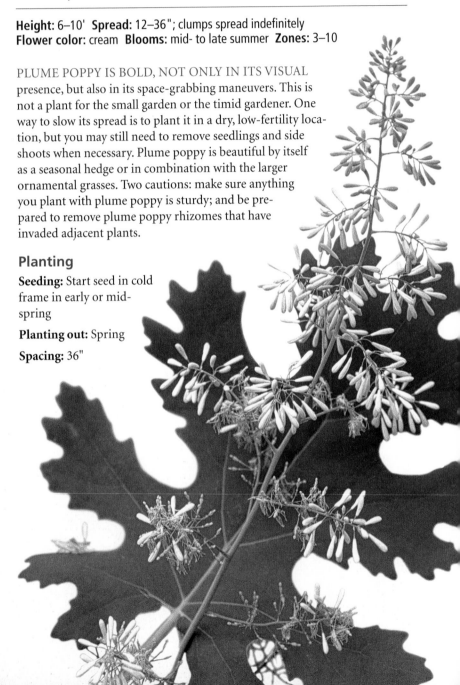

Growing

Plume poppy prefers **full sun** but tolerates partial shade. The soil should be of **average fertility, humus rich** and **moist**. Plume poppy tolerates dry soils and is less invasive in poorer conditions. Divide every two or three years in spring or fall to control the size of the clump.

Deadhead if you want to avoid having too many self-sown seedlings popping up all over. Pull up or cut back any overly exuberant growth as needed. Planting in a heavy-duty, bottomless pot sunk into the ground will slow invasive spreading.

Tips

Plume poppy looks impressive as a specimen plant or at the back of the border. Be sure to give it lots of room, because it can quickly overwhelm less vigorous plants. Drought tolerant and easy to care for, plume poppy makes a nice summer screen and is also a good choice for the center of a cement-bordered median or large island bed.

Recommended

M. cordata is a tall, narrow-growing, clump-forming plant with attractive, undulating, lobed leaves and plumes of creamy white flowers. Each clump easily spreads to 36" and needs this much space to be healthy. If given the room, however, clumps may spread indefinitely.

Problems & Pests

Slugs may attack young growth. Anthracnose can be a problem in warm, humid weather.

The flower plumes of these unusual members of the poppy family add a dramatic flair to fresh or dried arrangements.

Primrose
Primula

Height: 6–24" **Spread:** 6–18" **Flower color:** red, orange, yellow, pink, purple, blue, white **Blooms:** spring, early summer **Zones:** 3–8

THESE BRIGHT, CHEERFUL HARBINGERS OF SPRING ARE AMONG the first flowers to become available in garden centers in late winter. I plant polyantha primroses in containers to create spots of color by my front door. Primroses revel in cool locations, which unfortunately often dooms them in our hot, humid summers. By mid-summer, I am replacing my polyanthas with other plants. But if you can find a cool, moist setting, these plants will reward you with a long bloom. For those fortunate enough to have a shady wetland area, the world of primroses is yours.

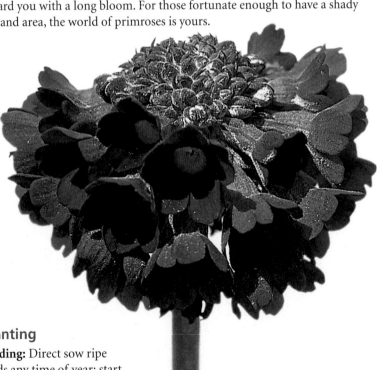

Planting
Seeding: Direct sow ripe seeds any time of year; start indoors in early spring or in a cold frame in fall or late winter

Planting out: Spring

Spacing: 6–18"

Growing

Choose a location for these plants with **light or partial shade**. The soil should be **moderately fertile, humus rich, moist, well drained** and **neutral or slightly acidic**. Primroses are not drought resistant and will quickly wilt and fade if they are not watered regularly. Overgrown clumps should be divided after flowering or in early fall. Pull off yellowing or dried leaves in fall for fresh new growth in spring.

Tips

Primroses work well in many areas of the garden. Try them in a woodland area or under the shade of taller shrubs and perennials in a border or rock garden. Moisture-loving primroses may be grown in a bog garden or in almost any other moist spot.

The species with flowers on tall stems look lovely planted in masses. Those with solitary flowers peeking out from the foliage are interesting dotted throughout the garden.

P. x polyanthus

P. japonica

If your primroses always look faded by mid-summer, you may wish to grow them as annuals and just enjoy them in spring and early summer.

Recommended

P. auricula (auricula primrose) forms a rosette of smooth, waxy foliage. Large flowers are clustered at the tops of stout stems. The plant grows up to 8" tall and spreads 10". The flowers are usually yellow or cream, but there are many cultivars with flowers in various colors.

P. denticulata (drumstick primula, Himalayan primrose) forms a rosette of spoon-shaped leaves that are powdery white on the undersides. The plant grows 12–18" tall and spreads 10–12". The flowers, which may be purple, white, pink or red and usually have yellow centers, are borne in dense, ball-like clusters atop thick stems.

P. eliator (oxslip) is a meadowland species from Europe. It grows about 12" tall and 6" wide. The yellow, tubular flowers are clustered at the ends of long stems.

P. japonica (Japanese primrose) grows 12–24" tall and 12–18" wide. It thrives in moist, boggy conditions and does poorly without enough moisture. It is a candelabra flowering type, meaning that the long flower stem has up to six evenly spaced rings of flowers along its length.

P. x *polyanthus* (polyantha primrose, polyantha hybrids) usually grows 8–12" tall, with about an equal spread. The flowers are clustered at the tops of stems of variable height. It is available in a wide range of solid colors or bicolors and is often sold as a flowering potted plant.

P. veris (cowslip primrose) forms a rosette of deeply veined, crinkled foliage. Small clusters of tubular

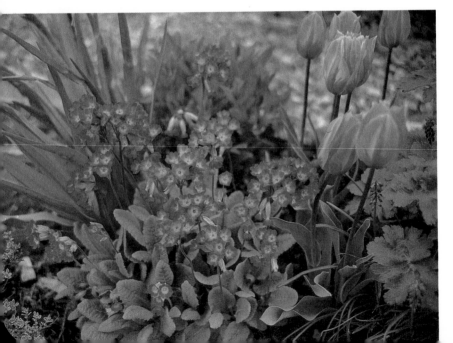

yellow flowers are borne at the tops of narrow stems. The plant grows about 10" tall, with an equal spread.

P. vialii (Chinese pagoda primrose) forms a rosette of deeply veined leaves from which small spikes of flowers emerge. Each spike has a two-toned appearance as the red buds open to reveal light violet flowers, starting with the lowest flowers. The plant grows 12–24" tall and spreads about 12".

P. vulgaris (English primrose, common primrose) grows 6–8" tall and 8" wide. The flowers are solitary and are borne at the ends of short stems that are slightly longer than the leaves.

Problems & Pests

Slugs, strawberry root weevils, aphids, rust and leaf spot are possible problems for primroses.

P. vialii

Primrose flowers can be made into wine or candied as an edible decoration. The young leaves of P. veris *are also edible and can be added to salads for a hint of spice.*

P. veris

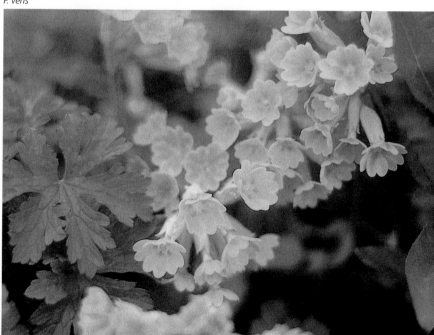

Purple Coneflower
Coneflower, Echinacea
Echinacea

Height: 2–5' **Spread:** 12–18" **Flower color:** purple, pink or white, with rust orange centers **Blooms:** mid-summer to fall **Zones:** 3–8

PURPLE CONEFLOWER POSSESSES MANY VIRTUES. IT IS A VISUAL delight, with its mauve petals offset by a spiky orange center. (The genus name is derived from the Greek word for 'hedgehog,' and one touch quickly confirms the appropriateness of the name!) For wildlife, it offers pollen, nectar and seeds from summer into early winter. It offers us medicinal benefits as an immune system booster. A caution: the herbal medicine echinacea does not work for everyone, and it should not be used for an extended period of time. And, as with any medicine, make sure that you consult with a qualified medical practitioner before using it.

Planting
Seeding: Direct sow in spring

Planting out: Spring

Spacing: 18"

Growing

Purple coneflower grows well in **full sun** or very **light shade**. Any **well-drained** soil is tolerated, though an **average to rich** soil is preferred. The thick taproots make this plant drought resistant, but it prefers to have regular water. Divide every four years or so in spring or fall.

Deadhead early in the season to prolong flowering. Later you may wish to leave the flowerheads in place to self-seed and provide winter interest. To prevent self-seeding, remove all the flowerheads as they fade. Pinch plants back or thin out the stems in early summer to encourage bushy growth that is less prone to mildew.

Tips

Use purple coneflower in meadow gardens and informal borders, either in groups or as single specimens.

The dry flowerheads make an interesting feature in fall and winter gardens.

Recommended

E. purpurea is an upright plant 5' in height and up to 18" in spread, with prickly hairs all over. It bears purple flowers with orangy centers. The cultivars are generally about half the species' height. **'Magnus'** bears flowers like those of the species but larger, up to 7" across. **'White Lustre'** bears white flowers with orange centers. **'White Swan'** is a compact plant with white flowers.

The Chicago Botanic Garden is field testing some exciting new hybrids with flowers in shades of deep pink, peach, sunset orange and yellow. Keep an eye open for them.

Problems & Pests

Powdery mildew is the biggest problem for purple coneflower. Also possible are leaf miners, bacterial spot and gray mold. Vine weevils may attack the roots.

'White Lustre'

Purple coneflower seeds are a significant food source for goldfinches and chickadees.

'Magnus' with 'White Swan'

Rockcress
Wall Rockcress
Arabis

Height: 2–12" **Spread:** 12–18" **Flower color:** white, pink
Blooms: spring, early summer **Zones:** 4–7

A GEM IN THE ROCK GARDEN, THIS EARLY-BLOOMING GENUS features white flowers that sparkle in the soft spring sun. Rockcresses are perennials that prefer a well-drained soil of low fertility. Like other members of the mustard family, they resent wet feet at any time of the year. Variegated rockcress (*A. ferdinandi-coburgi* 'Variegata') adds interest to the summer garden with its white-splashed leaves. Rockcresses combine well with the smaller speedwells, basket-of-gold *(Aurinia saxatilis)* and Carpathian bellflower.

Planting

Seeding: Start in containers in early spring; seeds need light to germinate

Planting out: Any time during growing season

Spacing: 12"

Growing

Rockcresses prefer **full sun**. The soil should be of **average or poor fertility, alkaline** and **well drained**. These plants do best in a climate that doesn't have extremely hot summer weather; they may be short-lived otherwise.

Divide in early fall every two or three years. Stem cuttings taken from new growth may be started in summer.

Cut plants back by up to half after flowering to keep them neat and compact and encourage a possible second flush of blooms. Before winter tidy them up but do not cut them back. Remove dead leaves and tatty growth in spring.

Tips

Use rockcresses in rock gardens, in borders or on rock walls. They may also be used as ground-covers on exposed slopes or as companions with small bulbs. Don't plant rockcresses where they may overwhelm slower-growing plants.

Species of the genus Arabis *resemble those of* Aubrieta. *Both are commonly known as rockcress, so write down the scientific name of the plant you want before you head to the garden center.*

Recommended

A. alpina subsp. *caucasica* (*A. caucasica*) forms a low mound of small rosettes of foliage. White flowers are borne in early spring. '**Compinkie**' has pink flowers. '**Snow Cap**' ('Schneehaube') produces abundant white flowers.

A. ferdinandi-coburgi (*A. procurrens*) forms a low mat of foliage. Small white flowers are produced in spring and early summer. This species is more shade tolerant than *A. alpina* subsp. *caucasica* and can therefore be planted where it will be shaded from the hot afternoon sun. '**Variegata**' (variegated rockcress) has white-edged foliage.

Problems & Pests

White rust and downy mildew are possible problems. Aphids are occasionally troublesome, along with *Arabis* midge, which causes deformed shoots that should be removed and destroyed.

Rockrose

Sunrose

Helianthemum

Height: 6–12" **Spread:** 12–18" **Flower color:** red, pink, yellow, cream, orange and bicolored **Blooms:** late spring to mid-summer **Zones:** 4–7

BOTANICALLY SPEAKING, ROCKROSES ARE CONSIDERED LOW-growing shrubs or subshrubs, but somehow they are usually grouped with herbaceous perennials. They create a green to gray-green carpet under taller plants in my rock garden. The tiny species do very well in containers and troughs, but do protect them from our freeze-thaw cycles. Since snow cover is unreliable in much of Ohio, use straw or some other loose material to insulate the sides of the container. 'Wisley Primrose' is lovely combined with speedwell (*Veronica spicata* 'Icicle') and dwarf lavender.

Planting

Seeding: Not recommended

Planting out: Spring

Spacing: 12"

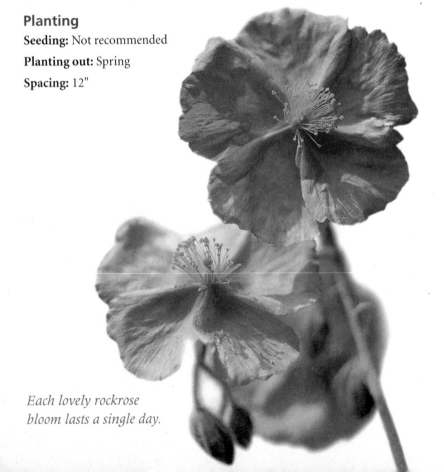

Each lovely rockrose bloom lasts a single day.

Growing

Rockroses grow best in **full sun.** The soil should be of **average fertility, neutral to alkaline** and **well drained.** Winter protection, such as a mulch of evergreen boughs, will guard against excessive cold and fluctuations in temperature.

Once the spring bloom is finished, shear the plants back to within an inch of the previous year's growth, and you may be rewarded with a second flush of blooms in fall. Do not divide rockroses because they grow from a single stem.

Tips

Rockroses can be used in rock gardens, as groundcovers and at the front of a border. These plants are actually shrubs but are often treated as perennials.

Recommended

H. nummularium is a low-growing evergreen plant with gray-green foliage. It grows 6–12" tall and spreads 12–18". The species is rarely grown, but it is a parent of many hybrids, which bear red, pink, yellow, cream, orange or bicolored flowers from late spring until mid-summer.

H. **hybrids** include the following popular selections. **'Raspberry Ripple'** bears white flowers streaked raspberry red from the petal bases. This low grower is 8" high and spreads 12". **'Rhodanthe Carneum'** ('Wisley Pink') forms a low, spreading mound 12" tall and 12–18" in spread. The leaves are a soft gray color and the flowers are pink with yellow centers. **'Wisley Primrose'** ('Wisley Yellow') grows 12" tall and spreads 12–18". It bears bright yellow flowers with deeper yellow centers. **'Wisley White'** is a rounded, spreading plant 12" tall and 18" wide. It bears creamy white flowers with yellow centers.

Rockroses rarely suffer from pest or disease problems.

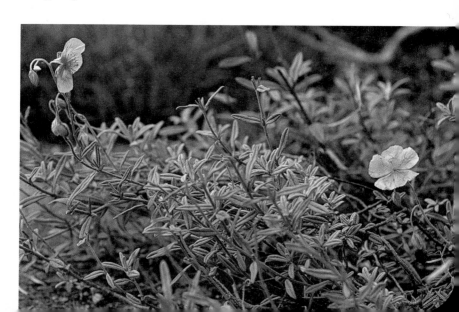

Russian Sage

Perovskia

Height: 3–4' **Spread:** 3–4' **Flower color:** blue, purple
Blooms: mid- or late summer to fall **Zones:** 4–9

RUSSIAN SAGE OFFERS FOUR-SEASON INTEREST IN THE GARDEN.
In spring it produces soft, gray-green leaves on light gray stems. In summer
the upper half of each stem is clothed in fuzzy, violet blue flowers.
Then, in fall, the stems becomes silvery white and last until late
winter. Russian sage is pettable, and when you stroke it you
will be rewarded with a pleasant herbal scent and a satiny
touch. A perfect blender, it provides a filmy backdrop for
just about any other plant. For starters, try combining it
with purple coneflower, *Sedum* 'Autumn Joy,' balloon
flower, speedwells and garden phlox.

Planting

Seeding: Not recommended;
germination can be very erratic

Planting out: Spring

Spacing: 36"

*The airy habit of this
plant creates a mist
of silvery purple in
the garden.*

Growing

Russian sage prefers a location with **full sun**. The soil should be **poor to moderately fertile** and **well drained**. Too much water and nitrogen will cause the growth to flop, so avoid growing this plant next to heavy feeders. Russian sage should not be divided because it is a subshrub that originates from a single stem.

In spring, when new growth appears low on the branches, or in fall, cut the plant back hard to about 6–12" to encourage vigorous, bushy growth.

Tips

The silvery foliage and blue flowers combine well with other plants in the back of a mixed border and soften the appearance of daylilies. Russian sage may also be used to create a soft screen in a natural garden or on a dry bank.

Russian sage blossoms make a lovely addition to fresh bouquets and dried-flower arrangements.

Recommended

P. atriplicifolia is a loose, upright plant with silvery white, finely divided foliage. The small, lavender blue flowers are loosely held on silvery, branched stems. **'Filagran'** has delicate foliage and an upright habit. **'Longin'** is narrow and erect and has more smoothly edged leaves than other cultivars.

P. **'Blue Spire'** is an upright plant with deep blue flowers and feathery leaves.

Russian sage is rarely troubled by pests or diseases.

'Filagran' (this page)

Sea Holly
Eryngium

Height: 1–5' **Spread:** 12–24" **Flower color:** purple, blue, white
Blooms: summer, fall **Zones:** 4–8

SEA HOLLIES ADD STRUCTURE TO THE GARDEN. THEIR SPIKY
umbels of silvery blue flowers create angular silhouettes in front of such
perennials as Joe-Pye weed, white mugwort and boltonia. A favorite of
mine is our native rattlesnake master *(E. yuccifolium)*. It allegedly repels
rattlesnakes and cures their bites, but I wouldn't want to depend on it!
Rattlesnake master emerges in spring looking like a yucca, but then it sends
up towering stems topped with small, cream-colored globes. It's not only
drought tolerant, it keeps my friends guessing: is it a weed or a perennial?

Planting

Seeding: Not recommended, though direct sowing in fall will produce spring seedlings

Planting out: Spring

Spacing: 12–24"

Growing

Grow sea hollies in **full sun**. The soil should be **average to fertile** and **well drained**. These plants have a long taproot and are fairly drought tolerant, but they will suffer if left more than two weeks without water. Sea hollies are very slow to re-establish after dividing. Root cuttings can be taken in late winter.

The leaves and flower bracts of these plants are edged with small spines, making deadheading a pain—literally. It is not necessary unless you are very fussy about keeping plants neat.

E. x *tripartitum* (below)

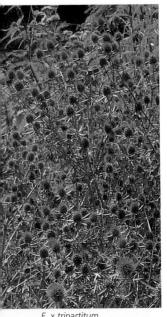

Tips

Mix sea hollies with other late-season bloomers in a border. They make an interesting addition to naturalized gardens.

Recommended

E. alpinum (alpine sea holly) grows 2–4' tall. This species has soft and feathery-looking but spiny bracts, and its flowers are steel blue or white. Several cultivars are available in different shades of blue.

E. giganteum (giant sea holly) grows 4–5' tall. The flowers are steel blue with silvery gray bracts.

E. x tripartitum grows 24–36" tall. The flowers are purple and the bracts are gray, tinged with purple.

E. varifolium (Moroccan sea holly) grows 12–16" tall. It has dark green leaves with silvery veins and gray-purple flowers with blue bracts.

E. x tripartitum

E. alpinum

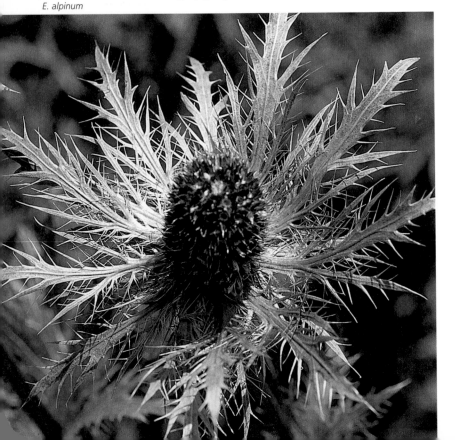

E. yuccifolium (rattlesnake master) is native to central and eastern North America. It grows 3–4' tall and forms a rosette of long, narrow, spiny, blue-gray leaves. From mid-summer to fall, it bears creamy green or pale blue flowers with gray-green bracts.

Problems & Pests

Roots may rot if the plants are left in standing water for long periods of time. Slugs, snails and powdery mildew may be problems.

The steel blue, globe-shaped flowerheads come in a variety of sizes and are prized for use in fresh and dried flower arrangements. Long lasting but short stemmed, these distinctive blooms must be mounted on florists' wire.

E. giganteum

E. x tripartitum

Sedum
Stonecrop
Sedum

Height: 2–24" **Spread:** 18" to indefinite **Flower color:** yellow, white, red, pink; plant also grown for foliage **Blooms:** summer, fall **Zones:** 3–8

EVERYONE KNOWS 'AUTUMN JOY,' BUT THERE ARE MANY OTHER sedums to discover. Some 300 to 500 species are distributed throughout the Northern Hemisphere. Many sedums are grown for their foliage, which can range in color from steel gray-blue to green to red and burgundy. A good number of these plants are well-behaved garden residents, but be forewarned that many of the low, rhizomatous species will ramble at will. They also root easily from single leaves and small cuttings. Although this tendency ensures that you will never lack plants to share, it can increase your maintenance load. Always ask how quickly any gift of sedum will spread.

Planting

Seeding: Sow indoors in early spring. Seed sold is often a mix of different species; you may not get what you expected, but you may be pleasantly surprised.

Planting out: Spring

Spacing: 18"

Growing

Sedums prefer **full sun** but tolerate partial shade. The soil should be of **average fertility,** very **well drained** and **neutral to alkaline.** Divide in spring when needed. Prune back 'Autumn Joy' in May by one-half and insert pruned-off parts into soft soil; cuttings root quickly. Early-summer pruning of upright species and hybrids gives compact, bushy plants but can delay flowering.

Tips

Low-growing sedums make wonderful groundcovers and additions to rock gardens or rock walls. They also edge beds and borders beautifully. The taller types give a lovely late-season display in a bed or border.

S. spurium

Low-growing sedums make an excellent groundcover under trees. Their shallow roots survive well in the competition for space and moisture.

S. spurium 'Dragon's Blood'

S. 'Autumn Joy' (this page)

'Autumn Joy' brings color to the late-season garden, when few flowers are in bloom.

Recommended

S. acre (gold moss stonecrop) grows 2" high and spreads indefinitely. The small yellow-green flowers are borne in summer. Plant this species only if you want it forever.

S. **'Autumn Joy'** (Autumn Joy sedum) is a popular upright hybrid. The flowers open pink or red and later fade to deep bronze over a long period in late summer and fall. The plant forms a clump 24" tall, with an equal spread.

S. **'Mohrchen'** forms an upright clump of stems about 24" tall, with an equal spread. Bronzy red summer foliage brightens to ruby red in fall. Clusters of pink flowers are borne in late summer and fall.

S. spectabile (showy stonecrop) is an upright species with pink flowers borne in late summer. It forms a clump 16–24" tall and wide. **'Brilliant'** bears bright pink flowers. **'Neon'** has deep rosy pink flowers.

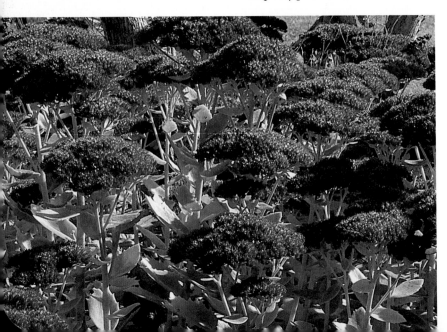

S. spurium (two-row stonecrop) forms a mat about 4" tall and 24" wide. The mid-summer flowers are deep pink or white. **'Dragon's Blood'** has bronze- or purple-tinged foliage and dark pink to dark red flowers. **'Fuldaglut'** bears red or rose pink flowers above orange-red or maroon foliage. **'Royal Pink'** has dark pink flowers and bright green foliage.

S. **'Vera Jameson'** is a low, mounding plant with purple-tinged stems and pinkish purple foliage. It grows up to 12" tall and spreads 18". Clusters of dark pink flowers are borne in late summer and fall.

Problems & Pests

Slugs, snails and scale insects may cause trouble for these plants. Plants may rot in wet locations.

S. 'Vera Jameson'

Perennial bed edged with *S. spectabile* 'Brilliant'

Shasta Daisy
Leucanthemum

Height: 10–40" **Spread:** about 24" **Flower color:** white with yellow centers
Blooms: early summer to fall **Zones:** 4–9

WHENEVER I HEAR 'DAISY,' I THINK OF THE SHASTA DAISY.
This old-fashioned perennial has never gone out of style. A real winner is
the newer cultivar 'Becky.' It blooms the longest of any of the Shasta daisies
in my garden, with little care other than deadheading and watering during
extended dry periods. Many Shastas will self-seed, but the seedlings often do
not share the attractive traits of the parent. Divide your plants or propagate
by tip cuttings to ensure you have the same plant. Try combining Shasta
daisy with other members of the aster family, with speedwells and with ornamental grasses.

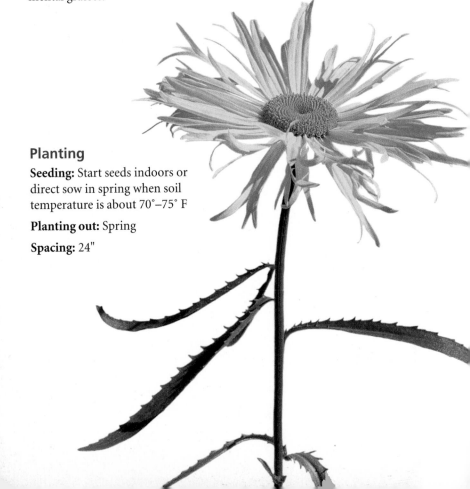

Planting

Seeding: Start seeds indoors or
direct sow in spring when soil
temperature is about 70°–75° F

Planting out: Spring

Spacing: 24"

Growing

Shasta daisy grows well in **full sun** or **partial shade**. The soil should be **fertile, moist** and **well drained**. Divide every year or two, in spring, to maintain plant vigor. Fall-planted Shasta daisy may not establish in time to survive the winter. Plants can be short-lived in Zones 4 and 5.

Pinch or trim plants back in spring to encourage compact, bushy growth. Deadheading extends the bloom by several weeks.

Tips

Use this perennial in the border, where it can be grown as a single plant or massed in groups. The large, showy flowerheads—some 2–5" across—can be cut for fresh arrangements.

This classic perennial daisy lends itself well to the 'loves me, loves me not' game played by children and the lovesick.

Recommended

L. x *superbum* forms a large clump of dark green leaves and stems. It bears white daisy-like flowers with yellow centers all summer and often until the first frost, especially if deadheaded. **'Alaska'** bears large flowers and is hardier than the species. **'Becky'** grows about 36" tall and bears many single flowers. It is drought tolerant and one of the best choices for hot summer climates. **'Marconi'** has large semi-double or double flowers. It should be protected from the hot afternoon sun. **'Silver Spoons'** grows to about 40" tall and bears spidery flowers with long, narrow petals. **'Snow Lady'** is a dwarf 10–14" tall with single flowers. **'Wirral Pride'** bears double flowers composed of layers of fine, shaggy petals.

Problems & Pests

Occasional problems with aphids, leaf spot, leaf miners and powdery mildew are possible.

Soapwort
Saponaria

Height: 3–24" **Spread:** 12–18" **Flower color:** pink, white, red
Blooms: spring, summer, fall **Zones:** 3–7

SOAPWORTS ARE ATTRACTIVE AND
a bit rowdy. In an informal herb garden,
bouncing Bet will quickly form a large
mass. The beautiful double-flowered
cultivar 'Rosea Plena' is a bit more
well mannered than the parent
species, and it can bloom for
most of the summer and fall.
For charm, you can't beat rock
soapwort for the larger rock garden. It forms a dense mat that is
covered with small pink stars for
most of May and June. *Saponaria* species
contain foaming compounds (saponins) and
can be used as a kind of soap; however, there
have been reports of skin reactions to the
gooey sap. So, as always, be careful
when playing with plants.

Planting

Seeding: Start seeds indoors in
early spring. Keep the planted
seeds in a cool, dark place at
about 60°–65° F until they germinate. Move into a lighted room as
soon as germination begins.

Planting out: Spring

Spacing: 18"

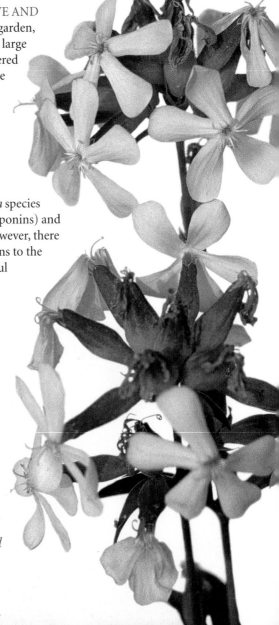

*Soapworts are rarely troubled
by pests and diseases.*

Growing

Soapworts grow best in **full sun**. The soil should be of **average fertility, neutral to alkaline** and **well drained**. Poor soil is tolerated, but rich, fertile soil encourages lank, floppy growth. Divide in spring at least every two to three years to maintain vigor and control spread. Cut rock soapwort back after flowering to keep it neat and compact. Bouncing Bet requires regular deadheading to keep it looking tidy after its initial bloom.

Tips

Use soapworts in borders, in rock gardens and on rock walls. Soapworts self-seed with enthusiasm and can overwhelm less vigorous plants.

Recommended

S. **'Bressingham'** grows up to 3" tall and spreads about 12". Its green foliage is topped with bright pink flowers in spring. This alpine type works well in the rock garden; it is not as invasive as some of the other soapworts.

S. ocymoides (rock soapwort) forms a low, spreading mound. It grows 4–6" tall and spreads about 18". The plant is completely covered in bright pink flowers in late spring and continues to flower sporadically all summer. **'Alba'** has white flowers. **'Rubra Compacta'** is very low growing, with dark pink flowers.

S. officinalis (bouncing Bet, soapwort) is an upright plant up to 24" tall and about 18" in spread. This species is aggressive and can quickly spread even farther with good growing conditions. Pink, white or red flowers are borne from summer to fall. Cultivars are not as invasive as the species. **'Rosea Plena'** bears fragrant, pink double flowers in early summer and sporadically until fall.

S. officinalis 'Rosea Plena'

Speedwell
Veronica
Veronica

Height: 6"–6' **Spread:** 12–24" **Flower color:** blue, white, pink, purple
Blooms: late spring, summer, fall **Zones:** 3–8

THE PREDOMINANT FLOWER COLOR OF *VERONICA* IS BLUE, SO this genus quickly became one of my favorites. A number of mat-forming species are available and perform beautifully at the front edges of beds. They wend their way through the legs of other plants and do their part to suppress weeds. The taller speedwells punctuate the front or middle of the bed with their spikes of white, pink or violet flowers. Speedwells accentuate the vertical in the garden, so they contrast well with plants that are rounded or more diffuse. Mix them with purple coneflower, Russian sage and garden phlox for a beautiful summer combination.

The genus name honors St. Veronica, who is said to have wiped the brow of Jesus as he marched to Calvary.

Planting

Seeding: Not recommended; seedlings do not always come true to type. Seeds germinate quickly when started indoors in early spring.

Planting out: Spring

Spacing: 18"

Growing

Speedwells prefer **full sun** but tolerate partial shade. The soil should be of **average fertility, moist** and **well drained.** Once established, culver's root tolerates short periods of drought. Lack of sun and excessive moisture and nitrogen may be partly to blame for the sloppy habits of some speedwells. Frequent dividing ensures strong, vigorous growth and decreases the chances of flopping. Divide in fall or spring every two or three years.

When the flowers begin to fade, remove the entire spike where it joins the plant to encourage rapid re-blooming. For tidy plants, shear back to 6" in June.

Tips

Hungarian speedwell is a beautiful plant for edging borders. Prostrate speedwell is useful in a rock garden or at the front of a perennial border. Spike speedwell works well in masses in a bed or border. Culver's root and its cultivars are good plants for the middle or back of the border and in situations where tall, narrow plants are needed.

V. spicata cultivar

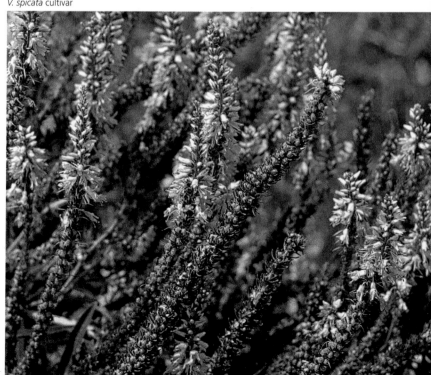

Recommended

V. austriaca subsp. *teucrium* (Hungarian speedwell) forms a clump 6–24" tall and 12–24" in spread. It bears spikes of bright blue flowers from late spring to mid-summer. 'Crater Lake Blue' grows 12–18" tall and bears deep blue flowers.

V. prostrata (prostrate speedwell) is a low-growing, spreading plant 6" tall and 16" in spread. Its flowers may be blue or occasionally pink. Many cultivars are available.

V. spicata (spike speedwell) is a low, mounding plant with stems that flop over when they get too tall. It grows 12–24" tall, spreads 18" and bears spikes of blue flowers in summer. Many cultivars of different colors are available. 'Blue Bouquet' is a low-growing cultivar, to 12", with spikes of bright blue flowers. 'Blue Charm' is a bushy cultivar growing 12–18" tall. It bears spikes of light purple-blue flowers. 'Icicle' ('White Icicle') bears spikes of white flowers. Subsp. *incana* has soft, hairy, silvery green leaves and deep purple-blue blooms. 'Red Fox' has dark red-pink flowers.

V. virginica (Culver's root) has been placed in a genus of its own as *Veronicastrum virginicum*, but it is still

V. spicata 'Red Fox'

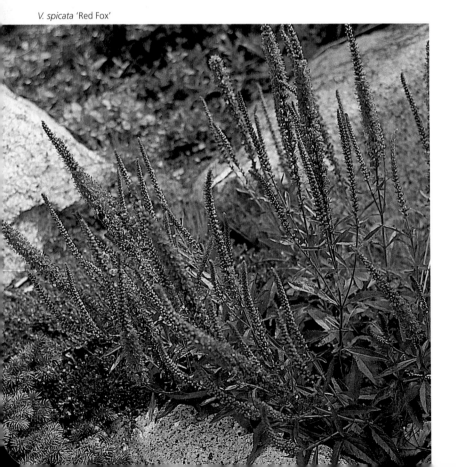

often grouped with the speedwells. An eastern
U.S. native, this close relative of the veronicas is
similar but much taller, with late-summer and fall
blooms. It grows 3–6' tall and spreads 12–24".
Excessive shade will cause the plants to flop over.
The flowers are borne on tall spikes and are most
often white but may also be pale pink or pale purple. 'Album' has attractive white flowers. 'Rosea'
has pale pink flowers.

Problems & Pests

Problems with scale insects are possible, as are
fungal problems such as downy and powdery
mildew, rust, leaf smut and root rot.

V. virginica (below), *V. spicata* cultivar (right)

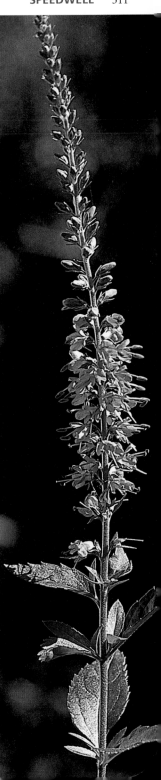

Spiderwort

Tradescantia

Height: 12–24" **Spread:** 18–24" **Flower color:** purple, blue, pink, red, white
Blooms: early summer to fall **Zones:** 3–9

WHEN GROWN ALONG THE EDGE OF A MOIST WOOD OR BESIDE
a water feature, spiderwort is one of our longest-blooming perennials. It
offers the subtle beauty shared by many of our native woodland plants. If
you look closely, you will see the buds that are waiting to bloom, clustered
under the open flowers. Newer cultivars tend to be more intensely colored
than the species. The flowers of 'Red Cloud' and 'Purple Dome' glow like tiny
jewels, especially when backlit by morning sun.

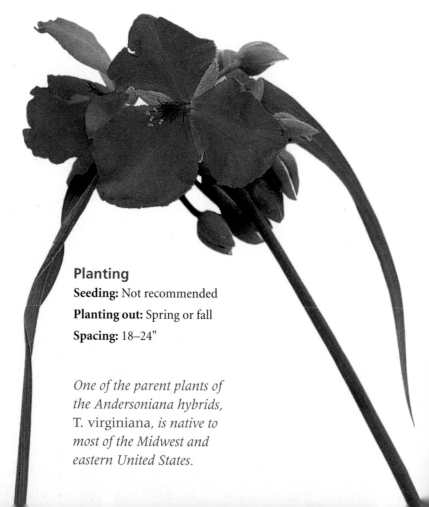

Planting

Seeding: Not recommended

Planting out: Spring or fall

Spacing: 18–24"

*One of the parent plants of
the Andersoniana hybrids,*
T. virginiana, *is native to
most of the Midwest and
eastern United States.*

Growing

Spiderwort grows equally well in **full sun, light shade** or **partial shade**. The soil should be **fertile, humus rich** and **moist**. Divide in spring or fall every four or so years.

After flowering has ceased and the leaves fade, cutting the plants back will produce fresh foliage and possibly a second round of blooms late in the season. Deadheading is not required during the flowering flush.

Tips

Spiderwort grows nicely in a well-watered border, and it looks very attractive next to a pond or other water feature, where the grassy foliage softens the sometimes unnatural edges of the pond. This plant is also attractive in a lightly shaded woodland or natural garden. Once established, spiderwort will grow almost anywhere.

Recommended

T. **Andersoniana Group** (Andersoniana hybrids) forms a large clump of grassy foliage. Clusters of three-petaled flowers are produced on long stems. 'Charlotte' has pink flowers. 'Isis' has bright blue flowers. '**Purple Dome**' has dark purple flowers. '**Red Cloud**' has red flowers. 'Snowcap' has white flowers.

Problems & Pests

Problems are rarely severe enough to warrant control. Aphids, spider mites, caterpillars, rot and leaf spot may afflict plants from time to time.

The name spiderwort apparently arose because the sticky sap of these plants can be drawn out from a broken stem to resemble a cobweb-like strand.

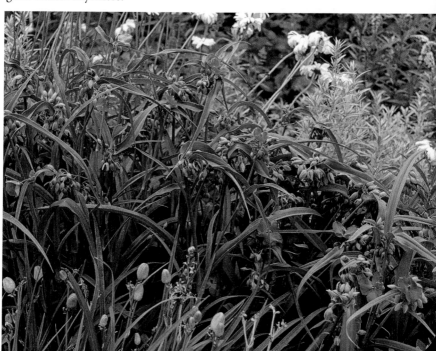

Sunflower

Helianthus

Height: 3–8' **Spread:** 36" **Flower color:** yellow and brown
Blooms: late summer, fall **Zones:** 4–8

SUNFLOWERS HIGHLIGHT THE LATE-SUMMER GARDEN, AND THEIR
golden faces have a way of lifting the spirits. While on a trip through Kansas
in summer, I passed by fields and fields of annual sunflowers. It was an awe-
some sight. Although most of us can't get that effect of masses of gold in our
smaller gardens, we can still create a sunny corner of joy with perennial sunflowers. For something a bit different, plant *H. salicifolius*, the willow-leaved
sunflower. Before it blooms, it creates a tall, mop-like column of very slender
leaves, adding an interesting texture to the garden.

Planting

Seeding: Start in spring;
seedlings may not come true
to type

Planting out: Spring

Spacing: 24–36"

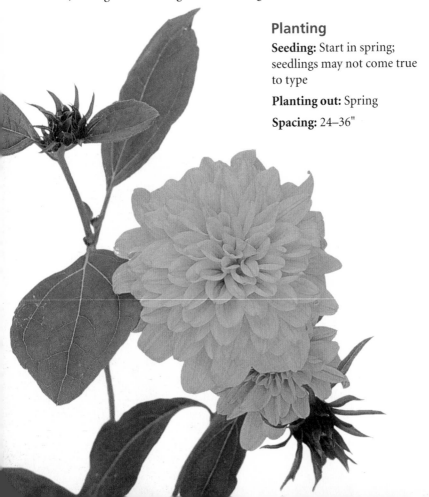

Growing

Sunflowers grow best in **full sun**. They flower less and become lanky in shaded conditions. Ideally, the soil should be of **average fertility, neutral to alkaline, moist** and **well drained**. *H.* x *multiflorus* prefers a constantly moist soil, while *H. salicifolius* is drought tolerant.

Cut plants back hard after flowering. You can also cut them back in early summer to produce shorter but later-flowering plants. Divide every three or so years in spring or fall.

Tips

These impressive perennials deserve a spot at the back of the border or in the center of an island bed. Sunflowers are tall plants that can provide a quick privacy screen in an exposed garden. The water-loving *H.* x *multiflorus* can also be planted near a pond or other water feature. *H. salicifolius* can be used in dry and underwatered areas.

Recommended

H. x *multiflorus* (perennial sunflower) forms a large, upright clump 3–6' tall and about 36" in spread. Many daisy-like flowers with yellow petals and brown centers are borne in late summer and fall. '**Loddon Gold**' bears golden yellow double flowers. '**Soleil d'Or**' bears yellow double flowers.

H. salicifolius (willow-leaved sunflower) is a large, clump-forming plant with narrow leaves. It grows up to 8' tall, spreads 36" and bears daisy-like yellow flowers with brown centers in fall.

Problems & Pests

Rare problems are possible with powdery mildew, downy mildew, fungal leaf spot and leaf-chewing insects such as caterpillars, beetles and weevils.

These plants are in the same genus as the annual sunflowers (H. annuus), *but the perennial versions have smaller, more plentiful flowers.*

H. x *multiflorus* 'Loddon Gold'

Sweet Woodruff

Galium

Height: 12–18" **Spread:** indefinite **Flower color:** white
Blooms: late spring to mid-summer **Zones:** 3–8

ONE OF THE PLEASANT SCENTS OF FALL IS THE MOWN-HAY SMELL of drying sweet woodruff. Your nose is detecting the presence of coumarin, a substance that can act as a blood thinner. Perhaps, then, it's a bit odd that sweet woodruff is used to flavor May wine, but apparently a little bit won't affect a healthy person. Sweet woodruff is also used as a fixative, or scent holder, in potpourri. Horticulturally, the plant is a small, unassuming ground-cover with subtle but lovely white flowers. A white-flowered crabapple under-planted with sweet woodruff makes a beautiful late-spring combination.

Planting

Seeding: Not recommended

Planting out: Spring or fall

Spacing: 12"

Growing

This plant prefers **partial shade**. It will grow well, but will not bloom well, in full shade. The soil should be **humus rich** and **evenly moist**. Keeping the soil moist will encourage plants to fill in more quickly, but don't let them sit in water. Divide in spring or fall.

Shear back after blooming to encourage plants to fill in with foliage and crowd out weeds.

Tips

Sweet woodruff makes a wonderful woodland groundcover. It forms a beautiful green carpet and loves the same conditions in which azaleas and rhododendrons thrive.

Recommended

G. odoratum is a low, spreading groundcover. Clusters of star-shaped white flowers are produced in a main flush in late spring, with sporadic blooming in summer.

Problems & Pests

Sweet woodruff may have occasional problems with mildew, rust and fungal leaf spot.

The dried leaves of sweet woodruff were once used to freshen stale rooms and stuff mattresses, leading to the alternative common name, bedstraw.

Thrift

Sea Pink, Sea Thrift

Armeria

Height: 8–24" **Spread:** 12–24" **Flower color:** pink, white, purple, red
Blooms: late spring, summer **Zones:** 3–8

ROCK GARDENERS CALL THRIFT A CUSHION
plant or bun plant, which means that it forms cute
hummocks or mounds. Thrift also features curious
lollipop-shaped flowerheads. Deer have not eaten it
in my garden, but they often tramp through it to get
to more succulent plants. One deer was kind enough
to chop a thrift plant into many smaller pieces. As an
experiment, I replanted the pieces, and most survived, showing how tough thrift can be. It is also
known for its salt tolerance, so you can place it near
a walk that gets salted in winter.

*It has been
suggested that
this plant is
called thrift
because it has
one root
supporting
many stalks, so
it's 'thrifty'
with its roots.*

Planting

Seeding: Start seeds indoors or out in spring or fall. Soak for a few hours before planting.

Planting out: Spring

Spacing: 10"

Growing

Thrift requires **full sun**. The soil should be of **poor to moderate fertility, sandy** and **well drained**. Thrift is very drought tolerant once established. Too fertile a soil or too much fertilizer reduces flowering and can kill the plant. Divide in spring or fall. Prompt deadheading extends the bloom.

Tips

Thrift is a useful plant for rock gardens or the front of a border.

If your thrift seems to be dying out in the middle of the clump, try cutting it back hard. New shoots should fill in quickly.

Recommended

A. 'Bees' is a group of large hybrids 18–24" tall, with an equal spread. The large white, pink or red flowers are borne in late spring and summer and are some of the showiest thrift blooms.

A. maritima forms a clump of grassy foliage. Ball-like clusters of pink, white or purple flowers are borne at the ends of long stems in late spring and early summer. The plant grows up to 8" tall and spreads about 12". 'Alba' has white flowers. 'Rubrifolia' has burgundy leaves, especially in early spring and in fall when temperatures are lower.

Problems & Pests

Problems are rare with this durable plant. It may occasionally come under attack by rust or aphids.

Attract bees and butterflies to your garden with clumps of thrift.

A. maritima 'Alba'

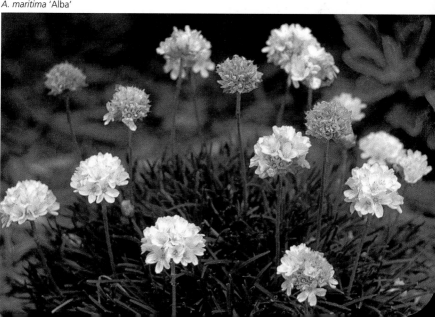

Thyme

Thymus

Height: 2–18" **Spread:** 4–16" **Flower color:** purple, pink, white;
plant grown mainly for foliage **Blooms:** late spring, summer **Zones:** 4–8

I CANNOT DO WITHOUT THYME IN MY GARDEN OR MY KITCHEN.
These plants are bee magnets when blooming; thyme honey is pleasantly
herbal and wonderfully complements biscuits. Thymes have two distinct
habits—upright, or low and creeping. Most of the stronger-flavored thymes
feature an upright form and are better candidates for use in cooking. The
creeping thymes make wonderful groundcovers for sunny slopes and flag-
stone terraces. In less-traveled areas, they can even replace grass. Imagine the
fragrance that would surround you as you strolled across a lawn of thyme.

Planting

Seeding: Many popular hybrids, particularly those with variegated leaves, cannot be grown from seed. Common thyme and mother of thyme can be started from seed. Start indoors in early spring.

Planting out: Spring

Spacing: 16–20"

Growing

Thymes prefer **full sun.** The soil should be **neutral to alkaline** and of **average to poor fertility. Good drainage** is essential. It is beneficial to work leaf mold and sharp limestone gravel into the soil to improve structure and drainage. Divide plants in spring.

It is easy to propagate thyme cultivars that cannot be started from seed. As the plant grows outwards, the branches touch the ground and send out new roots. These rooted stems may be removed and grown in pots to be planted out the following spring. Unrooted stem cuttings may be taken in early spring, before flowering.

T. x citriodorus 'Argenteus'

In the Middle Ages, it was believed that drinking a thyme infusion would enable one to see fairies.

T. x citriodorus 'Golden King'

Tips

Thymes are useful plants for sunny, dry locations at the front of borders, between or beside paving stones, on rock gardens and rock walls, and in containers.

Once the plants have finished flowering, it is a good idea to shear them back by about half to encourage new growth and prevent the plants from becoming too woody.

Recommended

T. x *citriodorus* (lemon-scented thyme) forms a mound 12" tall and 10" wide. The foliage smells of lemon, and the flowers are pale pink. The cultivars are more ornamental. '**Argenteus**' has silver-edged leaves. '**Aureus**' has leaves variegated with golden yellow. '**Golden King**' has leaves with yellow margins.

T. praecox subsp. *arcticus* (*T. serpyllum*) (mother of thyme, creeping thyme, wild thyme) is a popular low-growing species. It usually grows about 5" tall and spreads 12" or more. The flowers are purple. There are many cultivars available. '**Albus**' (white creeping thyme) bears white flowers.

T. praecox subsp. *arcticus* (this page)

'Elfin' forms tiny, dense mounds of foliage. It grows up to 2–3" tall and spreads 4". It rarely flowers. **'Lanuginosis'** (woolly thyme) is a mat-forming plant up to 3" high and 8–10" in spread, with fuzzy, gray-green leaves. It bears pink or purplish flowers in summer. **'Minimus'** grows 2" high and 4" wide. **'Snowdrift'** has white flowers.

T. vulgaris (common thyme) forms a bushy mound of dark green leaves. The flowers may be purple, pink or white. It usually grows about 12–18" tall and spreads about 16". **'Silver Posie'** is a good cultivar with pale pink flowers and silver-edged leaves.

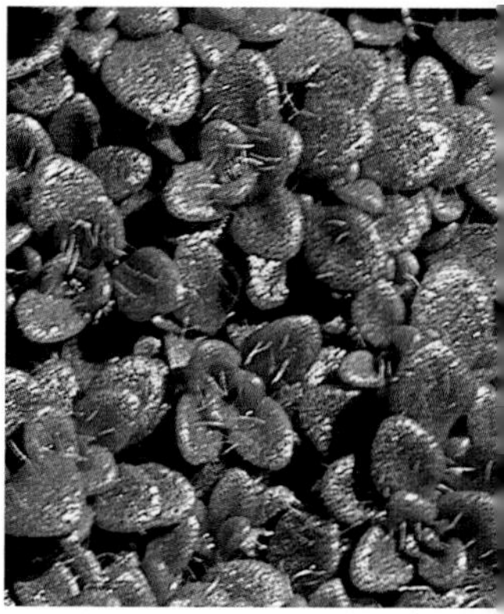

'Lanuginosis'

Ancient Egyptians used thyme in embalming, the Greeks added it to baths and the Romans purified their rooms with it.

Problems & Pests

Thyme plants rarely have problems unless they are subjected to poor drainage or overhead irrigation. Seedlings may suffer damping off and older plants may get gray mold or root rot. Good circulation and adequate drainage are good ways to avoid these problems.

T. praecox subsp. *arcticus* 'Lanuginosis' with *Achillea* & *Alchemilla*

Trillium
Wake Robin
Trillium

Height: 16–20" **Spread:** 12" or more **Flower color:** white, yellow, pink, red, purple **Blooms:** spring **Zones:** 4–7

THE SIMPLE BEAUTY OF TRILLIUMS ATTRACTS ALL THOSE WHO see them during their brief spring appearance. When pressed to explain this phenomenon, I can only say that simplicity is the essence of any garden. Unfortunately, many species of trillium are threatened or endangered because they have been excessively collected from the wild. The species listed here are all native to Ohio, and if you add any of them to your garden, get them from a reputable nursery. Pamper them for the first two seasons, and you will be rewarded with their ephemeral beauty for years to come.

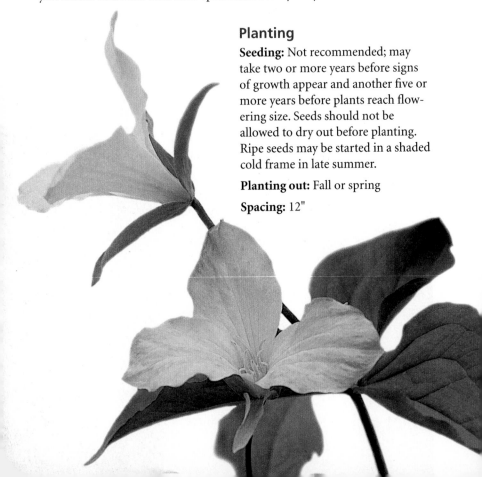

Planting

Seeding: Not recommended; may take two or more years before signs of growth appear and another five or more years before plants reach flowering size. Seeds should not be allowed to dry out before planting. Ripe seeds may be started in a shaded cold frame in late summer.

Planting out: Fall or spring

Spacing: 12"

Growing

Locate trilliums in **full or partial shade**. The soil should be **humus rich, moist, well drained** and **neutral to acidic**. Rhizomes should be planted about 4" deep. Add organic matter, such as compost or aged manure, to the soil when planting, and add a mulch of shredded leaves to encourage rapid growth. Division is not necessary. Apply compost every year.

Tips

These plants are ideal for natural woodland gardens and for plantings under spring-flowering trees and shrubs.

Trilliums are best left alone once planted. New transplants may take a year or two to adjust and start flowering. The amount of moisture they receive after flowering greatly influences how quickly the plants establish. Plentiful moisture in summer prevents the plants from going dormant after flowering. Instead, they send up side shoots that increase the size of the clump and the number of flowers the following spring.

Recommended

T. erectum (purple trillium, red trillium) has deep wine red flowers. It grows up to 20" tall and spreads up to 12".

T. grandiflorum (great white trillium, snow trillium) is Ohio's official wildflower. Its large white flowers turn pink as they mature. It grows 16" tall and spreads 12" or more. **'Flore Pleno'** has double flowers but is slower growing.

T. recurvatum (purple wake robin, purple trillium, bloody butcher) has dark purple or occasionally yellow or white flowers. It grows up to 16" tall and spreads 12".

Problems & Pests

Trilliums have few pest problems, but the young foliage may be attacked by slugs and snails.

T. grandiflorum (this page)

The name trillium comes from the three-parted leaves and flowers of these plants. 'Wake robin,' a rather more colorful moniker, reflects their spring bloom.

Wild Ginger
Asarum

Height: 3–6" **Spread:** 12" or more **Flower color:** burgundy or green, inconspic-uous; plant grown for foliage **Blooms:** late spring to early summer **Zones:** 4–8

WILD GINGERS ARE GROWN PRIMARILY FOR THEIR FOLIAGE EFFECT, but their flowers, though hard to see beneath the foliage, have value as con-versation starters. They have a unique shape and are an unusual brown-maroon color. And, if you get *very* close, you may notice a slightly fetid odor, which is unpleasant to us but attracts the wild gingers' beetle pollinators. Later in the season, ants harvest the seeds for the tasty seed covering, or aril. After they remove the aril, the ants toss the seed out of their mound, and next season a seedling sprouts.

Planting

Seeding: Not recommended

Planting out: Spring or fall

Spacing: 12"

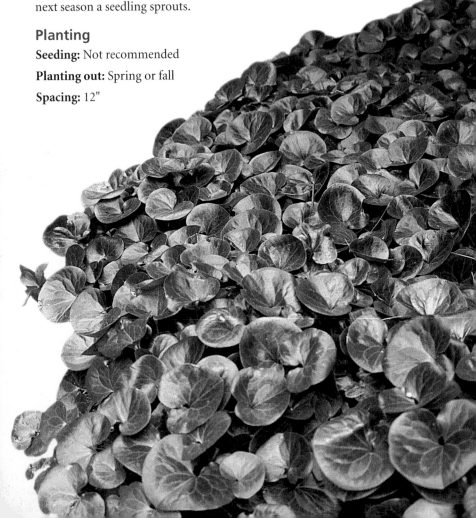

Growing

Wild gingers need **full or partial shade**. The soil should be **moist** and **humus rich**. All *Asarum* species prefer acidic soils, but *A. canadense* will tolerate alkaline conditions. Wild gingers tolerate dry conditions for a while in shade, but prolonged drought eventually causes wilting and dieback. Division is unlikely to be needed, except for propagation.

A. canadense (this page)

Tips

Use wild gingers in a shady rock garden, border or woodland garden. These plants spread to cover ground readily, but they are also relatively easy to remove from places they aren't welcome.

You can easily propagate or share wild gingers. The thick, fleshy rhizomes grow along the soil or just under it, sprouting pairs of leaves. Cuttings can be made by removing sections of rhizome with leaves growing from them and planting each section separately. When you take cuttings, be careful not to damage the tiny thread-like roots that grow from the stem below where the leaves attach.

Canada wild ginger rhizomes have a distinctive gingery scent. They are not related to the common culinary ginger (Zingiber officinale), but they may be used as a similar flavoring in many dishes.

Recommended

A. canadense (Canada wild ginger) is native to the Midwest and eastern North America. The heart-shaped leaves are slightly hairy.

A. europaeum (European wild ginger) is a European species with very glossy leaves, often distinctively silver-veined. It forms an expanding clump. This species is not as heat tolerant as *A. canadense*.

Yarrow

Achillea

Height: 4"–4' **Spread:** 12–36" **Flower color:** white, yellow, red, orange, pink, purple **Blooms:** early summer to fall **Zones:** 3–9

MY FIRST YARROW, *A. FILIPENDULINA* 'CORONATION GOLD,' CAME from a plant exchange. It lived happily in my garden for several years before I became entranced with some of its cousins. Because I have limited space, I had to banish 'Coronation Gold' so I could try *A.* 'Anthea' and *A.* 'Moonshine.' Their silvery foliage and soft yellow flowerheads combine beautifully with any other plant in a sunny garden. If your taste runs toward small, *A.* x *lewisii* 'King Edward' is charming and fuzzy. It must have excellent drainage or it will fade in the summer humidity. It has lived in my rock garden for eight years, intertwined with golden moneywort (*Lysimachia nummularia* 'Aurea').

Planting

Seeding: Direct sow in spring. Don't cover the seeds; they need light to germinate.

Planting out: Spring

Spacing: 12–24"

Growing

Yarrows grow best in **full sun.** The soil should be of **average fertility, sandy** and **well drained.** These plants tolerate drought and poor soil. They will also tolerate, but not thrive in, a heavy, wet soil or very humid conditions. Excessively rich soil or too much nitrogen results in weak, floppy growth. Good drainage is key to getting the best growth from these plants. Divide every two or three years, in spring.

The species *A. millefolium* and *A. filipendulina* often need staking. Many of the cultivars are less floppy.

Once the flowerheads fade, cut them back to the lateral buds. Yarrows flower longer and more profusely if deadheaded. Basal foliage should be left in place over the winter and tidied up in spring.

Tips

Yarrows are informal plants. Cottage gardens, wildflower gardens and mixed borders are perfect places for them. They thrive in hot, dry locations where nothing else will grow.

These plants make excellent groundcovers, despite being quite tall. The plants send up shoots and flowers from a low basal point and may be mowed periodically without excessive damage to the plant.

A. ptarmica 'The Pearl'

The ancient Druids used yarrow to divine seasonal weather, and the ancient Chinese used the stems to foretell the future.

A. millefolium cultivar with *Phlox*

Mower blades should be kept at least 4" high. Keep in mind that you are mowing off the flowerheads. Do not mow more often than once a month, or you will have short yarrow with no flowers!

Use yarrows in dried or fresh arrangements. For drying, pick the flowerheads just before the flowers are fully open. For fresh bouquets, pick once the pollen is visible, or the plants will die very quickly once cut.

Recommended

A. 'Anthea' bears bright yellow flowers that fade to creamy yellow. It will flower all summer if kept deadheaded. The foliage is silvery gray. Plants grow 12–24" tall and spread 12–18".

A. filipendulina has yellow flowers and grows up to 4' tall. It has been used to develop several hybrids and cultivars. Cultivars come in various heights, with flowers in shades of yellow. 'Coronation Gold' has bright golden yellow flowers and fern-like foliage. It grows about 36" tall, with a 12" spread. This cultivar is quite heat tolerant.

A. x *lewisii* 'King Edward' is a low-growing hybrid that reaches 4–8" in height and about 12" in spread. has woolly gray leaves and bears clusters of yellow flowers in early summer.

A. millefolium (common yarrow) grows 12–36" tall, with an equal spread, and has white flowers. The foliage is soft and finely divided. Because it is quite aggressive, the species is almost never grown in favor of the many cultivars. 'Cerise Queen' has pinkish red flowers.

A. millefolium cultivar

'Fireland' bears red flowers with yellow centers; the flowers mature to coppery salmon and then soft gold. 'Summer Pastels' has flowers of many colors, including white, yellow, pink and purple. This cultivar tolerates heat and drought very well and has fade-resistant flowers. 'Terra Cotta' bears flowers that open orangy pink and mature to rusty orange.

A. 'Moonshine' bears bright yellow flowers all summer. The foliage is silvery gray. The plant grows 18–24" tall and spreads 12–24".

A. ptarmica (sneezewort) grows 12–24" tall, with an equal spread. It bears clusters of white flowers all summer. 'The Pearl' bears clusters of white, button-like double flowers. This cultivar can become invasive. It can be started from seed, but not all the seedlings will come true to type.

Problems & Pests

Rare problems with powdery mildew and stem rot are possible.

A. filipendulina

Yarrows have blood-coagulating properties that were recognized by the ancient Greeks. Achillea *is named after the legendary Achilles, because during the battle of Troy he is said to have treated his warriors' wounds with this herb.*

A. filipendulina cultivar with Artemisia & Echinacea

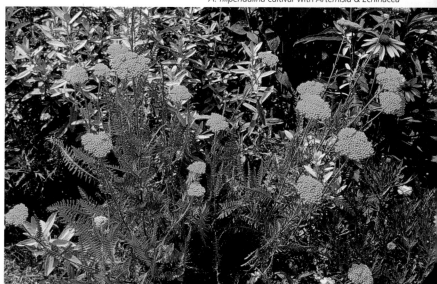

Other Perennials to Consider

Basket-of-Gold

Aurinia saxatilis

Vigorous, mound-forming plant with intense golden, spring-blooming flowers. Grows 8–12" tall and spreads 12–18". Short-lived in areas with hot summers but self-seeds, providing gardeners with replacement plants as older plants die out. Shear back after blooming, but leave a few flower-heads in place to provide the needed seeds. Basket-of-gold grows best in **full sun** with **poor to average, sandy, well-drained** soil. Plant is drought tolerant and can rot in poorly drained soil. Basket-of-gold can be included in borders, along pathways and in rock gardens, but avoid placing it near slow-growing plants because it will overwhelm them.

Aurinia saxatilis

Bugbane

Cimicifuga racemosa & *C. simplex*

Both species are large, clump-forming plants that spread about 24". *C. racemosa* grows 4–7' tall; *C. simplex* grows 3–4' tall. Spikes of sweet-scented, white or cream flowers are borne in late summer and fall. Purple-leaved cultivars are also available. Bugbanes grow best in **partial or light shade** with **fertile, humus-rich, moist** soil. Plants may require support from a peony hoop. Don't divide, because the roots resent being disturbed, but small sections of the rhizomes can be carefully removed for propagation. Use bugbanes in open woodland gardens, shaded borders or pondside plantings, but keep in mind they don't compete well with trees or other vigorous-rooted plants. Place them where you will be able to enjoy the scent of the late-season flowers.

Cimicifuga racemosa

Delphinium x elatum

Delphinium

Delphinium x *belladonna* &
D. x *elatum*

Large, upright plants 12–18" in
spread; bloom in spring or early
summer. *D.* x *belladonna* is smaller;
grows 3–4' tall and bears loose,
branched spikes of purple, blue,
white or mauve flowers. *D.* x *elatum*
grows 4–6' tall and bears tall spikes
of purple, blue, white, pink or yellow flowers. The flower spikes, particularly of *D.* x *elatum*, should be
staked to prevent them from breaking in the wind. Grow delphiniums
in a **sheltered** location with **full sun**
and **fertile, humus-rich, moist, well-
drained** soil. Plants are heavy feeders and are often short-lived in hot
climates. Annual division can keep
them vigorous longer, but frequent
replacements may be required.
These classic cottage-garden plants
can be included at the back of the
border, where they make a good
backdrop for warm-colored flowers,
such as peonies and poppies.

False Sunflower

Heliopsis helianthoides

Forms an upright clump of stems
3–5' tall and 18–36" in spread. Bears
yellow or orange, daisy-like flowers
from mid-summer to mid-fall. Cultivars are generally preferable to the
species because they are less floppy
and weedy-looking. Deadheading
will prolong the bloom, and plants
can be cut back once all flowering is
finished. False sunflower prefers **full
sun** but tolerates partial shade. Soil
should preferably be **average to fertile, humus rich, moist** and **well
drained,** but most soil conditions are
tolerated, including poor and dry
soils. This easy-to-grow plant can be
included at the back or in the middle
of herbaceous and mixed borders.

Heliopsis helianthoides

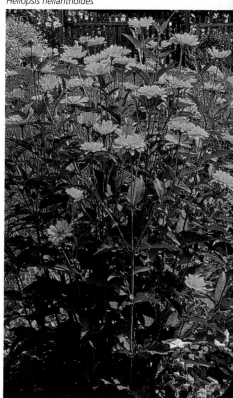

Gas Plant

Dictamnus albus

Large, clump-forming plant that grows 18–36" tall and spreads 12–36". Bears spikes of pink-veined, white or pink flowers; flowers and leaves both have a lemon scent. Can take several years to become established and flower. Gas plant prefers **full sun** but tolerates partial shade. Soil should be **average to fertile, dry** and **well drained**. Don't divide this plant; it resents being disturbed. Makes an attractive addition to a border. Avoid touching the leaves: when foliage oils left on the skin are exposed to sunlight, they can cause rashes, itching and burning.

On hot summer evenings, gas plant flowers excrete a gas that may ignite if exposed to fire, a curiosity that gave the plant its common name.

Ligularia

Ligularia dentata

Forms a clump of rounded, heart-shaped leaves. Clusters of daisy-like, orange-yellow flowers are held above the foliage in summer and early fall. Foliage can look wilted on hot days, even when soil is moist. The leaves will perk up at night, but plants that wilt frequently should be moved to cooler, more shaded locations. Ligularia prefers **light or partial shade,** with protection from the afternoon sun, and **humus-rich, moist** soil of **average fertility**. Division is rarely required but can be done to propagate new plants. Use ligularia alongside a pond or stream, in a well-watered border or naturalized in a moist meadow or woodland garden.

Lupine

Lupinus hybrids

Forms a mound of basal foliage from which spikes of colorful, pea-like flowers emerge. White, cream, yellow, pink, red, orange, purple, blue or bicolored flowers are borne from early to mid-summer. Plants are short-lived in hot-summer climates and are treated as annuals or biennials by some gardeners. Lupines grow best in **light or partial shade** with **fertile, sandy, well-drained, slightly acidic** soil. They resent having their roots disturbed and shouldn't be divided. Dead-heading prolongs blooming, but

Lupinus hybrid

Ligularia dentata

leave a spike or two in place toward the end of the flowering season to self-sow new plants as the older ones die out. Lupines are most attractive mass-planted in borders and cottage-style gardens. They also make stunning specimen plants.

Potentilla

Potentilla atrosanguinea & P. nepalensis

Most gardeners know the common shrub potentilla *(P. fruticosa)* but are not as familiar with the attractive perennial species. These plants are mounding or spreading in habit; some can be invasive spreaders. *P. atrosanguinea* forms a large clump of sprawling stems and foliage 12–36" tall and about 24" in spread. It bears yellow, orange or red flowers in summer and fall. *P. nepalensis* forms a loose clump of trailing stems 12–18" tall and 24" in spread. It bears pink or red flowers in late spring or early summer. Potentillas grow well in **full sun** or **partial shade** with protection from the hot afternoon sun. Soil should be **well drained** and of **poor to average fertility**. Plants are drought tolerant. Divide when they begin to thin out in the center. Add potentillas to borders, rock gardens and rock walls.

Potentilla atrosanguinea

Rosinweed

Silphium laciniatum & S. perfoliatum

Both species form large clumps of stems and bear clusters of yellow, daisy-like flowers in late summer and fall. *S. laciniatum* grows up to 10' tall and spreads 3'. It is commonly called compass plant because the flat sides of the leaves always face east or west. The flowers also face

Silphium perfoliatum

east, so be sure to plant this species on the west side of your garden. *S. perfoliatum* grows about 8' tall and spreads 4–5'. The leaves form a cup around the stem, giving this species the alternative common name cup plant. Birds and insects are often attracted to the moisture that collects in the cup. Rosinweeds grow well in **full sun** or **partial shade,** with **moist, neutral to alkaline** soil of **average fertility.** They tolerate heavy clay soils. Plants can be divided in spring, but it may take two people to separate the huge root masses. These tall plants can be used in meadow plantings, at the back of borders, along the edges of woodland gardens, in bog gardens and in waterside plantings.

Snow-in-Summer

Cerastium tomentosum

Forms a low mat of silvery gray foliage and bears white flowers in late spring. Plants grow 2–6" tall and can spread 36" in one year. Cut plants back after blooming is finished to encourage new growth and keep excessive spreading in check. Snow-in-summer grows well in **full sun** or **partial shade** with protection from the hot afternoon sun. **Poor to average, well-drained** soil is best. Plants will rot in heavy, poorly drained soil and spread invasively in rich soils. Divide when plants begin

Cerastium tomentosum

to thin out in the middle. Snow-in-summer can be used as a groundcover under taller plants, to edge borders and to prevent soil erosion on sloping banks. It can overwhelm less vigorous plants.

Sundrops

Oenothera fruticosa & *O. speciosa*

Lanky, upright or sprawling plants. *O. fruticosa* grows 18–36" tall, spreads 12–18" and bears yellow flowers in summer. The foliage turns red after a light frost. *O. speciosa* grows 6–24" tall, spreads 12–18" and

bears white or pink flowers in summer. Both species are prolific self-seeders and may turn up in unlikely places. Sundrops prefer **full sun** with **well-drained** soil of **average fertility**. Plants become invasive in too fertile a soil. These plants enjoy hot and humid weather, making them ideal for Ohio gardens, except for their somewhat invasive nature. They will brighten up borders, gravelly banks and rock gardens.

Turtlehead

Chelone obliqua

Upright plant that grows 18–36" tall, spreads 18–24" and forms a dense mound of foliage. Bears pink or purple flowers in late summer and fall. Pinch tips in early summer to encourage bushy growth. Turtlehead grows well in **full sun** or **partial shade** with **fertile, humus-rich, moist** soil. Tolerates clay soil and boggy conditions, but becomes floppy in too much shade. Divide in spring or fall, or propagate from early-summer stem cuttings. An attractive and useful addition to a pondside or streamside planting. Can also be used in a bog garden or in a poorly drained part of the garden where plants requiring better drainage won't grow.

Oenothera speciosa

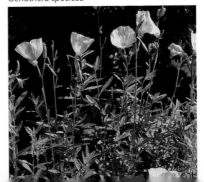

Gardens to Visit in Ohio

AKRON
Stan Hywet Hall and Gardens
(330) 836-5533
www.stanhywet.org/

BELLVILLE
Wade and Gatton Nurseries
(419) 883-3191
www.palmetto.com/hosta/
wade/wade.html

CANFIELD
Fellows Riverside Gardens
(330) 702-3000
www.millcreekmetroparks.com/
riversidegarden.htm

CLEVELAND
Cleveland Botanical Garden
(216) 721-1600
www.cbgarden.org/

Gardenview Horticultural Park
(Strongsville)
(440) 238-6653
www.geocities.com/heartland/
cottage/9303/

CINCINNATI
Cincinnati Zoo and
Botanical Garden
(513) 281-4700 / (1-800) 94-HIPPO
www.cincinnatizoo.org/

COLUMBUS
Chadwick Arboretum and Learning
Garden (Ohio State University)
(614) 688-3479
http://chadwickarboretum.osu.edu/

DAYTON
Cox Arboretum
(937) 434-9005
www.metroparks.org/

Wegerzyn Gardens
(937) 277-6545
www.metroparks.org/

KIRTLAND
Holden Arboretum
(440) 946-4400
www.holdenarb.org/

MANSFIELD
Kingwood Center
(419) 522-0211
www.kingwoodcenter.org/

TOLEDO
Toledo Botanical Garden
(419) 936-2986
www.toledogarden.org/

WESTERVILLE
Inniswood Metro Gardens
(614) 895-6216
http://metroparks.co.franklin.oh.us/
inniswood.htm

Jacob's ladder

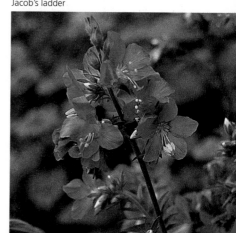

Height Legend: Low: < 12" • Medium: 12–24" • Tall: > 24"

SPECIES by Common Name	COLOR								BLOOMING			HEIGHT		
	White	Pink	Red	Orange	Yellow	Blue	Purple	Foliage	Spring	Summer	Fall	Low	Medium	Tall
Ajuga	*	*				*	*	*	*	*		*		
Anemone	*	*				*			*	*	*	*	*	*
Angelica	*				*	*	*			*				*
Artemisia	*				*			*		*	*	*	*	*
Aster	*	*	*		*	*	*			*	*	*	*	*
Astilbe	*	*	*				*	*	*	*		*	*	*
Balloon flower	*	*				*				*				*
Baptisia	*					*	*		*	*				*
Beebalm		*	*							*				*
Bergenia	*	*	*				*	*	*				*	
Black-eyed Susan				*	*					*	*		*	*
Blanket flower			*	*	*					*	*		*	*
Blazing star	*						*			*			*	*
Bleeding heart	*	*	*					*	*	*			*	*
Boltonia	*	*					*			*	*			*
Brunnera						*		*	*			*	*	
Butterfly weed	*	*	*	*	*		*		*	*	*		*	*
Campanula	*					*	*			*	*	*	*	*
Candytuft	*								*		*	*		
Cardinal flower	*	*	*			*	*			*	*			*
Catmint	*	*				*	*		*	*	*	*	*	*
Chrysanthemum	*	*	*	*	*		*			*	*		*	*
Clematis	*	*	*		*	*	*			*	*		*	*
Columbine	*	*	*		*	*	*	*	*	*		*	*	*
Coreopsis		*		*	*					*		*	*	*
Cornflower	*	*				*	*		*	*			*	
Corydalis	*				*	*		*	*	*		*	*	
Crocosmia			*	*	*					*		*	*	*
Cupid's dart	*					*	*			*	*	*	*	*

LIGHT				SOIL CONDITIONS						USDA Zones	Page Number	SPECIES by Common Name
Sun	Part Shade	Light Shade	Shade	Moist	Well Drained	Dry	Fertile	Average	Poor			
	*	*	*		*		*	*	*	3–8	68	Ajuga
*	*	*		*		*	*	*		5–8	72	Anemone
*	*			*			*			4–8	76	Angelica
*					*			*	*	3–8	78	Artemisia
*	*			*	*		*			3–8	82	Aster
	*	*	*	*	*		*			3–9	86	Astilbe
*	*			*	*		*	*		3–8	90	Balloon flower
*	*				*			*	*	3–9	92	Baptisia
*	*	*		*	*			*		3–9	94	Beebalm
	*			*	*		*	*		3–8	98	Bergenia
*	*				*			*		3–9	102	Black-eyed Susan
*					*	*				3–10	104	Blanket flower
*				*	*			*		3–9	106	Blazing star
*	*	*		*	*		*	*		3–9	108	Bleeding heart
*	*			*	*		*			4–9	112	Boltonia
	*	*		*				*		3–8	114	Brunnera
*			*	*			*			4–9	116	Butterfly weed
*	*	*			*		*	*		3–7	118	Campanula
*				*	*			*	*	3–9	122	Candytuft
*	*	*		*			*			3–9	124	Cardinal flower
*	*				*			*		3–8	128	Catmint
*				*	*		*			5–9	132	Chrysanthemum
*	*			*	*		*			3–8	136	Clematis
	*	*		*	*		*			2–9	140	Columbine
*					*			*		3–9	144	Coreopsis
*		*		*	*			*	*	3–8	148	Cornflower
	*	*			*		*	*		5–7	150	Corydalis
*				*				*		5–9	152	Crocosmia
*	*				*	*		*		3–8	154	Cupid's dart

Height Legend: Low: < 12" • Medium: 12–24" • Tall: > 24"

SPECIES by Common Name	COLOR								BLOOMING			HEIGHT		
	White	Pink	Red	Orange	Yellow	Blue	Purple	Foliage	Spring	Summer	Fall	Low	Medium	Tall
Daylily		*	*	*	*		*			*			*	*
Dead nettle	*	*			*		*	*	*	*		*	*	
Dwarf plumbago						*				*		*	*	
Euphorbia				*	*				*	*			*	
False solomon's seal	*							*	*					*
Foamflower	*	*						*	*	*		*		
Foxglove	*	*	*		*		*		*	*				*
Gaura	*	*							*	*	*			*
Globe thistle						*	*			*				*
Goat's beard	*									*		*	*	*
Golden Marguerite	*			*	*					*		*	*	*
Goldenrod					*					*	*			*
Hardy geranium	*	*	*			*	*	*	*	*	*	*	*	*
Helen's flower		*	*	*			*			*	*			*
Hens and chicks	*		*		*		*	*		*		*		
Heuchera	*	*	*				*	*	*	*		*	*	*
Hosta	*						*	*		*	*	*	*	*
Iris	*	*	*		*	*	*	*	*	*	*	*	*	*
Jacob's ladder	*					*	*	*	*	*		*	*	*
Joe-Pye weed	*	*				*	*			*	*			*
Jupiter's beard	*	*	*							*				*
Lady's mantle					*			*		*	*	*	*	
Lamb's ears		*					*	*		*		*	*	
Lavender		*				*	*			*	*	*	*	*
Lenten rose	*	*			*		*		*				*	
Lily-of-the-valley	*	*						*	*			*		
Lungwort	*	*	*			*	*	*	*			*	*	
Lychnis	*	*	*	*						*				*
Mallow	*	*				*	*			*	*	*	*	*
Meadow rue	*	*			*		*	*		*	*			*

SPECIES
by Common Name

| LIGHT | | | | SOIL CONDITIONS | | | | | | | | |
Sun	Part Shade	Light Shade	Shade	Moist	Well Drained	Dry	Fertile	Average	Poor	USDA Zones	Page Number	Species by Common Name
*	*	*	*	*		*	*			2–9	156	Daylily
	*	*		*	*			*		3–8	160	Dead nettle
*	*	*			*		*	*		5–9	164	Dwarf plumbago
*		*		*	*	*		*		4–9	166	Euphorbia
	*	*		*	*			*		3–9	170	False solomon's seal
	*	*	*	*				*	*	3–8	172	Foamflower
	*	*		*			*			3–8	174	Foxglove
*	*			*	*		*			5–8	178	Gaura
*	*				*	*		*	*	3–8	180	Globe thistle
	*	*	*	*			*			3–7	182	Goat's beard
*				*	*		*			3–7	186	Golden Marguerite
*	*				*			*	*	2–8	188	Goldenrod
*	*	*		*	*	*		*		3–8	190	Hardy geranium
*				*	*		*			3–9	194	Helen's flower
*	*				*	*		*	*	3–8	196	Hens and chicks
	*	*		*	*		*	*		3–9	198	Heuchera
	*	*	*	*	*		*			3–8	202	Hosta
*		*		*	*		*	*		3–10	206	Iris
	*	*		*	*		*			3–7	210	Jacob's ladder
*	*			*			*			3–9	212	Joe-Pye weed
*					*			*		4–8	214	Jupiter's beard
	*	*		*	*		*			3–7	216	Lady's mantle
*				*	*		*	*		3–8	220	Lamb's ears
*				*	*	*	*	*		5–9	222	Lavender
	*			*	*		*			4–9	226	Lenten rose
*	*	*	*	*		*		*		2–7	228	Lily-of-the-valley
	*	*	*	*	*		*			3–8	232	Lungwort
*	*				*			*		3–8	236	Lychnis
*	*			*	*	*		*		4–9	238	Mallow
*	*	*		*	*			*	*	3–8	242	Meadow rue

Height Legend: Low: < 12" • Medium: 12–24" • Tall: > 24"

SPECIES by Common Name	COLOR								BLOOMING			HEIGHT		
	White	Pink	Red	Orange	Yellow	Blue	Purple	Foliage	Spring	Summer	Fall	Low	Medium	Tall
Meadowsweet	*	*	*					*	*	*	*			*
Monkshood	*					*	*			*				*
Obedient plant	*	*					*			*	*		*	*
Oriental poppy	*	*	*	*					*	*			*	*
Pasqueflower	*		*			*	*		*			*		
Penstemon	*	*	*			*	*		*	*	*	*	*	*
Peony	*	*	*		*			*	*	*				*
Perennial salvia	*	*				*	*		*	*	*		*	*
Phlox	*	*	*	*		*	*		*	*	*	*	*	*
Pincushion flower	*	*				*	*			*	*		*	
Pinks	*	*	*				*	*	*	*		*	*	
Plume poppy	*							*		*				*
Primrose	*	*	*	*	*	*	*		*	*		*	*	
Purple coneflower	*	*					*			*	*			*
Rockcress	*	*						*	*	*		*		
Rockrose	*	*	*	*	*				*	*		*		
Russian sage						*	*			*	*			*
Sea holly	*					*	*			*	*		*	*
Sedum	*	*	*		*			*		*	*	*	*	
Shasta daisy	*				*					*	*	*	*	*
Soapwort	*	*	*						*	*	*	*	*	
Speedwell	*	*				*	*		*	*	*	*	*	*
Spiderwort	*	*	*			*	*			*	*		*	
Sunflower					*					*	*			*
Sweet woodruff	*							*	*	*		*	*	
Thrift	*	*	*				*		*	*		*	*	
Thyme	*	*					*	*	*	*		*	*	
Trillium	*	*	*		*		*		*				*	
Wild ginger							*	*	*	*		*		
Yarrow	*	*	*	*	*		*	*		*	*	*	*	*

Sun	Part Shade	Light Shade	Shade	Moist	Well Drained	Dry	Fertile	Average	Poor	USDA Zones	Page Number	SPECIES by Common Name
	*	*		*			*	*		3–8	246	Meadowsweet
	*	*		*				*	*	3–8	250	Monkshood
*	*	*		*				*	*	2–9	254	Obedient plant
*					*		*	*		3–7	256	Oriental poppy
*	*				*		*			3–7	258	Pasqueflower
*					*	*	*	*		4–8	260	Penstemon
*				*	*		*			2–7	264	Peony
*		*			*			*		3–9	268	Perennial salvia
*	*	*		*	*		*			3–8	272	Phlox
*	*				*			*		3–7	276	Pincushion flower
*		*			*	*		*		3–9	278	Pinks
*	*			*		*		*	*	3–10	282	Plume poppy
	*	*		*	*			*		3–8	284	Primrose
*		*			*		*	*	*	3–8	288	Purple coneflower
*					*			*	*	4–7	290	Rockcress
*					*			*		4–7	292	Rockrose
*					*	*		*	*	4–9	294	Russian sage
*					*		*	*		4–8	296	Sea holly
*	*				*			*		3–8	300	Sedum
*	*			*	*		*			4–9	304	Shasta daisy
*					*			*	*	3–7	306	Soapwort
*	*			*				*		3–8	308	Speedwell
*	*	*		*			*			3–9	312	Spiderwort
*					*	*	*	*		4–8	314	Sunflower
	*	*	*	*				*	*	3–8	316	Sweet woodruff
*					*	*		*	*	3–8	318	Thrift
*					*	*		*	*	4–8	320	Thyme
	*	*	*	*	*		*			4–7	324	Trillium
	*	*	*	*				*	*	4–8	326	Wild ginger
*					*	*		*	*	3–9	328	Yarrow

Glossary

Acid soil: soil with a pH lower than 7.0

Alkaline soil: soil with a pH higher than 7.0

Basal leaves: leaves that form from the crown

Basal rosette: a ring or rings of leaves growing from the crown of a plant at or near ground level; flowering stems of such plants grow separately from the crown

Crown: the part of a plant where the shoots join the roots, at or just below soil level

Cultivar: a *culti*vated (bred) plant *vari*ety with one or more distinct differences from the parent species, e.g., in flower color, leaf variegation or disease resistance

Damping off: fungal disease causing seedlings to rot at soil level and then topple over

Deadhead: to remove spent flowers to maintain a neat appearance and encourage a longer blooming period

'Marshall's Delight': a cultivar of *Monarda didyma*

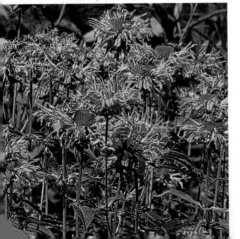

Direct sow: to plant seeds straight into the garden, in the location you want the plants to grow

Disbud: to remove some flowerbuds to improve the size or quality of the remaining ones

Dormancy: a period of plant inactivity, usually during winter or other unfavorable climatic conditions

Double flower: a flower with an unusually large number of petals, often caused by mutation of the stamens into petals

Genus: category of biological classification between the species and family levels; the first word in a scientific name indicates the genus, e.g., *Digitalis* in *Digitalis purpurea*

Hardy: able to survive unfavorable conditions, such as cold weather

Humus: decomposed or decomposing organic material in the soil

Hybrid: a plant resulting from natural or human-induced crossbreeding between varieties, species or genera; the hybrid expresses features of each parent plant

Invasive: able to spread aggressively from the planting site and outcompete other plants

Knot garden: a formal design, often used for herb gardens, in which low, clipped hedges are arranged in elaborate, knot-like patterns

Neutral soil: soil with a pH of 7.0

Node: the area on a stem from which a leaf or new shoot grows

Offset: a young plantlet that naturally sprouts around the base of the parent plant in some species

pH: a measure of acidity or alkalinity (the lower the pH, the higher the acidity); the pH of soil influences availability of nutrients for plants

Rhizome: a root-like, usually swollen stem that grows horizontally underground, and from which shoots and true roots emerge

Rootball: the root mass and surrounding soil of a container-grown plant or a plant dug out of the ground

Rosette: see Basal rosette

Self-seeding: reproducing by means of seeds without human assistance, so that new plants constantly replace those that die

Semi-double flower: a flower with petals that form two or three rings

Semi-hardy: a plant capable of surviving the climatic conditions of a given region if protected

Single flower: a flower with a single ring of typically four or five petals

Species: the original plant from which cultivars are derived; the fundamental unit of biological classification, indicated by a two-part scientific name, e.g., *Digitalis purpurea* (*purpurea* is the specific epithet)

Sport: an atypical plant or part of a plant that arises through mutation; some sports are horticulturally desirable and propagated as new cultivars

Subshrub: a perennial plant that is somewhat shrubby, with a woody basal stem; its upper parts are herbaceous and die back each year

Subspecies (subsp.): a naturally occurring, regional form of a species, often isolated from other subspecies but still potentially interfertile with them

Taproot: a root system consisting of one main vertical root with smaller roots branching from it

Tender: incapable of surviving the climatic conditions of a given region; requiring protection from frost or cold

True: describes the passing of desirable characteristics from the parent plant to seed-grown offspring; also called breeding true to type

Tuber: a swollen part of a rhizome or root, containing food stores for the plant

Variegation: describes foliage that has more than one color, often patched or striped or bearing differently colored leaf margins

Variety (var.): a naturally occurring variant of a species; below the level of subspecies in biological classification

Variegated cultivar of *Brunnera macrophylla*

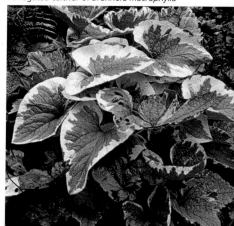

Index